This book is a gem! With warmth and transparency, Sandra Byrd invites you into her life, which will remind you of your own. Her engaging stories entwined with scriptural truth will touch your heart, while her practical tips will motivate you to action. You will smile, you will think, and you will deepen your walk with God through these inspired daily readings.

JUDY GORDON MORROW, author of *The Listening Heart: Hearing God in Prayer*

Turning to Sandra Byrd's devotions each day will feel as though you're going home—home to a friend's embrace and to God's welcoming arms as well. Each daily reading will give you rest, refreshment, and reminders of how to live well—and the monthly recipes and home ideas are delightful!

JANET HOLM MCHENRY, author of the best-selling *PrayerWalk*, *Daily PrayerWalk*, and *PrayerStreaming*

Sandra Byrd is absolutely one of my favorite writers, and this devotional proves exactly why! Her ability to weave story and truth together always impacts me and encourages me. I can't wait to keep this devotional on my bedside table and in the guest room and pretty much everywhere—anyone who picks it up and reads it will be blessed!

ANNIE F. DOWNS, author of *Let's All Be Brave: Living Life with Everything You Have*

THE ONE YEAR®

HOME&GARDEN
DEVOTIONS

Sandra Byrd

Tyndale House Publishers, Inc.
Carol Stream, Illinois

Visit Tyndale online at www.tyndale.com.

TYNDALE, Tyndale's quill logo, *The One Year,* and *One Year* are registered trademarks of Tyndale House Publishers, Inc. The One Year logo is a trademark of Tyndale House Publishers, Inc.

The One Year Home and Garden Devotions

Designed by Jacqueline L. Nuñez

Edited by Jane Vogel

Published in association with the literary agency of Browne & Miller Literary Associates, LLC, 410 Michigan Avenue, Suite 460, Chicago, IL 60605.

ISBN 978-1-4143-9186-1

Printed in the United States of America

21	20	19	18	17	16	15
7	6	5	4	3	2	1

WELCOME!

I live a busy life, just like most people I know. God is the most important person in my life, and yet it seems like he gets so little of my time. I often think of the passage in Deuteronomy 11 that warns us not to fall away, become distracted, and worship other gods or there will be unpleasant consequences. God urges those of us who are parents to teach our children his truths throughout the day—when we are sitting at home or walking along the road, when we wake up and when we lie down. He's asking us to invite him and his truths into our seemingly mundane routines because those moments are often when he draws near. God, as the perfect parent, illustrates his truth and love through the day-to-day situations we encounter. So many of us yearn to hear from God. He's there, talking to us throughout the banalities of everyday life, if we just tune our ears to hear.

This devotional is a collection of thoughts and truths that God has impressed on me as I have journeyed with him through daily life in the home. When I let the dog out in the morning, already worrying about what the hours ahead might hold, I may spy a tiny sparrow hopping along the ground. *See how I care for that sparrow?* he asks. *How much more valuable to me are you!* And then I relax into his peace, looking and listening for him throughout the day.

I'd love to hear the stories of how God works in your everyday life too. We're down on the ground together, planting flowers and pulling weeds. Please contact me at my website, www.sandrabyrd.com, and bless me with the insights God has given you.

Yoked together,
Sandra

JANUARY

Scented Linen Water

I don't know what makes clean sheets so comforting, but the first night spent sleeping on them feels like an absolute luxury. You can reproduce that feeling all the time by spritzing linen water on your sheets after turning down the bed. Spray from a few feet above the bed and allow the sheets to dry for a minute or two before you climb in. The spray also works well when ironing clothes or even just to refresh a room.

WHAT YOU'LL NEED

4 ounces distilled water

25-30 drops of essential oils of your choice (my favorites are pre-blended "unwind" or "sleep inducing" mixes)

A small, clean bottle with a spray nozzle

DIRECTIONS

Blend all ingredients together, then test the spray on a blanket or towel, or just mist into the air and walk into it as it falls. You may like to add more essential oil if you prefer a stronger scent.

Be sure not to add coloring; I did that once and stained my sheets!

For this month's free printable, go to http://tyndal.es/homeandgarden.

YOU CAN'T DIY

One holds the ladder while another one screws in the lightbulb. One chops the vegetables while another makes the rice. One offers advice on a project she's already finished while her friend listens and picks up tips. One mother shares her completed parenting journey with a woman who has just put her feet upon the path. John Milton, author of *Paradise Lost*, wrote, "Loneliness is the first thing which God's eye named not good." God has provided us with family, friends, colleagues, and ultimately himself so we need not go through this life on our own.

I love working in my home and garden, and I enjoy watching all of the do-it-yourself shows on TV. I've noticed, though, that rarely is anyone on any of those shows "doing it yourself," as in, alone. There is a team of workers, craftsmen, friends, spouses, and all manner of helpers pitching in to get the job properly done. This is exactly right! Any project, as well as life itself, is not meant to be accomplished on our own. Grief divided, joy shared, and all that.

Whether your goal is to replace the flooring in your front room, put some drapes up in your first apartment, plant an herb garden to experiment with cooking, or just learn how to be a better friend, wife, mother, sister, or worker, you'll find guidance in your everyday life as God meets you—as he always does—right where you are.

A new year has begun, and a fresh start, like fresh sheets, ushers in a sense of renewal and comfort, a sense of being happy at home—even a home under remodeling, renovation, and upgrading. During our lives, we are under continual renovation. Welcome home!

May the God of hope fill you with all joy and peace as you trust in him,
so that you may overflow with hope by the power of the Holy Spirit.

ROMANS 15:13

BARED SOLES

A few years back I bought a small, cheerful plaque and installed it just outside our front door. It teases, "Please, bare your soles!" Although most guests are okay with this request, some (especially short people like me, who lose precious inches in the process) are uncomfortable at first. Bare feet make us feel vulnerable somehow. Humble. But also, perhaps, more intimate with those we then spend time with inside.

The reason behind the policy, of course, is to protect our home from the mud and muck that shoes inevitably pick up during daily life. Streets are dusted with dirt or iced with dirty snow. Sidewalks are pasted with chewed gum, and the car's carpet is littered with old french fries.

Even if you don't have a "Shoes off, please" sign, most people have a mat outside their front doors. Very often it says, "Welcome." Welcome, friends. Welcome, family. Welcome, strangers. It may have a lovely fleur-de-lis design or a sun painted on it, but it is also usually made with stiff bristles or tough rubber for serious cleaning. Considerate guests scrape their shoes against the mat before entering as a sign of respect for the home.

We read in Scripture that Joshua and Moses were commanded to remove their sandals as a gesture of respect in the presence of God. It's good to realize that God is near and personal, but we sometimes forget to treat him and his house with appropriate reverence. Sunday mornings can be a rush out the door. Before I leave for church, or at least on the way, I try to take a quiet moment for confession and repentance, scraping off the mud and muck of the week. Taking off my shoes before entering the building. Approaching God's house with humility, respect, and "clean feet." Not criticizing his family, his decor, or the music once I arrive in his house.

I want my guests to feel welcome, but I want them to respect my home too. How much more should I show respect when God welcomes me into *his* house!

When the Lord saw Moses coming to take a closer look, God called to him
from the middle of the bush. . . . "Do not come any closer," the Lord
warned. "Take off your sandals, for you are standing on holy ground."

EXODUS 3:4-5, NLT

HOUSEHOLD IDOLS

You might be surprised to know that I, a committed Christian of many years, have a household idol. Well, *I* don't say it's an idol, but my husband does. He says that my day goes according to what the idol tells me. If it gives me good news, I'm happy, and if it gives me bad news, I'm grumpy. I tend to visit it several times a day. You might think of it as a Magic 8 Ball for grown-ups.

I dance with my idol. Well, not really, but kind of. The hokey pokey. I put my left foot on, I move my left foot back, I put my right foot on, then I lean way forward or back, trying to get my idol to say what I want it to say.

You've guessed, haven't you? It's my scale.

I care about my health, and I know my weight affects that. This is the time of year when most of us think about weight and health. I'd rather be one size smaller next year than one size larger, and I want to be around to enjoy my family and friends for a good long time. To be healthy enough to do every good work that God has prepared for me would be wonderful. I've come to realize, though, that when I spend too much time fretting about my weight, I use up time and energy that might have been available for those good works, and I become vulnerable to self-condemnation, which makes me question my goodness, my beauty, or my abilities.

I still check my scale once in a while, and that's okay. But I'm not letting it guide my day or my mood anymore. Instead, I focus on the eternal tasks and values first, and on the God who tells me I am of great worth to him regardless of my earthly, gravity-bound weight.

For physical training is of some value, but godliness has value for all things, holding promise for both the present life and the life to come.

1 TIMOTHY 4:8

MEASURE TWICE, CUT ONCE

I sat in the guest room, alone, carefully taking measurements of my new distressed dresser so that I could precisely fit each drawer with a beautiful black-and-white French toile liner. I had purchased only two rolls, so if I measured incorrectly and came up short, one drawer would be—horrors!—unlined. What would my guests think? What would Martha do? Hubs had just told me that perhaps he himself would become as distressed as the dresser if I spent much more time and money fixing up the room. "It's only this one room," I told him. He looked at me skeptically. He'd heard that before.

While I took the measurements of the drawers, I also took measure of myself. Was that a promise I intended to keep—it's only this one room? Or would I break it? When I said things like that, did I really mean them, or had they become meaningless conversational patter, easily discarded when the stress of the moment had passed?

"If this medical test turns out okay, I really will start exercising every day."

"If I get this job/raise/bonus, we'll use the money only to pay off debt. And tithe."

"Once this room is finished, I'm done."

"After the holidays, I'm going to eat healthier."

The best of intentions often leads to the worst of follow-through. We make these "promises" to ourselves, to our loved ones, to the Lord. But when we don't hold ourselves to the words we say, something breaks. I took a long time to measure the pretty drawer liners because they cost me something. If I cut them too short, I could patch them together, but I could not make them whole again. "Measure twice, cut once," a seamstress friend once told me. Think things through before promising. Once cut, most things are not easily made whole again.

Don't trap yourself by making a rash promise to God
and only later counting the cost.

PROVERBS 20:25, NLT

January 5
ALWAYS IN HOT WATER
Part 1

We were fortunate to buy a house built by a master plumber. He'd installed brushed-nickel fixtures and high-quality toilets. (Honey, please remember to put the seat down.) But the most exciting element to discover was the radiant heat installed throughout the house.

Radiant heat uses a large water heater in the garage to send hot water coursing constantly through yards and yards of copper tubing underneath the flooring. The heat rises and heats the entire room. Best of all? Warm feet when you pad about on a cold winter's morning.

However, there is one catch. There must always be hot water available. If the water heater breaks down, it means not just cold showers, but a freezing house. So we have to make sure that water heater is always kept in running condition. If the water goes lukewarm, it's good for nothing.

Scripture speaks of that too. When we are cold, we realize (even if we don't always admit it) that we need to be warmed somehow. It's been said that agnostics and perhaps many atheists are simply people who have gone cold with disappointment or anger toward God. On-fire believers are called just that because they burn with passion to share the hope that lives within them. Lukewarm, however, is good for little. Washing delicates, maybe. Rinsing out your mouth. But who wants to be spit out? Not me.

Keeping the water in the tank hot requires regular maintenance (attending church), periodic inspections (accountability), and upgrading (study, exhortation) from time to time. It's all worth it, though, because these actions enable us to share warmth with everyone who enters our homes.

I know your deeds, that you are neither cold nor hot. I wish you were either one or the other! So, because you are lukewarm—neither hot nor cold—I am about to spit you out of my mouth.

REVELATION 3:15-16

January 6
ALWAYS IN HOT WATER
Part 2

So about that wonderful in-floor heating system. I still love it, and I'm glad we have it, but after fifteen years of use, it broke. (It was supposed to last twenty-five years.) We knew the system was expensive, so we prayed like mad that it would be repairable. Several hundred dollars for a fix seemed better than many thousands of dollars for a replacement. And after praying, I had peace about it. I just knew that it was going to be fixable. But it wasn't.

We got the bad news that the whole system needed to be replaced and that it would take a week—and a short-term loan—to do it. Later that evening, while I was waiting for an appointment, I kept praying. *Why didn't you just let it be repairable?* I asked God. *Or at least give us a big chunk of money to pay for it?*

As I sat there, praying and thinking, it came to me that when I pray, most often I ask God to forestall bad things or, if it's too late for that, to provide an immediate fix. But neither of those requests really requires me to have faith that God will work things out for good. He will work for good in whatever circumstance appears on my horizon, whatever trouble I must undergo—and he usually does it in such a clever, creative, superhuman manner that there is no doubt it was God at work.

Hebrews tells us that without faith, we cannot please God. So why would he remove every opportunity we may have to please him by trusting him, to knit our hearts ever more tightly with his? He won't, which means we have plenty of time to build that love and faith while in the midst of the muddle.

Without faith it is impossible to please God, because anyone who comes to him must believe that he exists and that he rewards those who earnestly seek him.

HEBREWS 11:6

January 7

LOST DOG

My heart always clutches a little when I spot a poster about a lost dog in our neighborhood. Usually the poster displays a picture of the beloved pet, the pet's name, and a plea to everyone who sees the poster to keep their eyes open for the missing pooch. At the bottom of the poster, the owner's phone number is always included with an appeal to please call if the dog is seen or found.

After driving by such a poster, especially in cold winter, I am more watchful. No, it's not my dog, but I have a dog, and I know what heartache it would cause if she were lost. I wouldn't have a moment of rest till she was found. She's a house dog, you see, and the dark, wet conditions of winter would not be conducive to her well-being. We'd miss her companionship. She'd wonder if we were looking for her. Of course we would be looking for her; we love her. It's easy for me to sympathize with the unknown owner of the lost dog, and so I reach out to help however I can.

Scripture tells us that Jesus came to find the one in one hundred who is lost. It's not that he doesn't care for the other ninety-nine—of course he does—but he knows they are safe and whole and warm. The lost one, though, may be cold, hungry, or frightened. She cannot live long on her own under such conditions. She must be found. Christ has invited us to help him in his work, to help him seek those who belong to him but who are lost. We are not his dogs, of course, but his beloved children. It is a cause for great rejoicing when the beloved is finally found and brought home.

The Son of Man came to seek and to save the lost.

LUKE 19:10

KEEPING RECEIPTS

One of the coolest gadgets I've bought for my office in a long time is a portable receipt scanner. Sure, you can take pictures with your smartphone and send them to your computer; I've done that. But the scanner has a really clear resolution, and best of all, it allows me to automatically send the receipts to various files on my computer. Otherwise, I'd likely end up with the digital equivalent of the cardboard box full of unsorted papers.

I like to keep receipts for returns, of course, but the main reason I keep them is for tax purposes. As a small-business owner and as the wife of a chaplain, I have a lot of odd tax categories and need to provide this information for my accountant. It brings me peace to know that the documentation is all there to prove my complete compliance with the law. If audited, I'm ready!

I'd love to think that most of us pay our taxes in full because we're good people. But I'm pretty sure it also helps that there is a slight, er, threat of an audit looming. Knowing that we may be called to account keeps us on the straight and narrow in case we are ever tempted to depart from it.

As Christians, we know that we will be asked by our Lord to account for the things we've said and done here on earth. We will be, in a very real sense, audited. How have we spent the resources we've been given? Whom have we loved? Did we seek the good of others or mostly our own? No heavenly scanner will be required; it will all be right at his fingertips. I try to be a good person, and I'll bet you do too. But it still helps keep me on the straight and narrow to remember that one day my accounts will be lovingly scrutinized.

We must all appear before the judgment seat of Christ, so
that each of us may receive what is due us for the things
done while in the body, whether good or bad.

2 CORINTHIANS 5:10

POLISHED AND PERFECT

One rainy day while I was doing a New Year's cleaning out of the garage, I happened upon a stash of toys I'd saved from my kids' childhoods. One favorite—the rock tumbler—beckoned. It was a favorite not only because we'd had fun together fashioning agate key chains and quartz rings but because I, too, had cherished a rock tumbler in my own childhood.

I reached for it, and as I held it in my hands, I recalled the week we'd purchased it as a treat—and a distraction. We'd just learned that our children would have to leave the school they enjoyed, one where they felt safe and I felt they were in a protected environment. Financial pressures caused us to make some hard choices, and the school had to go. *It's not fair*, I told God. *They are safe there.*

But maybe he didn't want my children to be safe, necessarily; rather, he wanted them to be useful, satisfied, and fulfilled. Christlike. I'd looked down at our new rock tumbler. We'd soon throw a bunch of sharp-edged, broken stones into it with some grit and water, then start the motor. The action of those sharp stones bumping up against one another would produce the smooth, polished gems we desired. Till the rocks had been tumbled and scraped, they were rough and common.

Likewise, the Lord wanted my children to be the polished, beautiful, and useful gems he and I both knew they could be. That wouldn't come about without bumping up against some sharp circumstances, though. I am thankful that a trusted hand was turning and guiding the tumbler that would transform my kids into just who God wanted them to be.

Dear brothers and sisters, when troubles of any kind come your way, consider it an opportunity for great joy. For you know that when your faith is tested, your endurance has a chance to grow. So let it grow, for when your endurance is fully developed, you will be perfect and complete, needing nothing.

JAMES 1:2-4, NLT

BE THE BACON

My guests were due to arrive in thirty minutes. The last time we got together with these friends, at their house, my husband had bragged on my cooking skills. But the fresh-herb ranch dip I'd just mixed up was not going to make me any new fans. Yes, it had buttermilk and sour cream (full-fat!), along with some snips of parsley, chives, and good old dried onions. But it was still . . . bland. It needed a flavor punch. And something with salt.

My mind returned to a cooking class a friend and I had attended a month or so earlier. "Bacon is the duct tape of the kitchen," the teacher had reassured us. "The recipe rescuer. It can fix anything no matter what has gone wrong."

Bacon! The best of salt and savory seasonings combined. I opened the fridge and pulled out a bag of bacon crumbles and stirred a generous handful into the dip. Ten minutes later, a taste test confirmed creamy victory. The bacon was a complete game changer, bringing out the best in the other seasonings and adding life. The crumbles had, I suppose, saved my bacon and my culinary reputation!

You, my friend, are a bacon crumble in the dip of life. Scripture tells us that Christians are the salt of the earth, here to season with truth and wisdom, to bring out the best in others through grace and affection, to point the way for the spiritually lifeless. Of course, most of the problems we and our family and friends face are much more serious than a failed appetizer. Jobs that disappear and disappoint, difficult children, difficult parents, financial challenges, disillusionment, and health setbacks. These situations can seem overwhelming and, often, beyond repair.

Although we can't solve every problem (or even most problems) on our own or for those we love, we are on intimate terms with the one who can, Jesus Christ. We bring him with us wherever we go, into every situation we ourselves face or those we face hand in hand with a friend. He is the rescuer who can fix anything. He may change our circumstances, or he may give us the grace to persevere through them.

Salt is good for seasoning.

MARK 9:50, NLT

January 11
BLOSSOMS IN WINTER

Witch hazel trees are a hidden delight, although they are nondescript during spring and summer. When every other plant is flaunting blossoms and beautiful foliage, the witch hazel sends out leathery green leaves. Boring. Unremarkable. Not the horticultural eye candy that merits a stop on the city garden tour.

In autumn, things start to look up as those leathery leaves evolve into bright, coppery tongues. They are soon lost, along with every other deciduous tree's offerings, just as the chill sets in. But when the glory of Christmas has passed and we're in for a long, dull slog through mud and ice, the witch hazel proves its worth. In coldest January, it shoots out stunning flowers of red and orange confetti, like spent firecrackers. When all else is dormant, it releases brightness and joy.

Scripture speaks of things that blossom in difficult places—deserts; wildernesses; dry, cold patches of land and of soul. When everything is sunny and flowering, it's easy to overlook a particular plant or bud among the abundance. But when the landscape has gone dull and quiet, that one unusual bloom stands out as a ray of hope pointing toward what is to come.

God has sent kind souls into our lives to be those rays of optimism in dry, cold patches. He's also asked us to be a splash of joy in someone else's dismal day. I think I most appreciate those friends who are there for me when the sun is hidden and the ground is dry. It causes me to wonder, this winter day, to whom can I bring a word, a hug, a blossom of hope as a reminder of the promise of beauty just around the corner?

The desert and the parched land will be glad;
the wilderness will rejoice and blossom.
Like the crocus, it will burst into bloom;
it will rejoice greatly and shout for joy.

ISAIAH 35:1-2

GROWTH CHARTS

We were unloading the last boxes from the moving truck, stacking them all around the garage till they could be brought inside and unpacked. As I set one box on another, some markings on the garage wall caught my eye.

Each mark was a line, perhaps an inch in length, even and steady and clearly drawn against a straight edge. Next to each line was a name and a date. The markings made their way up a vertical line like the markings on a glass bulb thermometer. I smiled because I recognized them. They were growth marks.

The previous homeowners had recorded their children's heights over the years, and I saw how each child had grown from a wee sprite to a fully grown adult—a towering, six-foot adult in one case! Seeing this brought a pleasant wave of nostalgia. My grandmother had such a wall on her porch, marking the growth of each of her grandkids.

We all grow physically, so steadily and silently that, unless someone takes time to mark that growth, it happens almost without notice. Over the years when I'd looked at my grandmother's wall, I'd been surprised—and pleased—to see how I'd grown several feet, inch by inch.

Once we're adults, we no longer mark our physical growth, as we mostly stop growing (except in girth, but that's another story!). As Christians, though, we continue to grow, especially in grace toward ourselves and others and in knowledge of the Lord, whom we come to better understand and love. We might not mark our progress on the garage wall, but you can be sure that others will notice it. Although it's happening silently, with the Spirit's power it's happening steadily. Can you see it? Do you sense it? Look back a few years and compare. Your growth shows in the things you do and say, and in the way people turn to you for comfort and answers. You grow, girl!

Grow in the grace and knowledge of our Lord and Savior Jesus Christ. To him be glory both now and forever! Amen.

2 PETER 3:18

THERE'S AN APP FOR THAT

I bemoaned to a friend the other day that once an idea pops into my head, I have to write it down or I will forget it. My modern-day version of Post-it notes is to send myself a text and not delete it till I've done whatever I've reminded myself to do.

The Lord exhorts us many times in Scripture to remember what's important. We're to remember that he's coming soon and that he forgives us when we repent, so we must forgive others when they repent. The Israelites were to celebrate the Passover as a reminder that God had freed them from slavery. Christians are to celebrate the Lord's Supper as a reminder that Christ has freed us from sin through his death and resurrection.

The book of Numbers records the Lord's instruction that the people of Israel wear tassels on the hems of their clothing to remind them to obey him and be holy. When the Israelites walked, the tassels would rustle against their legs, a physical nudge. They'd see those tassels on other people, and it would bring his commands to mind.

Most Christians don't wear tassels today, but we have modern-day tools at hand that can remind us to be obedient to God. Wherever I go, I must admit, I bring my smartphone. While some decry our dependence on our phones, it is true that they can help us remember God's Word. There are Bible-memory apps to help me memorize verses and Scripture-of-the-day apps to exhort and encourage. I can listen to an audio Bible while I do housework. I'm so glad that God provides the means for us to do what he asks. The methods have changed, but the command to remember his instructions has not.

The LORD said to Moses, "Give the following instructions to the people of Israel: Throughout the generations to come you must make tassels for the hems of your clothing and attach them with a blue cord. When you see the tassels, you will remember and obey all the commands of the LORD instead of following your own desires and defiling yourselves, as you are prone to do."

NUMBERS 15:37-39, NLT

PIONEER WOMEN

We received a bread maker for Christmas, a shiny, muscular machine that promised warm loaves, chewy pizza crusts, and the smell of home-baked bread wafting through the kitchen any day at all. Paging through the booklet of recipes, I came upon one for sourdough bread and decided to start there. We'd first need sourdough starter, though—the pioneer woman's self-renewing equivalent of a modern-day packet of yeast.

The starter is a mother batch of sourdough from which you draw the natural leavening and which, in proper conditions and with some additions, regenerates itself continuously. Getting a bit of starter from friends or family is one way to start your own, but you can also create a starter from nothing but warm water, flour, and circulating air. Given the right conditions, yeast spores, which are all around us, will settle right in and begin to ferment.

Scripture talks about yeast too. Often, though, yeast is not portrayed positively; many times it represents sin. Like starter, sin grows when unchecked, and the potential for it is all around us in our everyday lives. If we give it a warm place to settle and land, it's sure to multiply. Soon it begins to take over and work its way into everything we do, or at least the parts of our lives we give it access to.

However, if we stop adding ingredients for it to feed on or remove the conditions that allow it to grow, sin, like the sourdough starter, will die. It's a strange truth of life that most of the things that are bad for us are often mixed up in things that are good for us. We can be thankful that the Spirit helps us discern which is which and then encourages us to remove the conditions in which sin thrives.

Your boasting is not good. Don't you know that a little yeast leavens the whole batch of dough? Get rid of the old yeast, so that you may be a new unleavened batch—as you really are. For Christ, our Passover lamb, has been sacrificed. Therefore let us keep the Festival, not with the old bread leavened with malice and wickedness, but with the unleavened bread of sincerity and truth.

1 CORINTHIANS 5:6-8

January 15
DIRTY DISHES

I don't know why, but unloading the dishwasher is one of my least favorite chores. My daughter's, too. She's been known to throw in a fresh detergent cube and start the machine up again just to delay the inevitable. I don't go that far, but sometimes I do walk away and ignore the chore for a while. But if the sink is full of dirty dishes, I'm left with two unpleasant options: unload the dishwasher or wash by hand. Eventually I have to do one or the other if I don't want the mess to expand.

Very often we take joy in our faith, but sometimes the working out of that faith on a practical basis seems more like a task than a calling. When things are falling apart, I often don't feel like offering praise and finding one (seemingly tiny) good thing to be grateful for while my scales are heavily balanced on the side of sorrow. I don't want to worship when I feel like crying, partly because I know worship brings those tears to the forefront. However, if I want to move forward and not let the mess expand, at some point I have to take a step, going through the motions even if I don't feel like it.

Praise is often a sacrifice, but God makes it clear in Scripture that he values our sacrifices, which, by definition, come at a cost. Soul work, like housework, takes discipline. But when I do what is right even when I don't feel like it, I discover that in the mysterious economy of God, praise unlocks my spirit to let the grief out and the sunshine in.

Soon enough, I have pushed through, cleaned up what needed to be cleaned up, and made it through the worst of it. My house is then in order, literally and spiritually. Joy is often the fruit of discipline, not the seed that produces it.

Through Jesus, therefore, let us continually offer to God a sacrifice of praise—the fruit of lips that openly profess his name.

HEBREWS 13:15

KIBBLES AND BITS

One day when my kids were young, I found them crouched, heads down, over our dog's food bowl. The dog stood a fair distance away from them, seemingly as confused as I was. I looked at her and she looked back; I could almost see her shrug. *Don't ask me, I have no idea what they're doing either.*

Being the calm, collected mom that I am, I shouted, "What in the world are you doing?" One child looked up at me and coolly said, "Eating dog food." Perhaps I was a little dull if that was unclear to me. The other said, "The Bible says that dogs eat what falls from the master's table, so we wondered what food that fell from the dog's bowl tasted like." But the looks on their faces indicated that they knew they'd been caught doing something they shouldn't.

I held back a smile. "What does it taste like?" Noses wrinkled. "Dusty graham crackers." I guessed that even if I hadn't interrupted them, the experiment would have soon been over and they would be rummaging through the pantry for Oreos to cleanse their dusty palates.

So often we wonder what it tastes like, that which is not intended for us. Is it good? Would we like it? Would it live up to our expectations? Sometimes we even act on the impulse and then, when caught, we feel guilty. Even though it may taste good for a moment, if it's not for us, it will always leave a bad taste, a sense that we are doing something we shouldn't. None of us, even a young child, believes that dog food is good for people. Better to turn away from it, toward the sweet, palate-cleansing property of Oreos—and the sweet Word.

I haven't turned away from your regulations,
for you have taught me well.
How sweet your words taste to me;
they are sweeter than honey.
Your commandments give me understanding;
no wonder I hate every false way of life.

PSALM 119:102-104, NLT

HAPPINESS IN A BOX

I lingered at the display in the big-box store. On special was the HappyLight Energy Lamp, promising relief from winter depression in a mere thirty minutes per day.

Most of us who live in the Northern Hemisphere understand seasonal affective disorder (SAD), the depression that comes with the clotting of winter clouds, the relentless months of darkness, and—at least in my hometown of Seattle—the 24-7 rain that waters our gardens. We laugh when people visit in the summer and pronounce the area an Eden. *Ah, but can you tough out six months of rain every year to pay for the lush growth in Eden?*

What can temper the gloom? The HappyLight lamp says it can help.

Thirty minutes each day, with the lamp box set behind a computer or a book so that you can catch the spectrum light in your peripheral vision, can make a difference for many people. You don't even have to focus on it! Just make sure it's there, you're there, and it's turned on.

Life, too, seems to be separated into periods of sun and periods of unrelenting clouds. When the gloom sets in, it sometimes sets in for months. Most of us can't afford to spend the six dark months in Mexico, nor can we leave a difficult job, a tiresome relative, or a persistent financial problem whenever it appears. We need something to help us right where we are.

Clinical depression needs clinical treatment. But if you're just feeling a bit "down," try some praise or upbeat music in the background. A verse of Scripture printed out and affixed to the bathroom mirror. A comical movie. A midday treat: tomato soup with cheese chunks or a cookie heated in the microwave. These are all in your peripheral "vision," nothing you need to concentrate on, but perhaps they will lift your spirits through a dark day. Soon, spring will arrive, the clouds will part, and things will look bright again. Those rains inevitably bring lush growth in your spirit, too.

*We who have fled to him for refuge can have great confidence
as we hold to the hope that lies before us. This hope is
a strong and trustworthy anchor for our souls.*

HEBREWS 6:18-19

January 18
FORCED BLOOMS

I love browsing the floral department in my grocery store in the wintertime. There are the usual assortments of cacti, cut flowers flown in from the south, and stunning forced-bloom forsythia. The forsythia are noble—long, leggy branches with yellow buds exploding through a skin of thin bark. Eye catching. Almost prideful.

Once while browsing, I began thinking about those forced blooms, considering which of my shrubs I could snip from to produce the same effect. But I quickly realized that while cutting branches from my bushes would provide one week's worth of beauty, it would deprive me of the years of enjoyment that the branch could give me if I left it on the shrub. Once cut and forced to bloom away from its natural environment, the branch slowly dies.

I'd been wrestling with one of my children that week about a personal choice. Nudged to Scripture, I read a familiar passage in Proverbs 22. I'd always taken it to be marching orders to train my kids in the faith, but this time I took a closer look. *The way they should go.* That did not necessarily mean the way I thought they should go.

My children are each uniquely created; they are not copies of me, or of my husband, or of anyone else. They have singular, God-given destinies, works he created in advance for them alone to do. Their schooling or career choices might not be what I'd thought they would be. They might choose different hairstyles or ink their skin. They may worship at a different kind of church or listen to different music. But if I help them to grow in their God-given direction, God will enjoy years—even decades—of them blooming for his glory. God does not want my children to be forced to bloom out of place for the sake of my enjoyment or pride. He wants them to be nurtured to maturity and bloom when and where he'd intended all along.

Start children off on the way they should go,
and even when they are old they will not turn from it.

PROVERBS 22:6

POWER BARS

One morning Hubs dug through the pantry before work.

"What are you looking for?" I asked.

"An afternoon snack," he said. "I'm dragging by the middle of the day, and I need to take a snack to work."

I told him I'd look for something appropriate when I was out shopping. He suggested lots of dark chocolate, which made me smile. I thought a protein bar might be more helpful. But when I got to the store, I found that many of the protein bars were worse, nutritionally, than candy bars. Lots of sugar, lots of trans fats, not enough protein to help him go the distance. Truth is, a candy bar masquerading as a power bar can fool our taste buds, but when it gets down to giving us the energy we need to push past three o'clock in the afternoon, that imposter doesn't have what it takes. We've got to build ourselves up inside in order to tackle challenges on the outside. After a little more searching, I found a handful of snacks that were good for us, as well as easily accessible during a busy day.

It takes a lot of energy to get through each day, whether we work at home, outside the home, or both. We need real sustenance to persevere, to make it through. This is true when it comes to feeding our spirits, too. Rather than relying on "candy bars" to power up my spirit—electronic distractions, empty TV treats, or excessive social media—I can pull on an unlimited supply of true nutrition, available day and night from our Lord. I'm definitely not against candy bars! I'm just learning how to enjoy them without relying on them instead of that which truly empowers.

I pray that from his glorious, unlimited resources he will
empower you with inner strength through his Spirit.

EPHESIANS 3:16, NLT

COMFORT

It's flu season, and I did not get a shot. Bad decision.

I've quarantined myself; I'm not seeing anyone except for my family and one faithful friend who has not been put off by my illness or even my potential contagion. Each day she stops by and makes sure I have what I need. Although I hate being sick, it's so nice to be cared for.

Sometimes, sickies young and old are tucked into a comfy bed or on the best couch in the house with a fuzzy blanket and a squished pillow. We get to pick what to watch on TV, or read some favorite books, or nap. My friend whipped up the only thing I wanted to eat: tomato soup with melted cheese. She also left hot chocolate in a pan on the stove, ready to be heated and sprinkled with tiny marshmallows.

Sometimes life's afflictions are simple and common, like a bout with the flu. Sometimes they are so difficult we're uncertain how, or if, we'll make our way through. We can't always change our circumstances; sometimes we just have to walk through them. But some things help—soothing rituals, calm friends, rest (wanted or not) that relieves and recharges. Best of all are our loved ones, whether family, or friends, or even pets. In his mercy, God, the author of all good things, sends others our way, knowing that when the rain falls, a shared umbrella can help. When the sun comes out again, we are to hold on to that umbrella and be watchful for a friend to invite underneath when it begins to rain in *her* world.

Every call or text received, pot of soup made, or hug offered reminds us that love will pull us through.

All praise to God, the Father of our Lord Jesus Christ. God is our merciful Father and the source of all comfort. He comforts us in all our troubles so that we can comfort others. When they are troubled, we will be able to give them the same comfort God has given us. For the more we suffer for Christ, the more God will shower us with his comfort through Christ.

2 CORINTHIANS 1:3-5, NLT

MRS. BEASLEY AND JESUS

When I was a kid, pretty much all my friends had a stuffed animal or a doll that was special to them, one that was so loved-on that it grew fragile over the years. We took our "love objects" with us wherever we went. When we were sad little things, they stayed right beside us, always listening, helping us to stop feeling bad. When we were worried, their cushy hugginess made us feel like everything was going to be okay. Love objects are faithful, no matter what.

Okay, confession time. My love object's name was Mrs. Beasley, and I still have her in my closet.

No, I don't take her out to hug anymore! But she meant a lot to me, and I keep her for nostalgic reasons as well as to help me remember what it was like to be a little girl.

Most of us outgrow our stuffed animals and dolls, but we never outgrow our need to have others to love and to be the recipients of their love in return. We'll always need someone to feel safe with, to share our deepest secrets with, to take with us when we go to new places and want to feel safe. And when we know Christ, we can have all that and more.

Not only is Jesus always there for us, he's always strong, and he loves us back, firmly, continuously—unlike our childhood love objects. We never outgrow him. In fact, as we get older, he can grow closer and more important to us than ever. He always listens, reassuring us in a way that an inanimate object never could, letting us know that everything will be okay and that we will never be alone.

Jesus is faithful, no matter what.

As you fall asleep tonight, think about the fact that you are the focus of great love from Jesus, a great love that will never diminish or be outgrown.

Be sure of this: I am with you always.

MATTHEW 28:20, NLT

January 22
CINNAMON ROLLS

One of the best smells in the world is the smell of cinnamon rolls baking in the oven. It's only fair, then, that it should be followed by one of the best tastes in the world: soft, gooey rolls (with butter!). But cinnamon rolls don't just magically appear, even if you buy them at the mall. Someone has to bake them. In my house, that would be me.

After mixing together all the ingredients, including that delightful cinnamon, I have a gloppy ball of speckled, white dough. This dough isn't like cookie dough; it doesn't taste good if you sneak a taste of it raw (I've tried). I have to divide the dough into pieces, then roll them out, brush them with cinnamon sugar and butter, roll them up, and let them sit on the cookie sheet to rise. And rise. And rise!

If I put the rolls into the oven before they are done rising, my family is treated to a doughy, deflated disk instead of a puffy roll. But if I wait the full time, then after baking . . . *mmm*!

I think this is what life is like. There are many good things ahead for each of us. God has promised a future and a hope. But each event in our lives, each privilege, each good time will come at just the right moment. Sometimes we have to wait for it. Look forward to it. Plan ahead for it. But don't force it too soon, unless you like dough disks instead of the tasty puffs you'll get if you wait upon his timing.

God blesses you who are hungry now, for you will be satisfied.

LUKE 6:21, NLT

January 23

TREADING WATER

Sometimes in the winter I stop by the YMCA near my house and use the pool to exercise. One day while waiting for the free swim, I watched some of the upper-division students. It brought back happy memories of the lessons of my youth.

One of the final tests, I recalled, was to jump into the water fully dressed to see how we would survive a highly stressful long-term stay in the deep. We were instructed to remove our backpacks, kick off our shoes and let them sink to the bottom, and strip off almost all our clothes. The pants we held onto, tying off each leg and blowing into them to create a flotation device, which we then wrapped around our necks. Then we turned onto our backs and calmly floated till we were "rescued."

The students who remained weighted down or who paddled furiously or tried to swim, no matter how skilled they were, soon ran out of energy. Tired and heavily burdened by their wet clothing, they risked sinking to the bottom of the pool just like those waterlogged shoes.

Often we women take on the problems and burdens of everyone around us—our friends, our kids, our loved ones—on top of all of our own burdens, till we feel like we're drowning.

In hard times, especially those that seem like they might include a long-term stay in the deep, our tendency is to *do* something. Anything! In fact, it's kind of an insult to be told you're treading water or floating through life while everyone around you seems to be kicking or swimming.

Relax. Turn onto your back and look, face up, for help. The Lord loves you. He not only holds the world in his hand, but he holds you: your life, your troubles, your worries. Next time you find yourself in the deep, release everything that burdens you, and let it sink. Slow down. Float. Wait for his rescue, because it will surely come.

Come to me, all you who are weary and burdened, and I will give you rest.

MATTHEW 11:28

MINISTRY OF A MESS

There was a pile of toys on the floor—I'd stepped on several building blocks and let out a loud cry of pain. Someone had taken a five-hundred-count box of tissues and pulled them out, one by one. Apparently no one had let the dog out. The shoes were reproducing themselves in the corner. Why is it that dirty clothes seem to generate spontaneously?

We'd had Bible study here the night before, and I hadn't gotten to the dishes yet. My home office was stacked with files and books that looked like multiple Leaning Towers of Pisa.

I like a clean house, I really do. I like my office tidy too. But as it has been said many times by many people, there are only so many hours in a day. I had to make some choices—which were more important? Comforting a child who'd been bullied or throwing away the rotting lettuce in my refrigerator? Taking a call from a friend whose mother had been diagnosed with terminal cancer or balancing the checkbook? Some rare days I'm caught up, but mostly, I'm not. And that's okay.

A messy desk is a sign of a productive mind. A kitchen with dirty dishes is being used. Toys all over the room mean kids are playing. Books splayed about on every surface prove we're reading and learning. A hug from my kid means that she believes she's going to recover.

Scripture tells us that a barn in disarray means that there are working animals present; things are happening there. Without the oxen, nothing gets done. At the end of the day, or the week, or our lives, no one will remember how clean (or not) our houses were, but they'll remember and feel, deep down, how we loved and cared for them there.

Without oxen a stable stays clean,
but you need a strong ox for a large harvest.

PROVERBS 14:4, NLT

January 25

MIRROR, MIRROR, ON THE WALL

My daughter had a friend who, I thought, had bladder issues. Every time she arrived at our house, she would immediately ask to use the bathroom. Of course we always said okay, and soon she no longer asked. She just headed into the powder room upon arrival, and nearly every hour on the hour thereafter.

One day she asked to use the upstairs bathroom. "Of course," I said, and after she headed up the stairs, I looked wonderingly at my daughter.

"She's addicted to mirrors," she whispered to me. "She doesn't think she's pretty."

There was currently no mirror in the powder room, which was being painted. So the friend had gone upstairs for her hourly hair check. "She's beautiful," I whispered back.

"She doesn't think so," my daughter answered.

So many girls, so many women, myself included, let their sense of self-worth be dictated by how pretty they think others perceive them to be. We can hardly help it—"ideals" of beauty are thrown at us everywhere, even in church, where heads in pews naturally turn toward the pretty and well dressed.

Just before that young lady came over the next time, we scrawled, with an erasable marker, on the mirror in each bathroom, "You are altogether beautiful." We plucked that passage from Song of Songs 4:7: "You are altogether beautiful, my darling; there is no flaw in you." She got a kick out of it and laughed, but I think it sank in. My daughter said it did. As for me, well, I didn't remove the phrase from the mirror in *my* bathroom. I struggle too. Each morning, that message brings a smile and a lightened step.

You are precious to me. You are honored, and I love you.

ISAIAH 43:4, NLT

AS SEEN ON TV!

Here's what I always wanted as a kid: sea monkeys. The comic books I bought promised that if only I would send in one dollar, they'd send me a packet of sea monkeys, complete with father, mother, and little monkeys—all wearing crowns! Now that I'm grown, I'm attracted to products that promise me an instant lawn, perfectly green, within weeks. Or products that promise to take pounds off of my frame without changing my diet or exercise habits. Want something to make your old beater look better than a new car? I can point you to an ad.

The truth is, we're blessed to live in an era in which there are so many products to entertain, assist, and encourage us. The trick is to find which ones genuinely work and which ones only want to part you from your money without giving you the hoped-for results. Usually I buy products from sources that offer a money-back guarantee. I can test them out for myself, prove them, use them, and then pass along the good news to my friends.

Likewise, many claims are made in the name of the Bible or the name of the Lord. Some of them sound, frankly, too good to be true. The way to sort theological truths from misleading errors is to test them yourself. Hold up claims against Scripture—the full counsel of Scripture, as the Bereans were praised for, not just cherry-picked verses—and you'll soon see that truth is proven and lies are exposed. I don't want to count on dropping the pounds effortlessly, and I don't want to pass along false hope to my friends.

The Berean Jews were of more noble character than those in Thessalonica,
for they received the message with great eagerness and examined
the Scriptures every day to see if what Paul said was true.

ACTS 17:11

READ THE DIRECTIONS

I couldn't figure out how the box for such a large piece of furniture could comfortably fit inside the back of our car, but it did! We happily made our way home, envisioning the television and books arranged on the new piece, thinking and talking about how it would enhance our lives. Once home, I understood how the box had fit into the car. When it was opened, dozens of pieces fell out, along with a hefty tome labeled "Assembly Instructions."

Now, I'm the person who scrolls all the way through the dozen pages of digital agreements for apps and websites, not reading, just clicking on "I Agree." I was not going to waste an hour reading directions, when putting part AA into part ZZ with screw HH and bolt 253 couldn't be that hard! An hour later, the piece was assembled. Two hours later, it wobbled and nearly collapsed, almost taking the TV with it.

I went back to the instructions. Surprising things can be found when one reads the directions. Humbled, I reassembled the piece of furniture in the proper order, thankful that I had not done any lasting damage.

Surprising things, too, can be found when we read sections of the Bible that we thought we knew. I find myself saying, much too often, "I know the Bible says _____, but I can't remember where." Or, "Memorization is my worst discipline." Or, "I remember it's something like . . ." Unfortunately, too often when I take the time to look up the exact verse, I realize I've forgotten some crucial points. I've learned that I'd better not quote the Sandra Paraphrase, because it's close enough to sound good but far enough off to do some real damage.

Read the instructions, and follow them closely, I tell myself. Structural integrity of the Word, passed on, is much more important than the security of the TV.

Do your best to present yourself to God as one approved, a worker who does
not need to be ashamed and who correctly handles the word of truth.

2 TIMOTHY 2:15

ADAM? EVE? SETH? CAIN? ABEL?

We have a running joke in my family involving a family member who can never remember names—especially the kids' and grandkids'. Instead, he just sits on the sofa and randomly calls out names one after the other, hoping someone will respond. We have learned not to answer, though, because the person he is looking for is usually in trouble of some sort. I will answer, eventually, but only to my own name.

A lot of times we parents think that our children—and their habits, their seeming "success," their grades, their jobs, their spouses, their manners, even their criminality or their unwise choices—reflect on us. If they are seen as successful, we're deemed good, effective parents who have done our jobs well. If they are seen as struggling, the silent questioning of where and when we might have done something different begins. Of course, parents have tremendous influence on their children, but God has gifted us with free will, too. My parents are not responsible for my failures, nor can they take credit for my success. This is true with my own grown children too. We are all accountable for ourselves.

Cain and Abel had the same parents. God is the parent of many children, some who may be seen as successful and some who may be seen as failures (though God, of course, looks at the heart and not the outward appearance). When my children struggle, I pray for them and offer counsel, but I don't own their struggle. When they are victorious, I celebrate with them, but I don't claim their victory.

To maintain your joy and sanity, remember: in the end, we answer only for ourselves!

Each of us will give a personal account to God.

ROMANS 14:12, NLT

A LIFE, FRAMED

A few years ago I received a digital photo frame as a gift. I love it! You can load digital photos into the lovely frame, then hang it on a wall or place it on a piece of furniture. All through the day the photos scroll, an ever-changing parade of very personal art. I've taken to loading the previous year's photos at the end of each year, a kind of review, if you will, of the highlights just passed. I enjoy looking back over the year just ended and looking forward to what the new year may hold.

As I look through the photos, I can see how my family has grown, how we've changed, and how we've been renewed or, sometimes, worn down by the circumstances that life has thrown at us during the year. A difficult good-bye is often followed by an unexpected hello. A painful passage through illness is often bookended by events planned to help us first persevere and then celebrate. As I review the previous year's highlights over and over, I realize that I have the opportunity to plan for the events this year will hold—or at least how I'll react to them.

Scrolling through a year in just a few minutes reminds me how fleeting life is. We are born, we grow, and soon we are gone. A seed becomes a shoot, then it flowers, and finally it withers. A house is bought, lived in, and then sold. The cycle of life continues; there truly is nothing new under the sun.

How will we spend this quickly passing life? What memories can I make today, what help can I offer, what blessing can I share that I will want to review? God will review my life with me, when my time comes. And that time is coming, no matter how young and vibrant we feel, before we know it.

LORD, what are human beings that you care for them,
mere mortals that you think of them?
They are like a breath;
their days are like a fleeting shadow.

PSALM 144:3-4

January 30
MISE EN PLACE

The rain sluiced the kitchen windows, sliding down the panes in gray rivulets. Turning on the oven, I was glad that I did not need to leave the house that day. I planned to spend it listening to music, taking care of a few household tasks, and baking cookies.

First, baking cookies!

I turned the oven on and began taking things out of the pantry. After mixing the dry ingredients, I set them aside and went for the wet. It didn't take me long to figure out something was wrong. I was out of vanilla. Completely. My choices were either to forget about baking and throw away the ingredients I'd already mixed or run out to the store (in that torrent!) to buy vanilla. This was becoming an unpleasant habit. A week earlier I'd had guests over for fondue and, since I had made it from scratch many times, I went ahead and did so without looking at the recipe. But I'd forgotten about cornstarch, which meant we had a giant glop of cheese instead of a smooth, creamy dip.

The French have a baking and cooking concept called *mise en place*, which means setting out all of the important ingredients, premeasured, before beginning. I didn't think I needed that ahead-of-time preparation, and I didn't want to wash extra dishes. But baking and cooking without preparation, even with familiar recipes, can lead to failure. Without an essential ingredient, no dish will be successful.

As I trudged to the car, a verse about preparation ran through my mind. Did I have my *mise en place* ready for sharing my faith? How long had it been since I'd run through the essential components: my life before and after, the saving grace of Christ, the verses that pointed the way? A long time.

I made it home and dried off, and while the cookies baked, I rehearsed my testimony once again. Even beloved recipes need a run-through now and again.

Always be prepared to give an answer to everyone who asks
you to give the reason for the hope that you have.

1 PETER 3:15

ON THE BOTTOM

My husband and I drove to the big-box store in stony silence, not really angry with one another but kind of mad that we were there at all. It was an hour after work. We were both tired, and rather than doing the shopping for the week, it would have been nice to rest, read, watch TV, take a walk, eat a cookie. Anything but errands. It seemed that there was never time to just relax; it was always one chore after another. Duty following duty.

We flashed our membership card, and I wielded the cart while he plucked things off shelves and added them to our growing pile. Chicken, check. Vegetables, check. Five-pound bag of coffee beans to power us through the next set of duties, check.

"Grab the toilet paper." I nodded toward the plastic-wrapped package of about thirty-six rolls. *That ought to last a month or two,* I thought.

"Where's that going to fit?" He eyed the cart, already packed full.

"Put it on the bottom," I instructed.

He started to laugh. "Where else would I put toilet paper?" And then I started to laugh, too, and neither of us cared if those around us stared. It turned the whole evening around.

Life often seems like duty following duty, crisis riding high on the crest of the crisis that just passed, with a few lulls in between to catch our breath. There's no getting around the storms or the busyness; the fastest way out is straight through, it's been said. But when you can make the journey with a joke and a smile, the trip is more enjoyable. Look for places to insert humor each and every day. It's healing. The ride home was filled with chatter—tired chatter, but pleasant, nonetheless.

A cheerful heart is good medicine.

PROVERBS 17:22

FEBRUARY

Boyfriend-Bait Beef Stroganoff

While this dish can be used to bait a boyfriend, it's an equally excellent recipe to prepare for friends and family on special occasions, to lure home a college kid, or to whip up for yourself when you're hankering something meaty and creamy.

WHAT YOU'LL NEED

1 1/2 pounds beef tenderloin, trimmed and cut into bite-sized pieces

4 tablespoons butter, divided

1 cup shallots, finely chopped

3 cups mushrooms, sliced

2 cups cold beef broth or stock

3 teaspoons cornstarch

1 cup sour cream

2 tablespoons Dijon mustard

DIRECTIONS

Over medium-high heat, melt 2 tablespoons of butter and add beef tenderloin. Cook, turning occasionally, for about 2 minutes until seared on all sides. You will still be able to see some red. Set aside.

Add remaining butter to a new pan and melt over medium-high heat. Add the shallots and mushrooms and cook until slightly browned, soft, and wilted, about 5 minutes.

Whisk together the cornstarch and beef broth. Pour mixture into the pan with the shallots and mushrooms and stir. Let the mixture simmer until thickened, about 2–3 minutes.

Add the sour cream, mustard, beef, and juices to the pan. Stir and reduce heat to medium. Cook until just warmed for rare beef, or continue cooking a few additional minutes to desired doneness. Add salt and pepper to taste. Serve over rice, riced cauliflower, mashed potatoes, or egg noodles.

For this month's free printable, go to http://tyndal.es/homeandgarden.

February 1

ARM'S REACH, NOT ARM'S LENGTH

Some friends from Europe were staying with us for a few days, resting and relaxing in our home and becoming a part of the family. Their children were grown; ours were still at home. I quickly learned that the cell phone revolution had happened after their kids had left home when I got a flurry of texts followed by a call one day as I sat downstairs with our guests in the family room.

"All right," I spoke into the phone after having texted back and forth for about five minutes. "I'll be right there." I clicked the phone off and stood.

One friend looked at me. "Who was that, then?"

I named my daughter.

"But she's . . . just upstairs."

I nodded. "Low-cost intercom system," I said, suddenly a little embarrassed that we'd resorted to texting and calling one another in our own home rather than taking a few moments to walk over and speak face to face. "And I'm going to talk with her in person now."

"Americans," our friend muttered with affection, turning back to his newspaper.

Technology has helped to connect us, certainly. Texting an "I love you" or "How is your day going?" is a quick way to check in without disrupting a day. Phoning to catch up with a friend while waiting for the tires to be rotated is a good way to keep in touch. But technology also allows us to remain at arm's length for conversations that would be better done in person, when facial expressions can be seen and shared. Connection at a distance can't foster the intimacy created by face-to-face discussions and the closure of a hug. Checkups are good via phone, but earnest love is best expressed with hands and arms and smiles, not fast-texting thumbs.

I hope to see you soon, and we will talk face to face. Peace to you.

3 JOHN 1:14

February 2

REPAIR, REPURPOSE, AND RENEW

We had a well-loved couch in our house; it had been around nearly as long as we'd been married. No matter where anyone sat on it, they would soon gently tumble to the center. To say that the springs and supports were shot would be an understatement. In addition, the fabric was worn and a little stained. It looked tired. Loved, but tired.

I had a friend who did custom reupholstering, and I asked him if it would be feasible to rework our old charmer. He assured me it was, so I chose some new stain-resistant fabric and dropped off our sofa at his workshop. A month later I picked it up. Our sofa had spring and bounce! It was stain free and like new on the outside. Inside, though, was the same frame that had carried us through movies and books and cuddles and arguments for decades. What was old was made new again, and we kept the best of both worlds (and saved money over buying new)!

Relationships, like couches and people, often need a little freshening up. We fall into bad habits or patterns of taking one another for granted. Our interactions might be stained with wrongs unaddressed or strained with hurt feelings left unforgiven. Christ promises he can regenerate us, and he can regenerate our relationships, too.

What can we do to partner with Christ in that regeneration? Consider these three *R*s of relationships:

- *Repair* by looking for broken pieces caused by careless words, lack of time or love, or a hardened or selfish spirit.
- *Repurpose* each important relationship to vibrancy with some new activities or times to connect as you pass into new seasons of life.
- *Renew* your commitment to the other person, be it a friend, a spouse, or a child.

If anyone is in Christ, the new creation has come:
The old has gone, the new is here!

2 CORINTHIANS 5:17

DIALING IN

It was a blustery Sunday afternoon, and we sat in the family room watching the football game. Tension was building just before the half, and there was an important play just ahead. Could our team keep their lead? Right at the important moment, something happened.

A cartoon station came on the screen, replacing the game channel!

"What in the world?" my husband asked, aiming the remote at the cable box and flipping back to the right channel . . . just in time to see the play.

"Must be a cable glitch," I mumbled. Crazily enough, during a critical moment in the third quarter, the TV switched stations again—to a foreign-language channel, a language we did not speak. Hubs looked at me and I looked back, and then we heard some giggling from the stairway. Our daughter held up her hands. "I'm innocent!" she proclaimed. Except she wasn't.

From three hundred miles away, our son had dialed into our cable account and was remotely changing the station, asking our daughter, via phone, to let him know what the response was. She sat on the stairs and reported our confusion. They shared a quiet laugh, the mad scientist and his trusty assistant.

Later that night, after having a good chuckle over it ourselves, I thought about how that remote assistance was very much like prayer. We don't understand exactly how prayer works; we send the signal up, and the action comes from a distance, mostly without our understanding how or why. Just like the changing of channels, prayer somehow activates power from afar, even if we don't know—yet—exactly how. Our God and his help are closer at hand than we think, and he always moves at the right time.

The LORD is far from the wicked,
But he hears the prayer of the righteous.

PROVERBS 15:29

February 4
PINE OIL CLEANER

When I was a young married woman, I returned home from work one day to a welcome fragrance. It was pine cleaner! I knew, then, that my new husband had taken time to clean the bathroom. I had chosen the right man! I smiled at him as I stepped into the bathroom, and he smiled at me. There was something behind his sheepish smile, though. I soon knew what it was: a guilty conscience.

I came out of the restroom a few minutes later. "Did you clean the toilets?" I asked. "Because it smells like it . . . but it doesn't look like it."

He hemmed and hawed, and I knew I was onto something. "No," he said. "I just poured some pine cleaner in there, swished it for a second, and let it sit for a while before flushing it down."

It smelled clean, but it wasn't clean.

We've all bumped up against situations where we—or others—were faking, pretending that something was what it wasn't. We tell someone we like their outfit, or a gift they gave us, when we don't. Our exaggerated enthusiasm often gives us away. Usually the motivation behind that kind of deception is good, even if we can't pull it off. More hurtful, though, is when people act as though they like us, but then leave us out. Tell us they love us, but then speak or act against us. I'm not suggesting that you should announce your dislike of anyone's clothing choices or personality in the interest of honesty; there is nothing wrong with kindness and social graces. But those you are called to love, truly love.

Don't just pretend to love others. Really love them. Hate what is wrong. Hold tightly to what is good. Love each other with genuine affection, and take delight in honoring each other. Never be lazy, but work hard and serve the Lord enthusiastically.

ROMANS 12:9-11, NLT

February 5
A THIEF IN THE NIGHT

A friend, the wife of a school principal, woke up one morning to find hundreds of plastic forks stabbed into her front yard, a field of white minisoldiers among the clover. She'd been forked!

A neighbor who had reported some pranksters woke up the next morning to find the trees in her front yard garlanded in toilet paper, some of it streaming wet. She'd been TP'd!

My daughter woke up on her birthday to find a large flock of pink plastic flamingos silently standing guard in her front yard. She'd been flamingoed!

These are all fun, lighthearted events that took place under the cover of darkness, but not all midnight occurrences are benign. Nighttime is often the favorite time for those who break into houses, hoping to steal things and then to steal away while residents are asleep and unaware. I recently read of a young couple who woke up and found a strange man sleeping on the couch of their new apartment—he'd had a key from the previous residents. I can imagine that those homeowners took precautions to ensure they had no more such surprises in the future!

The Day of the Lord—Christ's second coming, the beginning of the end of time—is something most Christians look forward to. But for those who don't believe, that day might bring more shock than awe. Get your house in order; don't be caught off guard!

Concerning how and when all this will happen, dear brothers and sisters, we don't really need to write you. For you know quite well that the day of the Lord's return will come unexpectedly, like a thief in the night.

1 THESSALONIANS 5:1-2, NLT

DEEP AND WIDE

A while back, I had a concern about my church. It pressed on my heart, and I had no peace for lack of a good solution. I wanted to seek counsel but did not want to gossip. I am thankful that I have a friend who is a wise, mature Christian who does not attend my church. I was able to ask her to guide me without worrying that she would guess who I was talking about. We sat together at my kitchen table, a place that has become not only where I share family meals but also where I pour my heart out to friends. We talked and prayed.

Everyone's workplaces present moral and ethical challenges at some time or other. Of course we hope that we'll know how to respond. But sometimes the answers are not easy. Sometimes we feel tempted to gossip or lash out in frustration or fear. If we have wise friends who are not in our workplaces, we can ask freely without concern that we're oversharing about coworkers.

As a wife and a mother, I want to seek wisdom on parenting from someone who has walked this path before me. Mostly, I want to talk with a woman who has weathered storms.

Scripture tells us there is wisdom in a multitude of counselors. With many opinions you're likely to get a well-rounded solution. But also, when you have many "counselors," you can choose to ask advice from someone who doesn't know the person or situation you are concerned about—and so be free of concern that you might start rumors or harm someone's reputation. Young girls often have one best friend, and that's okay. Women, however, are most successful when they have a circle of friends from many stages of life, backgrounds, and overlapping areas of interest.

Plans go wrong for lack of advice;
many advisers bring success.

PROVERBS 15:22, NLT

NO SOLICITORS

This past year we've had lots of people knocking on our door selling cleaning products, tree-trimming services, and the like. I'm often home alone. I don't think it's wise to open the door to everyone.

So I went looking for a tasteful *No Soliciting* sign. They came in every shape and size, from the inexpensive sticker at the hardware store to elaborate, cast-iron signs customized with your family name. My favorite was simple: *Please, No Solicitors, unless you're selling mint cookies.*

Yeah, definitely. I still want those cookies each spring!

Sometimes when we try to share our faith with others, people put out a metaphorical *No Soliciting* sign. We may try to explain that we're not selling anything, but on the other side it sure can feel like a sales pitch. My husband once had a friend who came to know the Lord through their time together. The next week, a mutual friend attacked my husband for "stealing his commission." What? There is no commission. The work is entirely that of the Holy Spirit. That knowledge frees us from having to drive home a sale, return time after time, or ask for referrals. We are not selling anything, ever.

Scripture tells us, instead, to be prepared to share why we have a hope that lives within us. Our testimony will be such that people will want to know why we have peace and joy. Our faith can be a natural part of our conversation with friends and colleagues, just like any other topic of importance in our lives, and we should listen respectfully, too.

Live a life of integrity, freely speak of your faith when it's appropriate, and make yourself open to questions. After all, we don't have anything to sell. We have something precious to give away.

Unlike so many, we do not peddle the word of God for profit. On the contrary, in Christ we speak before God with sincerity, as those sent from God.

2 CORINTHIANS 2:17

February 8
TEMPTING COOKIES

Everyone seems to be tempted by cookies—thin mint or otherwise! Yes, yes, sometimes chocolate chip or peanut butter, gingerbread, or the killers, Christmas cookies—frosted and sprinkled, please. However, there is a kind of cookie that actually follows you around, tempting you at work and at play. Computer cookies.

Most commercial sites register your computer, tablet, or phone when you browse the Internet and stop on their page. They note which products you linger on and which ones you actually place in a shopping cart but, after exercising your financial self-control, click away from without purchasing. I visit a few online stores quite often; one sells home goods in limited quantities, and they use a countdown clock to pressure you to make a decision—quick. Another sells clothing, and when I place something in my cart but don't buy it, those clothes, boots, and earrings follow me in the form of ads on social media and in my e-mail. It can be difficult to say no in the face of these ongoing temptations.

The interesting thing, of course, is that these are sites I have actually visited and financial temptations I myself began to engage with. We each have our own particular weaknesses, and Satan, being wily and wise, knows not to tempt me with what tempts my neighbor, my friend, or my sister. He tempts me with the cookie in the flavor I prefer, and he's noted my preference.

Scripture reminds us that God tempts no man, but Satan does. We're to keep watch so we don't fall into temptation, and we're to "close out the window" when temptation arrives, because "the spirit is willing, but the flesh is weak" (Matthew 26:41).

God blesses those who patiently endure testing and temptation. Afterward they will receive the crown of life that God has promised to those who love him. And remember, when you are being tempted, do not say, "God is tempting me." God is never tempted to do wrong, and he never tempts anyone else. Temptation comes from our own desires, which entice us and drag us away.

JAMES 1:12-14, NLT

LAUNDRY CHUTES

A favorite memory from childhood involves my grandparents' house. In their bathroom they had a "magical" tunnel. We kids could not slide through it, but we could slip all kinds of other items down and through it—stuffed animals, dolls, empty bottles, pictures, pencils. Few small things were spared from passage through the magical conduit of the laundry chute. A little push on the door and down the unsuspecting victim fell, through two stories, to end up in the padded bottom of my grandmother's laundry basket.

It's a good thing my grandmother was a tidy woman so that any unsuspecting objects did not have to rest too long in that basket with the dirty laundry. No chance of picking up that wet-towel smell.

I don't have grandchildren yet, but I'm ready if they come. We have a laundry chute, too, and I'm already giving it a good workout. Instead of letting my dirty clothes lie about gathering mold or must or that wet-dog smell after a towel has been draped on top of it, laundry goes shooting straight down to the laundry room to be washed, dried, and folded. I hope that someday stuffed animals will make their way down, too, though old soda cans, not so much.

Delivering dirty laundry right to where it needs to go is a good lesson for the spirit, too. So often we're tempted to bury our sins and poor choices, to hide them from others, draping a towel over the basket of that which needs to be cleaned. But just like those dirty clothes, our sins, mistakes, and wrong-doings will mold and smell till they are exposed to light, air, and detergent.

Done wrong? Me too. Shoot your sins straight to the laundry room, in prayer.

People who conceal their sins will not prosper,
but if they confess and turn from them, they will receive mercy.

PROVERBS 28:13, NLT

February 10

ASKING FOR THE RECIPE

When I was a teenager we lived next door to a woman who made the most wonderful cheesecake you could ever imagine. She was a New Yorker, and there's a reason there is no Minnesota-style cheesecake or New Mexico–style cheesecake, but there is a New York–style cheesecake. It was food fit for a king—or hungry neighbors, in our case.

We wanted to make that cheesecake ourselves, so we asked her for the recipe. Imagine our surprise when she declined to share it. A family secret, she said. But . . . she offered to make us a cheesecake anytime we wanted one. What a deal!

That was my first experience with someone unwilling to share a secret recipe, but it was certainly not the last time I'd heard someone ask for one. If you browse recipes online, you will find many comments such as "I took these to work and not only were they all eaten, but everyone wanted the recipe." It's satisfying to offer something that people devour, admire, and want to repeat. One friend has been asked so many times for the recipe of one of her dishes that she's printed it out and brings a stack of them whenever she serves the dish.

Wouldn't it be lovely if we could share our faith with as much pride and flourish as we do a treasured recipe? Wouldn't it be thrilling if, after an encounter in which we share or display our faith, a friend or stranger asks us for the "recipe" for facing difficulties, or for our joy, or for life? It's already printed out, you know. Easy to share!

Make the most of every opportunity. Let your conversation be always full of grace, seasoned with salt, so that you may know how to answer everyone.

COLOSSIANS 4:5-6

February 11
VENISON

Our neighborhood has a family or two of deer that call it home. They've been here a long time—longer than we have.

Because our house sits up high, the deer have always liked our yard, or so the neighbors have told us. Once on our lawn, they have a clear view of the entire area: what might be near, what might be coming, what might be stalking. Only after surveying the entire lawn do they lower their heads to eat. (Sometimes it's my flowers, which is unwelcome, but we'll save that for another time.)

Deer are prey species. They are hunted for their flesh, and so they are wary by nature. They know that predators of all kinds, both animal and human, pursue them. Somehow, as my husband says, they always know the first day of deer season, and they flee to safe ground till the last day. They also know where to find high ground. They have to be alert to the dangers that lurk, waiting to devour them and their young.

Although we don't often think of ourselves as such, we are prey species too. Satan hates what and whom God loves, and that would be you and me. Scripture says Satan looks for those he may devour, and that usually means the weak and unwary. Where are you vulnerable to fear, to inaction, to the voices that whisper and take you down? What scares you away from taking a step of faith? What fears do you allow to undo you? Take the high ground, be cagey and cautious when required, but then move forward. You don't need to live in paralyzing fear—our deer certainly don't—but be aware, because your faith depends on it.

Stay alert! Watch out for your great enemy, the devil. He prowls around like a roaring lion, looking for someone to devour.

1 PETER 5:8, NLT

UPSTAIRS, DOWNSTAIRS

Because I write fiction, much of it historical fiction, I spend a lot of time with my nose in history books and my eyes and ears engaged in historical movies. One notable difference between our time in the present and time gone by is that there was a great divide between people who were "downstairs," who served, and those who were "upstairs," who were served.

The servants were subject to the master and his family. The sons were accorded the privileges of family and were stewards, along with the head of the household, of all that they owned. When the fortunes of the family rose, so did the fortunes of the sons and daughters. When the family fell on tough times, so did the sons and daughters.

For the most part, I am the servant to my family, as is my husband, as are most of you. We serve the Kingdom, we serve our neighbors, we serve our friends. But we aren't just "downstairs" kinds of folks; we are also children and heirs. Which of us doesn't revel in a story of a commoner turned princess, of fortunes turned around?

It often feels like we spend much of our time scrubbing pots and clothes and taking food to others even when we're dead tired. But you have another identity, friend. You are an "upstairs" girl, too. God calls us his heirs—co-heirs with Christ. For a little while, we will suffer, earthbound, as he did. But later, we will be raised with him. Tiara, anyone?

If we are children, then we are heirs—heirs of God and co-heirs with Christ, if indeed we share in his sufferings in order that we may also share in his glory.

ROMANS 8:17

PUT IT IN INK

A friend came over for coffee, and as we sat on the couch and talked, I noticed the close attention she paid to our conversation. It wasn't the "hurry-up-I-need-to-check-my-phone" look I sometimes get (and, I fear, give). She didn't look as if she were eager for me to pause so she could interject her experience or opinion. She looked at me attentively and listened.

And then she followed up with the most remarkable comments. "I'll write your concerns down in my prayer journal. I have a page for you there, listing your prayer requests, so when I pray each day, I remember what to bring to the Lord for you."

In a hurry-scurry world where most of my jotted notes consist of things I must do or pick up at the grocery store, I admit I never used to write down prayer requests. But I felt so blessed, so loved, so attended to by the fact that someone did that for me that I started doing it myself.

Writing something down shows its significance. It means it matters. It means you're paying attention, and something and someone is so important that you are taking measures to ensure you won't forget. Someone's heartfelt prayer request really is more important to me than whether I remember butternut squash at the grocery store. If I write out my grocery list, how much more should I write down prayer requests!

My daughter sometimes uses a pen to write something on her wrist if she doesn't want to forget it during the day. Could I temporarily ink myself with "Pray"? Or with the tiny initials of someone who needed me to remember them throughout that day?

Jesus has written my name in his Book of Life. He thinks I'm significant. He says I matter, and he says you matter too. Hallelujah!

The glory and honor of the nations will be brought into [the city of God].
Nothing impure will ever enter it, nor will anyone who does what is shameful
or deceitful, but only those whose names are written in the Lamb's book of life.

REVELATION 21:26-27

CHOCOLATE FONDUE

When my daughter was planning her wedding, she decided she wanted chocolate fountains at the reception. Chocolate fondue has been a favorite tradition in our family since she was a child, and she wanted to bring it to another level and share it with friends and family on her special day.

You've probably seen these fountains at events: melted chocolate erupts from the top and gently flows over layers of glass plates. At the base of the fountain are cut-up strawberries, pound cake, cheesecake, maraschino cherries, bananas—and lots of dipping forks. Wedding guests pierce a treat with the fork and then hold it under the flowing chocolate, turning the fork till the sweet is completely coated. One man even held his coffee cup under the fountain to make a perfect (and perfectly rich!) mocha. The best part? The chocolate never runs out. Everyone can dip as many berries as they like without worrying about taking more than a fair share, and no one has to worry about getting to the fountain too late to have enough.

The bounty of good, delicious things was a perfect illustration for a wonderful day. It reminded us how sweet life can be—one day among many to share with loved ones. It was a delightful privilege for us to supply that never-ending cascade of chocolate for our daughter and her new husband as well as for their guests.

God, too, has an unlimited store of sweetness and goodness. He delights in showering us with excellent things, in celebrating with us, in being among us and our loved ones. Next time you have cause to rejoice, remember the hand that provides good things. Thank him today for his goodness, his provision, his rich blessings. Dip your cup into life and watch him fill it to overflowing.

Sweet!

My cup overflows with blessings.

PSALM 23:5, NLT

February 15
LETTING GO

My daughter and I were looking for fun alternatives to throwing rice or flower petals at her wedding reception. At my own wedding we threw birdseed, a little treat for the birds from the Byrds! Among the options my daughter and I found were sparklers for guests to hold to form a bridge for the newlyweds to walk under and Chinese lanterns to light and release to float free.

It was not easy to release my daughter; although she's living nearby, she's in a new phase of life. I realized that if she had a health crisis or an accident, my husband and I wouldn't be the first ones called; our son-in-law would be. It was a strange but happy transition.

Releasing is often hard. Whether it's letting go of a child into adulthood, relinquishing a beloved job, moving on to a new church, letting go of a bad relationship or one that has simply run its course, we have a hard time transitioning. We invest so much of our hearts in whatever we do and whomever we love.

Transitions can be good, though. None of us would want to have remained as children, so we must let our children progress too. New jobs follow old ones, even good old ones, with fresh challenges and insight. Although we let go of some relationships, there are other fine people in the world ready to meet us. Church families come and go, and though we move on, we will all be together again someday.

A wedding is a celebration of leaving and cleaving. Other transitions can be celebrations too, as we let go of the past with all it has held and reach toward the future. I'm happy to see my daughter so eagerly looking forward. God feels that way about you and me—his daughters.

"I know the plans I have for you," declares the LORD, "plans to prosper you and not to harm you, plans to give you hope and a future."

JEREMIAH 29:11

OF BIBLES AND LACE DOILIES

Sometimes you can learn something about a person as soon as you step into her house. (I'm not talking about untidiness—that just shows we're busy. Right?) How a woman decorates her home tells you something about her personality, what she values, what style she enjoys. I have friends whose breezy personalities are reflected in their "California casual" decorating style: not much on the coffee table, casual chairs to welcome lots of friends. I have an older friend who still has handmade doilies on the back of her sofa and underneath her many thriving plants. It's sweet and a little old-fashioned, like she is. I myself love French country, and I'd rather have a bare wall than something that doesn't fit!

Because many of my friends are believers, I see Bibles on a lot of end tables, coffee tables, and bedside tables. There's a Bible in every room in my house. I should say that with a sense of pride . . . and I guess I do. But what I'm really wondering is this: Is it a tool, like those in the garage? Or is it a lovely doily that is never touched—a tabletop fashion accessory?

In many countries around the world, a Bible would be a well-worn, beloved, and perhaps hidden possession. For most of history, Scripture was unavailable to the vast majority of Christians. Perhaps now, it is as Thomas Paine said: "What we obtain too cheap, we esteem too lightly."

I mean to ensure that dust does not coat the covers of my many Bibles, and I don't mean because of a weekly housekeeping routine!

All Scripture is inspired by God and is useful to teach us what is
true and to make us realize what is wrong in our lives. It corrects
us when we are wrong and teaches us to do what is right.

2 TIMOTHY 3:16, NLT

SIXTH SENSE

It's common knowledge that we humans have five senses by which we perceive the world. Supposedly, sight is the one we rely on most, followed by hearing, touch, smell, and taste. (I'm guessing that taste has led the way in my life, judging by the number of cookbooks and condiments in my kitchen.)

We've grown herbs in tiny kitchen gardens in most of the places we've lived. My son loved to tend those gardens. He has an excellent sense of smell, and after spending time distinguishing those herbs, he took the challenge one neighbor offered of identifying those herbs by scent alone—and won!

It's been said that if a person loses the ability to use one sense, the others will become sharper to compensate. With practice, people are able to use their remaining senses more effectively.

I would venture that we Christians have a sixth sense—no, not the kind described in creepy movies. Our sixth sense is the sense of discernment. I like this description from GotQuestions.org: "A discerning mind demonstrates wisdom and insight that go beyond what is seen and heard." Most simply, discernment is the ability to tell right from wrong, good from bad, evil from holy. It might help you understand situations, people and their intentions, or spiritual warfare. Scripture tells us that discernment is attained by constant practice.

We Christians are not missing the function of a sensory organ, but we have been given an extra—a bonus—through the power of the Spirit, to help those who have eyes to see and ears to hear. Don't lose your sense of discernment for want of practice! The consequences are more serious than misidentifying herbs.

*Solid food is for the mature, who by constant use have
trained themselves to distinguish good from evil.*

HEBREWS 5:14

February 18

SOFT CHAIRS

My husband and I were visiting our new friends' house for the first time to attend a small-group meeting. After some shuffling around, we all went to sit in their family room. Members made their way to the couches, the love seat, and the kitchen chairs brought in for the occasion. No one sat in the recliner, though, because as my husband said, "No one sits in another man's chair."

At our house, we each have our own special place. Hubs has his chair, and no one else sits in it, except the dog—if she can get away with it. Mostly she prefers any blanket pulled to the floor. My daughter is small and loves the love seat, especially now that she's a newlywed. Our son likes the soft couch in the man cave. And I like the little chair in a reading nook, complete with a warm blanket and a small table for my books and Bibles.

It's the place I go when everyone else has left the house, a place of quiet and peace, the place where I meet with God. I didn't always have a special place to meet with him, because I know he is with me everywhere. But when I set aside a place and made it cozy and left a Bible there, it beckoned to me to come away more often. And as I did, I drew closer to God and he to me.

As women, we spend so much of our time helping others and providing comfort. We love, we soothe, we give up what we want or need to meet the wants or needs of another. And for the most part, that's really fulfilling. But Scripture encourages us to love others *as we love ourselves*, which suggests we need to do loving things for ourselves as well. Find a place just for you, a place where you can read, rest, and get away to meet with God. You deserve that tender care too.

Come near to God and he will come near to you.

JAMES 4:8

February 19

GROW LIGHTS

We have lived next door to two different neighbors who used grow lights. Our first experience was the more unpleasant of the two.

We found out about their lights when we discovered rats . . . in our garage. First there was one, then another, and then there was one in our *house*. You can imagine our horror as the kids and I jumped up on the highest surface possible, leaving Hubs to chase the thing out with a broom. We finally trapped them all a few months before we were to move. We later came to find out that our neighbors had a marijuana-growing operation in their basement, full of moist, warm air for growing something illegal. And for breeding rats.

At another house, we had neighbors who used grow lights to start tomatoes early in the spring, allowing them to use heirloom seeds from which they could grow rare varieties. Their grow lights provided moist, warm conditions in order to grow something lovely. And they did not have rats!

Good growing conditions are the same no matter if you're cultivating something healthy or not, legal or not. The choice of what to plant and nurture is up to the grower. The grower must choose seeds wisely with the end result in mind.

We have seeds presented to us each day—choices on how to spend time and money; decisions about books, movies, and other forms of entertainment; habits to nurture or discard; arguments to pick or lay aside. We, too, must choose wisely. It may be helpful to ask yourself these questions: How will this affect my life? The lives of those around me? What crop do I want to harvest?

I'm hoping to be a wise grower. I do want tomatoes. I don't want rats!

Live a life worthy of the Lord and please him in every way: bearing
fruit in every good work, growing in the knowledge of God.

COLOSSIANS 1:10

UGLY REVEAL

I have a lovely friend named Leila who is a godly woman and teacher of the Word; she's also refreshingly honest. She had an experience one winter's night that I want to share with you, using Leila's own words.

"God always has a way of smacking me upside my head. Called the garbage company today, and I was so rude to the office lady as I demanded to know *why* our garbage was missed again . . . only to realize trash day is tomorrow. But that wasn't enough humiliation for me. I was working on ministry stuff this evening (with a headset on) and stopped to yell at the grandkids to be quiet. Went back to work, only to see my entire yelling rant in text on my screen. I didn't turn off the microphone option I was using before I started yelling. Nothing like reading your ugly heart in the written word. *sigh*"

Can you relate? I certainly can. It's so easy for us to use harsh words or take a rough tone and not even hear it. But if someone happens to be recording it and we hear it played back later . . . ouch!

I've got news. One day, our words will all be replayed right in front of us and right in front of the Lord. (As my friend Toni said, I hope I have a private audience!) I'd best be thinking right now about what I want to hear.

I tell you this, you must give an account on judgment day for every idle word you speak. The words you say will either acquit you or condemn you.

MATTHEW 12:36-37, NLT

UPGRADING TO GRATITUDE

You've probably read the Ten Commandments, even though it may have been a while. I reviewed them again recently, and I was feeling pretty smug. In no way do I covet my neighbor's donkey or ox. I am not aware that any of my friends have a servant for me to covet either, though I definitely grow a little wistful when I hear of people who have weekly housekeeping service. However, I admit to one area of covetousness.

I covet houses.

And the world is ready to help me do just that! On television there is show after show of remodeling, redoing, or reworking; buying, bidding, or selling. I sometimes watch them, yes, lusting for the houses I'll never have, mouth agape at the realization that people have that kind of cash to drop on decorating.

Then there are the websites that send me an alert when one of my neighbors is selling a house. Am I interested? You bet I am. There are times (head hangs here) I scroll through to see what the interiors of their houses look like and what upgrades they've made. *I'm collecting ideas*, I tell myself. But I envy. I really do, especially when I have to spend money on a broken water heater instead of replacing the threadbare carpet.

It's easy for me to rationalize that lusting after a house isn't as bad as lusting after my neighbor's husband. But the tenth commandment doesn't really distinguish between the two. They both involve desiring and lusting for what does not belong to me. Lust of any kind makes us discontent with what and whom we've been given . . . or not given. It makes us envious, which leads to questioning God's fairness and goodness. It fills us with bitterness, not with thanksgiving.

I've turned off the real estate alerts, because God has told me . . .

You must not covet your neighbor's house.

EXODUS 20:17, NLT

February 22

COMPANIONS

My daughter and son-in-law have a cat, and I'm telling you, that cat is very smart. She knows where everyone is, what time they are supposed to be home, what's for dinner, and how to solve difficult math equations. So it's hard to find toys that amuse her.

She does enjoy chasing string and the pretend bird that hangs from a stick. Her new trick is to jump up on the dryer, open the cabinet, lift the lid to the box of dryer sheets, and take one out to play with. And, of course, she loves boxes.

As much as she loves to play, though, it's clear that she's happiest when she's with her people. She'll follow them around every corner and into every room. She'll plop down in the center of the bed so she can't be ignored. She wants to be on the table when they're eating. (Forbidden. Bad kitty.)

And when they sit down to watch TV, she curls up on the couch with them, washing her face and watching TV too. She was created for and feels most fulfilled by the companionship of her owners, no matter how many toys she's given.

We, too, were created for companionship. We have a lot of "toys" in modern life, and while they amuse us for a time, they are never completely satisfying at a soul level. When we invite our friends, our family, our coworkers, and of course our Lord to join us each day in the things that we do, we are most content. It's a breathtaking truth, when you think of it, that God has deigned to dwell with and within us. Don't forget to enjoy his companionship and offer yours every day.

I will ask the Father, and he will give you another advocate to
help you and be with you forever—the Spirit of truth. The world
cannot accept him, because it neither sees him nor knows him. But
you know him, for he lives with you and will be in you.

JOHN 14:16-17

February 23
TEARING DOWN

My town is not old by European or East Coast standards, but it does have a number of homes that are nearly one hundred years old. Because there is a lot of land that fronts water, some of these houses were beach getaways of old, and now they are fairly tired, small homes on spectacular properties with eye-popping views.

When they are listed for sale, the properties often command much more than one would expect for a little old beach shack. That's because they're marketed as teardowns. These properties are purchased for the land, and the house is torn down to make way for something new. It's not much of a loss, because most of them are falling down anyway.

Sometimes, though, a perfectly good house is torn down simply because the owner doesn't like the style and has the money to start fresh. It's much harder to watch that happen. Hundreds of thousands, or in the recent case of a star athlete's Florida home, millions of dollars' worth of housing is torn down for no good reason except for a whim, and because the owners can.

We can tear down our "houses" too, only we usually use our mouths. We speak without thinking, or out of anger or self-righteousness. Sticks and stones may break bones, but words can do long-lasting damage. Children often have trouble controlling their impulses, but adults, too, need to be responsible stewards of their mouths. Take a few minutes, or hours, to cool off or think through the history of a relationship before speaking in haste. There is much more at stake than a tumbledown cottage. Our words can prove destructive to a job, a marriage, a relationship with a child, or a friendship.

Set a guard over my mouth, LORD;
keep watch over the door of my lips.

PSALM 141:3

BUILDING UP

On a street I often walk on, I've had the privilege of watching a family build their own home—mostly. They hired professionals to level the lot, pour the foundation, and build the frame. From there on, though, they did much of the work themselves. The older children helped with the drywall. The mother painted and did the landscaping. The father put up most of the siding. Perhaps he had construction experience—or perhaps he watched DIY shows!

I was not the only onlooker heartened by this display of cooperation. I noted others watching and listening and—when the front door was painted—clapping! The young family planted a fairy-garden hedge of tiny plants, and I found myself praying that they'd grow strong and tall. The family worked together through heat and rain and, I'm sure, financial and personal setbacks to accomplish their common goal. And when one of them had a project falter, the others all stepped up to help.

We believers can do likewise with our faith family. We can pitch in together on a project, cheering one another on in person, through text, or by e-mail. Using Scripture, we can shore up unsteady walls or the metaphorical leaky roof in a friend's life. We're supposed to encourage one another with songs, and I will—via CD, digital file, or link. Listening to me sing would not be uplifting!

I'm asking myself this morning, *What can I say, and to whom can I say it, to build someone up for the day or the project that lies ahead?*

Do not let any unwholesome talk come out of your mouths, but only what is helpful for building others up according to their needs, that it may benefit those who listen.

EPHESIANS 4:29

THE KING'S CRABS

I love the show *Deadliest Catch*. It follows the lives of Alaskan crab fishermen as they battle the Bering Sea while trying to trap pots of gold—figuratively speaking. A new deckhand can make eighty to one hundred thousand dollars in one season. I love to eat crab (my kids say that makes me a cannibal!). I especially like Dungeness or king crab, served with drawn butter or in eggs Benedict or a hot dip. We live near a lot of fishermen, and when my husband performed the wedding for a crab fisherman not long ago, it got me thinking and learning about crabs.

In order to grow, crabs have to shed their exoskeletons (a process called molting) and grow new ones. For the forty-eight hours or so between shedding the old shells and growing new ones, the crabs are extremely vulnerable to predators. They need to take refuge, if they can, in a safe place.

That's kind of like us, isn't it? If we don't grow, spiritually and emotionally, we become trapped in shells too small for what we were intended to be. But the step forward—shedding the past and venturing into the future—leaves us vulnerable for a little while. We mustn't be afraid to grow, either as people or as believers. We just need to take refuge in a safe place (with good friends, the Word, a supportive family) till our new shells have grown.

May we all be crabs for the King!

Dear brothers and sisters, I close my letter with these last words: Be joyful. Grow to maturity. Encourage each other. Live in harmony and peace. Then the God of love and peace will be with you.

2 CORINTHIANS 13:11, NLT

SMOOTH AIR

I pulled a suitcase out of the closet; I was going to Denver. The weather here was iffy, as it often is, but it was especially so in Denver, which is notorious for thunderstorms in the summer and blizzards in the winter. It's often bumpy flying in and out of Denver during its many seasons of weather change. The airport is often blanketed in clouds.

I pulled the suitcase to my room and nervously started to pack. I made a pact with God that I wouldn't complain about the person sitting ahead of me reclining his or her seat into my lap nor the child kicking my seat from behind, if only the air would stay smooth.

I often pray for smooth air when I'm about to fly. I don't really believe we're going to crash, but turbulence is so uncomfortable—and so out of my control. I'm ashamed to admit I have spent up to half an hour on a flight simply asking God, over and over, to make the air smooth. What I want is comfort and the reassurance that nothing is going to harm me.

I realized that we do this in our prayer lives quite a bit. Instead of praying for the welfare of others, or that people would draw near to Christ, or for any of a thousand worthy causes that need our intervention, we pray for smooth air. No financial worries, no relational difficulties, nothing at all to disturb the illusion that we are in control.

I got on the plane and spent just one minute praying for smooth air but then twenty-nine more praying for things that would matter, eternally, after I landed.

I urge, then, first of all, that petitions, prayers, intercession and thanksgiving be made for all people—for kings and all those in authority, that we may live peaceful and quiet lives in all godliness and holiness. This is good, and pleases God our Savior, who wants all people to be saved and to come to a knowledge of the truth.

1 TIMOTHY 2:1-4

SHOCKING

There is a dog at a house a few streets over who is the most perfectly self-controlled dog I have ever seen. Although he has a large front yard, and walkers and other dogs (even cats!) parade past him on a regular basis, he never goes beyond the edge of his property to chase or even befriend them. He stays put, where he belongs.

One day while his family was outside, I asked about it. "Oh, it's easy," said the dog's owner. "We've got an underground fence." A wire is buried along the perimeter of the lawn, and when the dog gets too close, his collar beeps and emits a tiny electric pulse. "It's for his own protection," the owner explained, almost apologetically. But yes, I understood. Better a tiny but noticeable warning than a dog who runs into oncoming traffic.

Truth is, we humans also need boundaries from the things that will harm us. Temptations. Vulnerabilities. We're all susceptible. James 1:14-15 tells us that often our temptations come from within; therefore our hearts and minds are the places where we need to erect protective fences, our boundaries for things we will let in and what we will keep out.

Dogs cannot erect their own protective fences, of course, but we can, with help from our Master. What area in your life needs more Spirit control, an inner fence, and perhaps a little zap in order to fill you with life and peace?

Those who are dominated by the sinful nature think about sinful things,
but those who are controlled by the Holy Spirit think about things that
please the Spirit. So letting your sinful nature control your mind leads to
death. But letting the Spirit control your mind leads to life and peace.

ROMANS 8:5-6, NLT

STAIRWAY TO HEAVEN

My in-laws came to stay with us for a few months, and one of the greater difficulties for them was walking up and down our steep staircase. We were happy to help them when they needed it, but I know it was frustrating for them. When they moved in with my sister-in-law, she was able to have a motorized stairlift installed. Mom and Dad would simply sit down on the chair, and it would safely whisk them upstairs. What fun it would have been to have such a gizmo around when we were kids!

In contrast, I've been looking for hills to climb in my quest for better health, even on cold winter days. Hills force my muscles to work harder and my heart to pump more efficiently, even hours after the walk. Also, hill climbing burns fat faster than easier walking does. I'm glad of the benefits, but I'm also glad when I'm at the top and can turn around and walk back down. Looking up that long hill from the bottom is daunting.

It's sometimes difficult to praise God and remember his help and goodness as we climb the daunting hills of life. When things get hard, I'd like to be whisked straight to the top, to the end of the problem. Going uphill is tough. But for most of us, it's necessary for spiritual health and endurance. And when we get to the top together, we celebrate, and then we have a victory to encourage us the next time we're looking up from the bottom.

The path we walk is charted by faith, not by what we see with our eyes.

2 CORINTHIANS 5:7, VOICE

MARCH

Cordon Rose Cheesecake

Although we've never met, Rosy Levy Beranbaum taught me to bake through her classic cookbook, *The Cake Bible*. Cordon Rose Cheesecake is both creamy and firm, and in more than twenty-five years I have never found one that offered competition in either flavor or presentation.

 Substitute any fruit you wish for the strawberries if you prefer. We love to use blueberries to mix it up. You can make this with a simple graham-cracker crust if you can't find ladyfingers. I almost prefer it that way.

WHAT YOU'LL NEED
1 package ladyfingers
2 (8-ounce) packages cream cheese, softened
1 cup sugar
1 tablespoon cornstarch, optional
3 large eggs
3 tablespoons lemon juice, freshly squeezed
1/4 teaspoon salt
3 cups sour cream
4 to 5 cups strawberries, hulled
1/4 cup currant jelly
1 tablespoon water
A 9-inch by 2½-inch (or higher) round springform pan
A 12-inch cake pan or roasting pan to serve as water bath

DIRECTIONS
Preheat oven to 350 degrees. Lightly grease the round spring-form pan and wrap the outside of it with a double layer of heavy-duty aluminum foil.

Slice each ladyfinger in half lengthwise. Line the sides of the pan with the ladyfingers, rounded sides against the side of the pan, so that you have a ring of ladyfingers resembling a picket fence. Line the bottom of the pan with more ladyfingers, rounded sides down. Set aside.

In a large mixing bowl, use a whisk beater (or a wire whisk or an electric mixer) to beat the cream cheese and sugar until very smooth, about 3 minutes). Beat in the cornstarch. Add the eggs one at a time, beating after each addition until smooth and scraping down the sides. Add the lemon juice and salt and beat until incorporated. Beat in the sour cream until just blended.

Pour the batter into the greased springform pan. Place the springform pan in the larger pan. Pour very hot water into the larger pan, about 1 inch high, so that the springform pan is surrounded by the water. Bake for 25 minutes, then cover the pan loosely with foil. Bake for an additional 15 minutes, then turn off the oven without opening the door and let the cake cool in oven for 1 hour. Remove the springform pan to a rack and cool to room temperature, about 1 hour.

Cover with greased plastic wrap and refrigerate overnight. To unmold, run a towel under hot water and wipe the sides of the pan several times. Run a thin metal spatula around the sides of the cake and release the sides of the springform pan. Place a plastic-wrapped plate on top and invert. Remove the bottom of the pan. Reinvert onto a serving plate.

Arrange strawberries or other fruit on top of the cake. If you have recently rinsed them, make sure they are thoroughly dry. In a small saucepan or microwave oven, heat the currant jelly until melted and bubbling. Strain it into a small cup and stir in the water. Brush it over the berries.

Refrigerate cake until shortly before serving.

Recipe used with the kind permission of Rose Levy Beranbaum.

For this month's free printable, go to http://tyndal.es/homeandgarden.

TABLE SERVICE

Over the course of time, when our kids were growing up, we noticed a distinct devolution in table manners. I'm not referring to talking with their mouths full or forgetting to use napkins. Instead, one child who was sitting down would ask someone else (also sitting down) to get up and procure something for them: salt, more milk, a second helping, whatever. Finally after much muttering about how each of us has our own two hands and feet, it was pointed out to this child that we do not live in a restaurant. We each serve ourselves, or one another, but we don't snap our fingers and call, "Garçon!"

Another child spent quite a bit of time pointing out what each of us was doing wrong. Elbows on the table. Fork in the wrong hand. Letting different foods touch one another on the plate. This child was gently told to remove her own elbow from the table.

It occurred to me that this is how the church has devolved too. Instead of serving one another, we spend a lot of time expecting people to serve us: church music must be just right, the sermon must resonate each and every week, people must be friendly—and if one of these things doesn't meet our expectations, we're not shy about tossing the comment card into the collection plate (sometimes in lieu of a check). We're quick to complain.

That is convicting. I need to tend to my own personal holiness, not others', and use the gifts God has given me to serve them.

God has given each of you a gift from his great variety of
spiritual gifts. Use them well to serve one another.

1 PETER 4:10, NLT

March 2
CROSS-TRAINING

A few months ago my husband and I bought a cross-trainer and some kettle bells for our house. We hadn't been very good about making it to the gym, so the gym had to come to us. After years of eating French pastries, it was time to work off the accumulated brioche.

Our workout plan consists of both cardio and weight training, and when we can work out together, one of us is on the cross-trainer while the other one does lifting, and vice versa—working side by side, though differently, in the same room (the man cave). He likes to watch a game while working out, and I normally have some music pumping, so we don't actually talk. But I recently noticed something.

If I slow down to fix my music or grab a towel, he'll automatically slow down a little to keep in time with me. And if he speeds up, trying to hit a target heart rate, I find myself pushing a little harder to match his efforts. Even if we aren't looking directly at each other, we adjust to keep in rhythm.

Isn't that a picture of what we're aiming for in marriage? Sometimes I am tired of life, of the struggles and the pain and the worries, and my man slows down his pace long enough to listen to me and encourage me to keep going. Sometimes he's racing toward something, pushing us to a goal that seems out of reach—but really isn't—and I speed up to make sure we both grasp it at the same time. Husbands and wives should try to work in tandem, difficult as that may be sometimes, if our marriages are to be healthy and in good shape.

May the God who gives endurance and encouragement give you the same attitude of mind toward each other that Christ Jesus had.

ROMANS 15:5

March 3
GREEN CHEESE

I love cheese: hard cheese, soft cheese, runny cheese, smelly cheese, good old American cheese. Even Velveeta is good in a Juicy Lucy. (If you don't know what that is, look it up because you're going to want to make one.)

Even if tightly wrapped, some types of cheese begin to brown and harden on the outside or sprout green and blue mold before I get to eat it all. I find it hard to throw the cheese out, though, because most of it is still good. Hence the fine art of trimming.

While the cheese is still firm, I slice off the bad part (plus a little margin, just in case). I pitch the moldy part and keep what is still healthy and tasty.

There are things in our lives, too, that may have started out good but somehow have begun to rot around the edges. Spending habits. Eating habits. Prayer requests that turn into gossip, or a friendship with someone of the opposite sex that has turned a bit more serious. (This is okay for the unmarried!)

Instead of tossing the cheese out with the mold, carefully examine it and then firmly cut out the bad part. Then keep an eye on it, and enjoy. Some habits, though, too easily turn into sin despite our best efforts. Nothing is worth that. It's best in that case to quickly throw the whole thing away.

If your hand or your foot causes you to stumble, cut it off and throw it away. It is better for you to enter life maimed or crippled than to have two hands or two feet and be thrown into eternal fire. And if your eye causes you to stumble, gouge it out and throw it away. It is better for you to enter life with one eye than to have two eyes and be thrown into the fire of hell.

MATTHEW 18:8-9

RSVP

Evites are fun—they arrive via e-mail, they're usually really attractive, and they promise a good time. They're easy to deliver and to respond to. Most times they ask, "Will you join us? RSVP and let us know if we can count you in."

Even better are mailed requests. I love receiving fancy embossed invitations, especially to weddings. The paper is elegant and top quality, in keeping with the significance of the occasion. Response cards are usually prestamped to make replying easy. I have a special cabinet in my kitchen in which I store invitations and greeting cards. Sometimes I thumb through them, grateful for the places and events I've been invited to.

A life of faith is one of constant invitations. God asked Abraham to trust him when he told Abraham to go to an unknown land. Moses and the Israelites were invited to the Promised Land; Joshua was challenged to lead them. Matthew, Peter, and Andrew were all invited by the Lord to follow him on a grand adventure, to lay aside their day-to-day concerns and fall in step with him.

When the Lord invites you to join him in a new venture, one filled with promise and possibilities, do you run? Do you stuff the invitation in a drawer without responding, or are you quick to RSVP? I want to be counted on to answer quickly. *Yes, I'll come along. Count me in!*

A large crowd came to [Jesus], and he began to teach them. As he walked along, he saw Levi son of Alphaeus sitting at the tax collector's booth. "Follow me," Jesus told him, and Levi got up and followed him.

MARK 2:13-14

March 5

DISPLACED

Although most of us have someplace we call home, we are definitely a people on the move. The world is becoming a global village: borders are porous, and airplanes can fly us almost anywhere in the span of a day. It used to take months to circumnavigate the globe; now we can circle it in about fifty hours. We can get from here to there quickly, but sometimes that makes the world even lonelier.

In some way, we are all displaced people. As Christians, we know we're displaced from our true home in heaven, which awaits us after death. Many of us live in the country in which we were born, but perhaps our parents or grandparents were immigrants. Or maybe our children will be! We move across the world, the country, the state, the city. It's a kind of footloose lifestyle now, where we're unsure if the place we call home today will be the same next month or next year.

Sometimes, because of economic instability, people move due to housing costs, new jobs, foreclosed homes, better opportunities. Some people are displaced emotionally from their families. Many people have no church. Some have no neighbors. Lots have few friends.

Believers have a home—a permanent home, something most of us crave—with Christ. Perhaps we might reach out a hand to those who feel adrift and offer them hope for that kind of belonging too. Who can you invite into the warmth of your friendship, your family, your church, your life, your faith?

We all remember a time when we were lost, lonely, or frightened, and someone held out a hand to say, *Mi casa es tu casa.*

Jesus says that, for sure.

We are citizens of heaven, where the Lord Jesus Christ lives.

PHILIPPIANS 3:20, NLT

JESUS IN THE DIAPER PAIL

Those of us of a certain age remember the show *Kids Say the Darndest Things*. The host would ask young children questions that the kids then answered in a spontaneous and amusing manner. One reason it's fun and funny to watch kids, on TV and off, is that they have no filter. Parents work hard to help children learn not to say things that hurt others, but sometimes their unfiltered observations are actually full of wisdom. Kids say what they think, and their wheels are always turning.

Our son was a little shy of three when his sister was born, and they shared a room—his captain's bed, her crib, their dresser, their toys and binkies . . . and a diaper pail. We'd taught our son that Jesus was everywhere with him; he needn't be afraid of a dark room or a new situation, because Christ was there to hold his hand. One night he called us into their room, which had been nearly turned upside down.

"Jesus is in the diaper pail!" he proudly proclaimed.

"What?" I asked, horrified.

"You said he was here, and I looked everywhere else," he said. Of course. The diaper pail was locked, the only space that couldn't be accessed.

But you know what? Jesus *is* in the diaper pail of life with us, in all the dirty, ugly, unpleasant situations we have to face. He doesn't shrink from them or from us. Instead of promising to merely meet us on the other side, he holds our hands and walks through those diaper-pail circumstances with us. He never leaves nor forsakes us.

Kids say the darndest things.

The LORD your God goes with you; he will never leave you nor forsake you.

DEUTERONOMY 31:6

March 7

BRING HOME THE BACON

My daughter is a devoted vegetarian, due to her great love of animals. Her first word was *dog*. She'd wanted to become a vegetarian since about the age of eight, and finally, when she was twelve, I agreed. I'd found her standing over a roasted chicken, crying, "It has a rib cage."

However, before she gave up meat, she loved bacon. Bacon and eggs; BLT sandwiches; bacon sprinkled on pizza. One day we were studying Scripture with our kids—I can't remember the passage now—and had come across a portion that called for worshipers to offer the fat portion of the meat as an esteemed offering to the Lord.

The next morning, I saw her kids' Bible on the coffee table. When I went closer, I could see something wedged inside, a most unusual bookmark. My daughter had gone into the kitchen and pulled a piece of bacon from the refrigerator, then slid it into her Bible.

"Why did you do that?" I asked.

"I wanted to give God what made him feel most special," she said. "To let him know I love him."

My heart was so touched. When was the last time I had read something in the Bible and taken immediate action to please the Lord? I'm sorry to say at that moment I could not remember, but I vowed then to follow her lead. I don't know if God loves bacon, but he does tell us a few things we can do to honor him. To love him with our all our hearts, souls, and strength. To love others as we love ourselves. To act justly, love mercy, and walk humbly with him.

Truly I tell you, unless you change and become like little children, you will never enter the kingdom of heaven.

MATTHEW 18:3

PASS IT ON

I love it when I move into a house and find an orderly garden that has been tended and loved. One house offered a wonderful surprise. We had moved in during the autumn, and in the spring we were delighted to see lovely fields of bulbs gracing the lawn with their flowery presence, drawing the eye and soothing the soul. I offered a silent prayer of thanks for the previous homeowner who had "paid it forward" in the garden for me. I vowed to do likewise.

Many of the homes we have lived in have been rented, and people would often ask, "Why are you spending money on that yard when it isn't yours?"

"But it *is* ours," we'd reply, "for now." And later it would belong to someone else who would surely appreciate the daffodils in the spring or enjoy harvesting the berries from the bushes in the back. I usually didn't know who would move into our homes after us, but—just as I did with the bulb planter—I felt connected to them through the land and the fruit of our mutual labor.

Kingdom work often involves planting good things into the life of someone you will know only for a short season. You may never see those seeds sprout, but you faithfully planted them, knowing God would cause them to grow. Perhaps you've had the pleasure of accompanying someone on the final leg of the journey to Christ, harvesting what others had planted, watered, and weeded. We are sometimes planters, often weeders, and occasionally harvesters. It's a pleasure to share the garden with our brothers and sisters and to rejoice in the fruit of our mutual labor, knowing that the Master Gardener plots it all.

It's not important who does the planting, or who does the watering.
What's important is that God makes the seed grow.

1 CORINTHIANS 3:7, NLT

CONTENTMENT

I had written a list. My house needed:

1. New windows. The double panes had failed, and there was condensation between them.
2. New flooring to replace the—I admit it—pet-stained and child-worn carpet currently in use.
3. Interior paint. The white showed the effects of thousands of fingerprints and vacuum bumps.
4. Exterior paint. Yes, I like vintage, but not gothic creepy.

I was about to mark down needs five through ten and beyond when I caught myself and laughed. Need? *Need?*

The things we need are those things that keep us alive—food, shelter, clean water, clothing, medical care. Almost everything else is a want. I would be ashamed to show the refugees of the world my "need" list. It's okay to want things, and it's okay to acquire and enjoy some of the things we want. But when we start treating wants as needs, doing everything we can do to satisfy them, trouble is knocking.

I can spend too much and fall into debt. I can work too many hours to earn ever more money and sacrifice time with friends and family. Aren't those friends and family the reason I want a welcoming house anyway? Will they really notice the shabby carpet? Maybe. Or maybe I'm just worried they will. Maybe instead they'll notice the food and hospitality I offered.

Some people will actually use the Internet to look up the addresses of new friends, just to make sure they are keeping up with the new Joneses. I've never done that; I'm just saying *some people* do. And when I—er, some people—do, I am never content.

I went back to my list and retitled it "Wants." I'm developing a better sense of the difference between a want and a need.

If we have enough food and clothing, let us be content. But people who long to be rich fall into temptation and are trapped by many foolish and harmful desires that plunge them into ruin and destruction.

1 TIMOTHY 6:8-9, NLT

LOCK YOUR WIFE AND YOUR DOG IN THE TRUNK

People have long called dogs "man's best friend." You don't have to be a man to know that dogs love their owners. Most people who have a dog understand the kind of love and devotion a dog gives to the people it lives with. There's an old joke: lock your wife and your dog in the trunk and see who is happy to see you when you open it up thirty minutes later!

Why are dogs called our best friends? Maybe because they are always glad to be with us. No matter if we've been gone for ten minutes or ten weeks, when we return, they're eager to see us, greeting us with wiggling and wagging tails. Maybe it's because dogs guard us—when anyone threatens us, they "speak" right up. Loudly, sometimes. Maybe it's because they seem to know when we are sick or sad, and stay particularly close or do funny things to try to cheer us up.

Pet dogs are domesticated: they are bred to want to serve their masters. They derive happiness and fulfillment from being loyal to those to whom they belong. They are faithful, devoted, trustworthy, and true to whatever is best for their masters, and good masters, in return, take good care of them.

Now, we are people, of course, and not dogs. We are made in the image of our Master, which gives us an honor our beloved pets don't have. I still wouldn't be happy after thirty minutes locked in a trunk, but I can seek to be as loyal, trustworthy, and true to my Master's causes as possible.

I will search for faithful people
to be my companions.

PSALM 101:6, NLT

SECOND-DAY SAVOR

Some things are just better later. Drive-in movies, for example, are much better when it's completely dark out than when there's even the tiniest bit of daylight. So are fireworks and sparklers. Anything made with tomato sauce, in my opinion, is better later; lasagna, spaghetti and marinara, even pizza taste better to me the next day. I love brownies . . . tomorrow. I think cake needs a day to settle in to perfect moistness. The trick is, you have to know that and plan ahead. It's tempting to skip the waiting, but we must remember when something will be better later.

We live in a world where now is better, where people seek the immediate gratification of every impulse. Buy now, pay later, and you may find yourself drowning in debt. Trade off school or training for a quick job today, and you may find out that job leads nowhere. On the other hand, parents routinely put off their own needs and wants for the sake of their children and then later find that they enjoy those things all the more for having waited for the right time. Some things are worth waiting for. The right spouse. The right church. The right house.

What are you wishing and hoping for? Is there something you fervently desire that seems just out of reach, not quite within your grasp? It's hard to hold out and believe when it seems like everyone else is getting what they want and need right now. Trust, though, that sometimes second-day savor is better than first-day immediacy. Delight in the Lord—right now—and trust that the future will bring his very best for you.

Trust in the LORD and do good;
dwell in the land and enjoy safe pasture.
Take delight in the LORD,
and he will give you the desires of your heart.

PSALM 37:3-4

UNDER PRESSURE

My son was home for spring break, and he had piled a stack of books on the coffee table—planning to study even while on vacation. I thumbed through one book and came to a section on cell biology. One of the great things about cells (one of the few things about cells that I recalled from my own schooling) is that they respond, on the inside, to pressure from the outside. That response is what allows them keep their shape, integrity, form, and usefulness. With even more outside pressure, they "bulk up" inside (technically, I believe it's called "hypertrophy") to meet the challenge.

In some loosely connected way, this is kind of like a home's furnace or air-conditioning system. When sticky summer heat builds up outside, the AC kicks in to cool the environments in which we live. When winter rages outside or the winds rattle the windows all night long, the furnace automatically kicks on to keep us warm.

I keep waiting for the day/week/month/year in which my life has no problems. I'm halfway through life now (at least), and that time still hasn't arrived. I know that such a day is coming, but not on this side of heaven. In the meantime, I have a secret super Power who helps me deal with whatever comes my way. Indwelt by the Holy Spirit, I am "bulked up" and strengthened to face the cold, the heat, all the pressures of life. By the grace of God, we have what we need to stand up to them all, made stronger on the inside to face what comes from the outside.

*My God will meet all your needs according to
the riches of his glory in Christ Jesus.*

PHILIPPIANS 4:19

OVERSTUFFED

I like to make the best use of time. I also dislike doing laundry. Therefore, in order to do the greatest amount of laundry in the least amount of time, I try to put as much laundry as I can into a given load.

This is known as washer stuffing.

Apparently I have passed this trait along to my daughter, who texted one day to ask her dad to come and look at her washer and dryer. Her clothes were ripping, and there were burn marks on some of her delicates. I could sense the panic in her words; as a newlywed, money was tight, and a new washer and dryer were definitely not in the budget.

Dad checked out her machines and diagnosed the problem. The rips? Washer stuffing—clothes were tangling in the agitator. The burn marks? Dryer stuffing—clothes were becoming overheated in an overcrowded dryer.

In my case, the clothes hadn't actually ripped. But, come to think of it, they weren't getting completely clean, either, because there was no room for them to move freely in the soapy water. "Partly clean clothes" kind of defeats the purpose of washing them in the first place, doesn't it? Once dry, they were wrinkly, too, because there was no room for them to tumble in the dryer. My efforts to get more done in less time was causing me to do it less well. Not a good trade-off.

Sometimes my daily, weekly, and monthly calendars are equally stuffed. I want to fit in as much as possible, but then there is no room to breathe. I've packed so much in that I end up doing all of it in a mediocre manner, which is not at all what I'd set out to do. I have come to realize that it is much better to choose fewer activities and do them well. Each of us has limited time; may we use it wisely and seek excellence.

Teach us to number our days,
that we may gain a heart of wisdom.

PSALM 90:12

DIM BULBS

It is generally understood that to be called a "dim bulb" is not, shall we say, the highest praise. And yet there are times when a dim bulb is exactly what is called for.

I like the under-cabinet lighting in my kitchen; it lends a nice ambiance to the room. I like the faint light that illuminates my stairway. It's not lit up like a runway, but it's bright enough so that no one will trip. Every woman of a certain age knows that candlelight is more becoming than the bright bulbs in her makeup mirror. And night-lights are just perfect for getting around in the dark.

God's Word illuminates every aspect of our lives. We understand that Scripture is profitable for teaching, correcting, rebuking, and training. We know how it sheds light on our paths and that it can help others. The problem is, there may be times when we who are farther along the path may be too eager to shine a spotlight of truth on others who are less mature in the faith.

Our ability to tolerate the brighter light of faith has increased over time. Others, younger in their faith or wounded or more vulnerable, may need the soft radiance of a muted light to begin with. We needn't, for example, point out every possible sin to avoid or offer suggestions for a dozen new spiritual disciplines to begin at once. Discipleship is a patient process. Sanctification is a gentle art. Gradually, over time, that dimmer switch can be turned up.

This command is a lamp,
this teaching is a light,
and correction and instruction
are the way to life.

PROVERBS 6:23

March 15

BEND OR BREAK

Short people—and I proudly count myself among them—often need a little lift to get things done around the house. I do have a handy step stool, but in the interest of saving energy (not to be confused with sloth), I don't always want to haul it upstairs.

One day I had to replace a lightbulb that was out of reach. No step stool was immediately at hand, so I improvised one. I laid a strip of laminate from a nearby closet across two stacks of books and tried to stand on it. It wobbled, it bowed, and it broke. Apparently, thin laminate is not meant for standing on.

Do you ever feel like that piece of laminate? Fragile, wobbly, and called upon to carry a burden that you were never designed to carry? I would bet that most of us have prayed, at one time or another, *Please, God—not one more thing right now. I don't think I can do it!*

The troubling news for me is that some of those unbearable difficulties are self-inflicted. Sometimes I say yes when I know I should say no. Sometimes I take on a project or a new relationship without counting the cost. More often than I care to admit, the burden I carry is simply worry. It doesn't lighten the load; it weighs me down.

In this world we will have troubles, but Christ will not give us more than we can handle yoked together with him. Under the weight of the cares assigned to us, we might bend, but we won't break. Be brave. I know it takes courage to stand up under your burdens; it does for me, too. But you must rid yourself of the self-inflicted weights you carry. After all, you don't want to snap!

My yoke is easy and my burden is light.

MATTHEW 11:30

March 16
PHONE STACKING

Out to dinner a few weeks back, I noticed that at the tables around us there were several diners who were on the phone. They were either talking into their phones or were bent over them, texting, seemingly unaware of the room around them, the food in front of them, and the person across the table.

Even more heartbreaking, I once drove past an outdoor cafe and saw a mother, father, and small child of perhaps three seated at a table for what one would have thought would be a special family outing. But Mom and Dad had their heads down over their phones, while the little one sat there quietly sipping her drink.

I'm not wagging a finger, trust me. My phone is always with me, day and night. Our phones have become indispensable aids to modern life, and in many ways, they really do help us keep in touch. But face-to-face time shouldn't turn into top-of-head to top-of-head time.

Maybe you're familiar with the phone stacking game. All the phones go facedown in the middle of the table. The first person to pick up a phone during the meal pays the check. At home, the first one to reach for a phone does the dishes. The game isn't meant to be punitive; it's just a friendly reminder in our technology-focused era that the age-old custom of breaking bread is meant to include talking, listening, and laughing with those right in front of us.

They devoted themselves to the apostles' teaching and to fellowship, to the breaking of bread and to prayer.

ACTS 2:42

TABLE TOPICS

All right, all right, I'm convinced. We're supposed to talk—and eat—when we're with one another. But sometimes it's hard to find something fresh to talk about.

We already know the rules about conversations with people we don't know well—no politics, no religion, no controversies. Sometimes limiting discussion of these topics with those we do know well is a good idea too!

Sometimes dinner conversations can fall into a stale pattern (or simply fall flat, if they are being held in front of the television). I truly believe that most of us want to share conversation with those we love and eat with, but beyond "How was your day?" or a discussion of looming or past problems, it can be hard to find topics to chat about.

One solution we found is "Table Topics"—boxes of questions designed to be conversation starters. They are sold in a variety of sets—one for families, one for teens, one for dinner guests, and so on. They include questions such as "What was the best and worst job you ever had?" and "Who do you most identify with in the Christmas story?"

Long-married couples will be surprised at the fresh answers and insights they get from listening to their spouses. Friends of many years will learn new and different reasons to love, and perhaps sympathize with, one another. For families, the topic cards provide a non-threatening way for children—and their parents—to reveal information to and about one another.

Don't want to buy the boxes? You don't have to! Do an Internet search for dinner-table conversations and make some conversation starters of your own. But do it soon. You'll be surprised and delighted to learn undiscovered truths about your loved ones; you'll grow closer as you delight in one another's interests. Much more satisfying than "How was your day?"

Don't look out only for your own interests, but take an interest in others, too.

PHILIPPIANS 2:4, NLT

PENCIL SKETCHES

After visiting a local museum, I became interested in a particular artist's work. I bought a tiny print to hang on my wall, went home, and looked him up. I read his bio, saw images of his other work, and learned about his creative process.

It looked like this. First, he would start with an idea. As the idea began to take shape, he would sketch it on paper—not art paper, just regular paper he carried around with him. Sometimes there was a lot of erasing, followed by new sketches. Later, he would darken the lines, and when the main subject looked as he wanted it to, he would begin to work on canvas. His goal was to bring into being the vision he had in his mind's eye.

Some time later, after the main idea had been fully developed on the canvas, the surrounding areas were ready to be painted—and often repainted—till his original vision had come to life at last. A fine work of art develops slowly: sketches into pictures, pictures into painting, bit by bit, filled in, erased, repainted. This is how the masters work.

You are an artistic creation too. And God is the Master who has created—and is still creating—you. He does not bring us out of the womb fully grown and mature. Likewise, when we are born again, he does not expect us to be fully mature at that birth either. Instead, bit by bit, over time, we develop into the work he has seen in his mind's eye from the beginning.

Be patient with yourself as you grow into that masterpiece. The Master is patient, for sure.

He who began a good work in you will carry it on to
completion until the day of Christ Jesus.

PHILIPPIANS 1:6

ROARING LIONS

My dog hides. My daughter's cat hides. If the pets across the street could hear and see it, they would hide too.

The vacuum cleaner is on.

I only have to open the closet where the beast is caged, and my dog runs for the hills. If the stairs are blocked for some reason, she'll jump up onto the fireplace hearth, the wimp. But is she a wimp? Really, the machine is about six times her size and is loud even to me, never mind to delicate canine ears. The machine seems to follow her around the house, or at least makes a sweep through every room (when I have time), seeming to leave no area as a sanctuary. When I shut it down and silence ensues, I can see my dog relax and return to her perch on the back of the couch, fearful no longer—till the next time, anyway.

Still, doesn't she know that, as fearsome and loud as the beast is, I am in control of it? I, her trusted and beloved pet parent? Have I ever once let it eat her? Harm her? Have I chased her with it on purpose? Of course not. She should trust me; she should know that even though it prowls the grounds from time to time, it is never out of my control, as scary as it may seem. I can easily turn it off and pull the plug, although I let it roar from time to time for purposes that only I can understand.

Thank you, Father, that although Satan roars and prowls, you are still in control, and I am in your hands—hands that have never done me wrong.

Be alert and of sober mind. Your enemy the devil prowls around
like a roaring lion looking for someone to devour.

1 PETER 5:8

A POISON TREE

I was angry with my friend;
I told my wrath, my wrath did end.
I was angry with my foe:
I told it not, my wrath did grow.
And I watered it in fears,
Night & morning with my tears:
And I sunned it with smiles,
And with soft deceitful wiles.

And it grew both day and night.
Till it bore an apple bright.
And my foe beheld it shine,
And he knew that it was mine,
And into my garden stole
When the night had veiled the pole;
In the morning, glad, I see
My foe outstretched beneath the tree.

WILLIAM BLAKE, 1794

I stood in line at the home improvement store, waiting to return some light-bulbs that did not fit. Ahead of me was a woman who had a cart filled with dead plants. The store promises that if the plants you buy from it die for any reason, your money will be refunded. It was clear to me that this woman simply had not planted or watered these plants, and they had died from willful neglect. The store honored its policy anyway.

So often, we do that to those we care about. We ignore the relationship, or we treat it—and others—poorly. We don't explain why we are angry, nor do we ask them to tell us why *they* are. If they do tell us the reason, we dismiss it. We do not own our sin. Sometimes relationships, too, die from willful neglect.

While I have time, I should think about the people I need to reconnect with, make amends with, or ask for forgiveness. Communication can restore a relationship to health. Time passes quickly, and unlike a home improvement store, it offers no money-back guarantee for damage due to negligence.

If your brother or sister sins, go and point out their fault, just between
the two of you. If they listen to you, you have won them over.

MATTHEW 18:15

REFLECTIONS

A friend of mine recently moved into a house that had several walls of mirrors. She understood the reason for them—they make the rooms look bigger, and they reflect the scarce light of a Northwest autumn and winter. And yet, it's kind of disconcerting to see yourself no matter which corner you turn or which room you walk into.

"Is my hair really that frizzy?" she asked me, patting the back of her head.

"Are my hips really that wide?" I asked in return, glad that it wasn't my house or I'd be walking sideways all day just to avoid confronting my worst features. Those mirrors brought to mind that old saying, "Wherever you go, there you are."

Initially, the phrase meant that you can't simply leave a problem behind. If you don't solve it, it will just follow you around. Sometimes, though, we see many more problems with ourselves than are really there. We are not lost causes! Christians, of course, know this on some level. Because we are "new" people in Christ, we are called to be on the move constantly, moving away from the old life and toward the new one. Much better than thinking, *Wherever I go, there I am*, is remembering that wherever we go, there Christ is too, working in and through us.

We don't look and act as we wish we did all the time, but we are growing every day. And someday, we'll see not the distorted image, but a perfectly clear picture, as Jesus sees us now.

Now we see things imperfectly, like puzzling reflections in a mirror, but then we will see everything with perfect clarity. All that I know now is partial and incomplete, but then I will know everything completely, just as God now knows me completely.

1 CORINTHIANS 13:12, NLT

ON HOLD

I got a new cell phone a couple of months ago. I love its touch screen, the way I can save favorites, the way I can use the scribble pad to make notes to myself. It's helpful to be able to check my e-mail when I need to, but it's a temptation to check it even when I don't need to. My kids keep in touch with me much more regularly, and I like the handy calculator and flashlight. It's got a lot of cool features, but one feature I was unaware of is that my phone plays enjoyable background music to my callers before I answer a call.

I usually pick up on the second or third ring, so it's not like people have to wait too long. But sometimes it's not the right time for me to answer, and I'm glad they can listen to good music instead of those irritating rings. It reminds me of how, sometimes, I wait on the Lord. I "call" him, so to speak, asking for something or just hoping to chat. Sometimes he picks right up, and I hear back from him immediately—maybe through impressions or words in my heart and mind, through another person, or through Scripture. But more often, from my perspective, it seems like I'm on hold.

And while I'm on hold, life goes on. But I realize the time spent waiting usually includes good friends, shared meals, fun times with my husband and kids, meaningful work, and other pleasant distractions. God has provided some background music for me to enjoy till it's the right time for him to answer.

This is the confidence we have in approaching God: that if we ask anything according to his will, he hears us. And if we know that he hears us— whatever we ask—we know that we have what we asked of him.

1 JOHN 5:14-15

March 23

SOFT WAX

I sat at the kitchen table one day, surrounded by bits of ephemera and photos from our family trip to London. I'd set aside the afternoon to scrapbook the pieces so we'd be able to page through them later.

I came across the ticket stub for Madame Tussauds. Madame Tussaud began her illustrious career making wax portraits just before and during the French Revolution. Afterward, she made her way to Great Britain, where she continued to make life-sized wax figures of the rich and famous. Wax is cheaper and easier to work with than, say, metal or stone. It can be colored and molded and altered, if need be, over time. It doesn't break as clay does, but molds perfectly, conforms exactly, to the shape it is pressed into. That's why, when you visit the museum, the celebrities look so lifelike.

(Yes, we had our pictures taken with the Beatles. And the Queen.)

We, too, are to be like wax. Soft and pliable in the hand of the one who made us, who conforms us to his pattern. From our perspective, each new day seems to bring an unexpected twist—good or bad—or situation we had not anticipated. God, though, saw all this coming and uses our circumstances to mold and shape us. According to Scripture, he does this by conforming us, over time, to the image of his Son.

Be soft and pliable. He who models you loves you.

Those God foreknew he also predestined to be conformed to the image of his Son, that he might be the firstborn among many brothers and sisters.

ROMANS 8:29

IT'S ALL IN THE SAUCE

I was trying to avoid doing some real work, so I decided that the day was perfect for cleaning out the condiments in my pantry. I'm kind of a condiment junkie, so I knew this task could easily help me delay the real work by at least an hour. While sorting, I found two treats I hadn't used in a while: reduced balsamic syrup (dreamy over tomatoes or sliced strawberries) and banana sauce. I have no idea what banana sauce is good for, but it's common in Filipino cooking, and I thought it looked interesting when I saw it in the store. At $1.79, I didn't have a lot to lose.

If I were to use a food analogy, my life is pretty, you know, roasted chicken. I have a job to do, I have a house to keep clean, I have kids to raise and a marriage to enjoy and maintain. So that doesn't leave a lot of time or money for crazy adventures, dream vacations, or wild expeditions. I think most of us have roasted-chicken (or hamburger) lives. So the zip has to come from the condiments.

One week, my friend and I might sneak out to see a chick flick in the middle of the work day. Another time, my husband and I may save up to eat dinner at a restaurant where couples sit together on a love seat. My kids and I are planning to go on a Chocolate City tour when everyone is home for the holidays—some months away, but I can look forward to it. I still have to come home and get to work and fold the clothes, but adding those "condiments" to my normal roasted-chicken routine keeps life full of zip and fun.

The banana sauce is really good on egg rolls, by the way.

A person can do nothing better than to eat and drink and find
satisfaction in their own toil. This too, I see, is from the hand of
God, for without him, who can eat or find enjoyment?

ECCLESIASTES 2:24-25

BUILDING NESTS

I took a work break one morning and sat on my back porch with an iced coffee, watching the birds flit about. Chirpy, cheerful birdsong early in the morning always heralds spring for me, and now I watched as my winged friends began to build their nests.

It was actually very time-consuming work. The birds would flutter to the ground and find twigs—not too heavy but big enough to add bulk—and then fly them back up to the nest-in-progress. Back and forth, back and forth, for some time. Then finally, when the structure was complete, they had made something they would have to live in, for better or worse.

That week I had been nursing a grudge (what an apt word—*nursing*!) against someone who had hurt my feelings. Day by day I would review things, in the privacy of my mind, that I thought helped build my case. She'd done this. She'd said that. She'd forgotten something else. I'd reach further and further for evidence to justify my resentment. But as I watched the birds that morning, I realized I had been building a nest of hurt, twig by twig—a home of bitterness and sorrow that I would have to live in.

I decided to call the other person, and we started a somewhat difficult conversation that ended with laughter and plans for the future. Just as a nest can be built twig by twig, it can be dismantled a piece at a time too. The same is true of a grudge. It's much easier to nurse a grudge and make war with some-one. But it's more life giving to build peace.

Turn from evil and do good;
seek peace and pursue it.

PSALM 34:14

MAKING PROGRESS

I have a friend who was finally realizing her dream—her own house, customized according to her tastes and needs, built from scratch. First she purchased the property she wanted to build the house on, and then she hired a contractor. It seemed like the proverbial marriage made in heaven, right? She moved into an apartment with a short-term lease and waited.

And waited. And *waited*!

Months after the construction was supposed to have been well under way, the only visible sign of progress on the property was the large gray foundation slab. My friend visited the site every week or two and was reassured that progress was being made. First, the foundation had to be reinforced, the contractor told her. Then another time she was told it was curing. But the building of the house itself still had not begun. With her lease running out, she decided to fire the contractor and hire another. This new crew started with that long-standing foundation, and they built a house on top of it. A great house, the dream house she'd wanted all along.

No one can live on a slab. You need to have a foundation to start with, of course, because a house cannot be built on the bare earth (or sand!), not if you want it to stand straight, strong, and true. But once the foundation is laid, the house itself needs to be built. A foundation is what it all rests on, but the actual living is done in the house. When you came to faith in Christ, your firm foundation was laid. Wonderful! But don't stop there. Grow, learn, serve, risk, trust. Move on to construct the "home" you were meant to live in, the life you were meant to live.

Let us move beyond the elementary teachings about Christ and
be taken forward to maturity, not laying again the foundation of
repentance from acts that lead to death, and of faith in God.

HEBREWS 6:1

I AM STILL ALIVE

The previous owners of our current house were people who loved decorating but hated gardening. So when we went to overhaul the backyard, we pulled out many plants that had become diseased or had died from neglect. Against the back fence, though, I found one long, straggly rose, twining herself to a small piece of careworn lattice.

She'd been planted in the wrong place, entirely. There was very little natural sunlight, and what was there was up high, so she'd been forced to push her vine up tall in order to reach it. The soil had not been amended, so it was thin and nutrient poor. Water came only when the skies provided it and not through drip or hose. Her leaves showed signs of bite marks. But the most remarkable thing about this rose was not all the hardships she had endured. It was her color and her perfume.

Her bloom was a pale lilac, ethereal, the color of the clouds at twilight. Her scent was distilled sweetness, ladylike, sugar and spice and everything nice. In spite of the conditions in which she was forced to live, she not only survived, she thrived.

Although she did not seem to fit into my garden plan, I could not cut her down. She seemed to say, *In spite of it all, I am still alive.*

So I kept her and planned my garden around her instead. More valuable to me than a perfect scheme was the lesson she brought, one I knew I had needed in the past and would no doubt need again. No matter where and how we're planted or how thin the soil seems to be, God will enable us roses to thrive.

Those who trust in their riches will fall,
but the righteous will thrive like a green leaf.

PROVERBS 11:28

WASHCLOTHS

Once you hit your teen years, exfoliating—that is, scrubbing the surface of your face to remove anything that would be clogging your pores—is supposed to be a must. Likewise, once you hit a "certain" age, women are advised to exfoliate in order to expose the soft, younger-looking skin under what one can assume is tough, older-looking skin, although the products don't explicitly say that.

I reviewed the array of exfoliation products at the beauty store with a friend, who muttered about exfoliants being called washcloths in her day. I chose one made of olive oil and salt that was supposedly good for the whole body, and so did she.

Later that night, I took my new product into the shower and used it. I was skeptical, I admit, especially because it was to be used all over the body. I took care to rub it into my elbows and knees and—why not?—the decades-old stretch marks. Couldn't hurt, right? Afterward, I have to admit, my skin felt softer, newer, fresher, and it definitely had a glow to it. I can't say if it looked younger—but maybe it did!

Exfoliating became a regular part of my routine, and I made sure the little olive-green jar had a permanent place on my shower shelf. Skin cells die, dirt builds up, and both need to be removed, again and again. Our spirits are like that too. All too easily our souls get polluted; we become calloused and hardened to what is going on around us. We need the blood of Christ to wash us clean, to slough off the old, constantly corruptible self so that we may be made soft, new, and glowing again. Younger? No. But cleaner? Definitely!

You were taught, with regard to your former way of life, to put off your old self, which is being corrupted by its deceitful desires; to be made new in the attitude of your minds; and to put on the new self, created to be like God in true righteousness and holiness.

EPHESIANS 4:22-24

THAT WRETCHED GRASS

I have a dry triangle of land between my garage and a walking path. It's in the hot sun, and it's a difficult place to water. I thought about putting rock in there and calling it good, but then I remembered how much I liked a friend's sedum, also called stonecrop. Perfect! It likes to be hot, dry, and neglected. Why can't all of my plants be so easy?

So I planted mats of sedum there—kind of like laying down a piece of carpet, only plants. A couple of months later, willowy strands of grass were poking their way up through the sedum mat. Pulling them out at the roots also pulled out the sedum, the very plants I wanted to keep. *I should have rocked this over*, I thought, exasperated. But no, I really loved the sedum. I decided that I'd just give the grass a haircut and hope the sedum got strong enough to crowd out the weeds.

One of the stories Jesus told was about a farmer who planted good seed in his fields. While his workers were sleeping, an enemy came in and planted weeds among the farmer's good crops. They grew up together, close, weed and plant. If the farmer's workers had pulled out the weeds while the good plants were still young, the good plants might have been pulled out as well.

It's easy for me to have strong opinions about which people are "good plants" and which are "weeds." And sometimes I wonder why God allows clearly evil people to survive and sometimes even appear to thrive. Perhaps the answer is in Jesus' parable and in the garden of sedum.

"An enemy has done this!" the farmer exclaimed. "Should we pull out the weeds?" they asked. "No," he replied, "you'll uproot the wheat if you do. Let both grow together until the harvest. Then I will tell the harvesters to sort out the weeds."

MATTHEW 13:28-30, NLT

March 30

LINING THINGS UP

Our front garden includes a long stretch that faces the street and is in full view of everyone. Because of that, it makes the first statement about our home. It was a lovely place to put hedges and shrubs, but because it was so visible, we wanted to ensure that everything was placed exactly right.

We capped off the ends with barberries (deer hate them) and then took a tape measure and marked off eight-foot sections in between them for all the other shrubs. A little squirt of chalk powder helped us to remember where to plant each one, and when we had finished, it was exactly as we had hoped and planned.

God takes the long view, too, especially with something so important to him and to the world as his plan for the redemption of mankind through Jesus. He carefully lined things up. Starting with Adam and Eve, we can see God's faithfulness—although sin had been introduced, a blood sacrifice was made to atone for it. In Genesis 22, Abraham was asked to sacrifice his only son, but then at the last minute God himself provided a different sacrifice, foreshadowing the death of Jesus. Leviticus 17 speaks of the blood sacrifice required for atonement. And John speaks of Jesus as the Lamb who came to take away the sins of the world, restoring our relationship with the Father.

God laid out all the events, in line, in the right order and at the right time, so we can see how it all relates. He has always required sacrifice to cover sin; he is the same yesterday, today, and tomorrow. But he has also always provided that sacrifice himself, sparing not even his own Son in his desire to restore his relationship with you and me.

God—who does not lie—promised them [eternal life] before the world began. And now at just the right time he has revealed this message.

TITUS 1:2-3, NLT

THE SWEETEST SCENT

When my daughter grew up and moved out, she wanted one thing of mine to take with her. No, not a kitchen appliance or the vacuum cleaner (although I'm sure she would have taken them if I had offered to let her). She wanted one of my old perfume bottles. The request brought tears to my eyes.

She was all grown up, and I was proud of my daughter, but I cherished the thought that even out on her own in the world she would want to pop the top of one of my perfume bottles and feel that I was close.

I remember my first perfume: Love's Baby Soft. I loved it. When my daughter was old enough for perfume, I bought her some Love's Baby Soft too, which she enjoyed. She and I don't wear the same scents anymore, of course, but we each have found a fragrance that we love, and they have become our signature scents.

Perfume played an important role in the Bible, too. Just before Jesus was to be crucified, a woman poured very expensive perfume over him as a way of giving him honor. Another time, Mary Magdalene, a follower of Jesus, washed his feet with her tears, wiped them dry with her hair, and then rubbed expensive perfume on his feet, also to honor and thank him.

God tells us that the knowledge of Christ is actually like a sweet perfume and that we, his followers, are to spread that wherever we go. In a sense, the discernible presence of Jesus is the signature scent of a Christian.

Thank God! He has made us his captives and continues to lead us along in Christ's triumphal procession. Now he uses us to spread the knowledge of Christ everywhere, like a sweet perfume.

2 CORINTHIANS 2:14, NLT

APRIL

Puddle Jumpers

April showers bring May flowers, but we can have April flowers too. I love to plant April flowers in containers that remind me that it's . . . April!

You can make fun planters out of repurposed wellies or rubber boots. Use boots that your family has outgrown, or visit the thrift shop and buy an inexpensive pair. Poke holes into the bottom of each boot so that they will properly drain. Fill with soil about three quarters of the way up the boot, then plant early bloomers such as pansies or snapdragons.

It's fun to do this in autumn, too, planting spring bulbs with sturdy stems such as crocuses or daffodils. Place in a protected area during the winter and then bring to the front steps or front entry in early spring.

It's fun to pop a small umbrella alongside of this display if you have one handy.

For this month's free printable, go to http://tyndal.es/homeandgarden.

BOILED EGGS

I peeled some eggs for dinner, thinking about my husband's great—if danger-ous—sense of humor. His mother was a nurse, and she would boil eggs to take to work for her lunch, marking them with an *H* on the outside of the shell to remind her, and the family, that they were hard-boiled. Because she had a good sense of humor, too, she would often peel them by first tapping them on the side of her head to crack the shell.

You see where this is going, don't you?

Her young and foolish son took some uncooked eggs and wrote an *H* on several of them, hoping his mother would tap one on her head at work and make a mess. Luckily for him, she'd had her hair done the previous day and didn't want to mess it up, so she cracked the egg on the arm of a chair instead. She told my husband later that he now understood the meaning of "divine intervention"; the Lord had clearly intervened on his behalf!

Who can find a spiritual lesson in eggs? Well, I can, and I'd bet you can too. The thing about those eggs is that in order to make them hard, you have to do something to them: boil them in water. They don't just harden on their own, with or without an *H* written on them. It takes decisive action.

Hardening our hearts is like that too. The book of Hebrews tells us that we have a choice when we hear what God is telling us to do—we can harden our hearts, or we can turn them toward him. It's not always easy to keep our-selves soft toward God—especially when he reproves us. But remember: even that reproof is really a loving form of divine intervention.

The Holy Spirit says, "Today when you hear his voice,
don't harden your hearts as Israel did when they rebelled,
when they tested me in the wilderness."

HEBREWS 3:7-8, NLT

LET THERE BE REST

I adore French style and French food, so I've tried to learn to cook and bake a few French treats, most with success. But I've struggled with croissants.

In order to get those flaky layers, the dough has to be given proper time to rest, or it will never become that buttery treat we enjoy.

We humans need rest too. So often we're on go-go-go, hounded by looming deadlines and bills. Every well-intentioned health care provider tells us more things we need to do to care for ourselves. Church wants more help for ministry. Work becomes more competitive, and we want to invest time in our relationships. There is a temptation to skip the rest that God commands—the Sabbath.

The Sabbath is one day each week set aside for no work. I admit that I struggle to keep it—I have so many important things to get done! I was thumbing through verses on the Sabbath a few weeks ago and came upon the passage about how the women who had gone with Jesus to his crucifixion wanted to prepare his body for burial. Since it was the Sabbath, though, they waited till the next day.

Wait a minute. What do I have to do that is more important than what those women had to do? Really . . . nothing. And yet they obeyed the command to honor the Sabbath. They took God at his word, even when caring for . . . God.

The Lord knows that a rest allows us to enjoy the life he has created for us as well as do our best work on the other days, and he has given us a day every week for just that purpose.

The women who had come with Jesus from Galilee followed Joseph and saw the tomb and how his body was laid in it. Then they went home and prepared spices and perfumes. But they rested on the Sabbath in obedience to the commandment.

LUKE 23:55-56

BROKEN VESSELS

I don't know where I first came across a piece of *kintsugi*, but it made an immediate impression, and from that moment on, I wanted to own some. Not just any piece of *kintsugi*, but a communion set, which made its symbolism even more poignant.

Kintsugi is the Japanese art of taking broken pottery and repairing it with seams of gold. The pottery itself is usually nothing spectacular—made of red clay, perhaps; small; fashioned by hand but without any features that call attention to it. What makes each piece one of a kind is that the broken parts aren't covered up and hidden; instead, they are celebrated. The very fact that the piece has been broken and then made whole again with the most precious materials is what gives each piece its unique beauty. The piece becomes more beautiful than when it was unbroken and common.

Isaiah prayed, "You, Lord, are our Father. We are the clay, you are the potter; we are all the work of your hand" (Isaiah 64:8). Sometimes the Lord allows circumstances to enter our lives, which break us, shatter us into pieces, ruin our hope or our sense of usefulness and wholeness. But even then we are not out of his hand. He takes us and mends us with the gold that is his love. The shattering and the mending are what make us unique. We are repaired by the gold of Christ, who himself was broken and mended.

On the same night the Lord Jesus was betrayed, He took bread in his hands; and after giving thanks to God, He broke it and said, "This is My body, broken for you. Keep doing this so that you and all who come after will have a vivid reminder of Me."

1 CORINTHIANS 11:23-24, VOICE

TO STIFFEN RESOLVE—
ADD STARCH!

As a young bride, I was eager to be a good wife and homemaker. (I'm not saying that's not true now, just that my enthusiasm may have dimmed a bit over the years!) I knew that my new husband liked his shirts well pressed, and I tried to do a good job. I made fine creases when I ironed; they were just in the wrong places.

Since my husband had been in the military, a neatly pressed shirt meant something entirely different to him than it did to me. So he took over the ironing, which was just fine. I was surprised to see him using spray starch—new to me—to give the clothes a crisp, firm look and feel. To add stiffness, add starch.

There aren't a whole lot of other places to use starch in our lives, but there are definitely places I would like to firm up, like the underside of my upper arms. The trouble is, I don't really like arm workouts. It takes all my willpower to get off the couch and into the gym. You might say that in order to firm up my arms, I need to firm up my resolve!

In the book of Daniel, the young Israelite men stiffened their resolve to eat only the food that they knew God had prescribed for them. Although it seemed impossible to those who opposed them, Daniel and his friends actually became healthier and stronger. Today, we need to make good choices for ourselves, too—body, mind, and soul. That very often involves firming up our commitment to choose only those things that are good for us, holy, and pure. Prayer, Scripture, and accountability are just the kinds of "starch" that help hold us up for the long haul.

Where does your resolve need to be stiffened?

Daniel resolved not to defile himself with the royal food and wine, and he asked the chief official for permission not to defile himself this way.

DANIEL 1:8

April 5

PART THE CURTAINS

One time I stayed in a small village in France, where one walks everywhere and the houses closely line the streets. I was a stranger, of course, not only to the town but to the country, and everyone could tell. As I would walk down the street on my way to the *boulangerie*, I could see the delicate lace curtains in the windows part just slightly. The people inside could see me, but I could take only a tiny peek at them. We were separated by that curtain.

Scripture tells us that there has always been a curtain between us and God, mainly to shield us from the power of his holiness, but also, perhaps, to represent the separation between him and us. Leviticus 16:2 says, "The LORD said to Moses, 'Warn your brother, Aaron, not to enter the Most Holy Place behind the inner curtain whenever he chooses; if he does, he will die. For the Ark's cover—the place of atonement—is there, and I myself am present in the cloud above the atonement cover'" (NLT). The people were separated from God by both a chasm—sin—and a curtain. God was always there but not seen.

With Christ's death on the cross, the veil between us and God was parted—actually, it was torn, a much more robust word. Christ has made a way for us to be in the presence of God's holiness. He has made a way for us to see God, in himself.

At the time, it seemed kind of romantic and mysterious to see those French lace curtains parting, and I still enjoy the privacy that curtains give me as I decide whether and when to answer my front door. But I'm glad there is nothing between me and God anymore. Now I can see him, although dimly. But the path has been paved for me to soon see him face to face.

Dear brothers and sisters, we can boldly enter heaven's Most Holy Place because of the blood of Jesus. By his death, Jesus opened a new and life-giving way through the curtain into the Most Holy Place.

HEBREWS 10:19-20, NLT

JAPANESE *WA*

The Japanese concept of *wa* is so integral to the culture and to the nation that the character used to write *wa* is the same one used to express the names *Japan* and *Japanese*. Disturbing *wa* in Japan is a social no-no.

Wa is the understanding that harmony with others—family, friends, colleagues, and society as a whole—is of highest importance. A person is expected to act in whatever way necessary to avoid disturbing peace and harmony. If disagreements need to be expressed, they are done so privately and with respect so as not to embarrass either party or make onlookers uncomfortable. According to *wa*, harmony is more important than self-expression. Although it has some shortcomings, in an age of increasing narcissism and me-first attitudes, *wa* is a refreshing concept.

This is a concept integral to the Christian experience, too. We are told to consider others as better than ourselves, to love one another as we love ourselves, to encourage one another in doing good works. We're exhorted to gently and privately confront those who sin against us and to refrain from any "self-expression" that is really gossip. This course of action can bring repentance and maintain peace. It does not give the opportunity for self-justification or self-pity, both of which are better left behind. Setting aside self for the good of others was modeled by our Savior, who now calls us to leave our current way of living and follow him.

Although I am not Japanese, I admire this concept of *wa*. I hope to carry it into my personal relationships and preserve peace and harmony in my communities, too.

∽

Live in harmony with one another.

ROMANS 12:16

WOUNDED BRIDES

I was recently thinking of a friend who was leaving the church. The church may be the bride of Christ, but it was a marriage our friend no longer wanted to be a part of.

I've known a lot of Christians who have stopped attending church—churches that were not true to Scripture, or churches where members were allowed to harm one another, or worse yet, where the shepherds helped themselves to a leg of lamb or used their power to pronounce judgment but not their ears to listen nor their arms to hug. Others left churches that overlooked suffering people while the church pushed forward with building programs. Some of those who left—both clergy and laymen—were used up, overworked, underappreciated, or burned out.

And yet, we can't simply blame "the church." *We* are the church. And sometimes we are the ones who are so rushed that we don't take time to offer a bit of love to someone who desperately needs it. Or we find petty, nitpicky things to be irritated about with the pastor, the music, or the person in the next pew, even though Scripture reminds us that love is not easily angered. We don't jump in and get involved, but then we complain that no one really knows us. Yes, the church has hurt me, too. But the church has also loved me, prayed for me, fed me, taught me, worshiped with me, cared for me, called me, led me.

Satan cannot remove us from God's hands, but he can drive us so far apart from one another that the church can become a very dysfunctional marriage indeed—a marriage in which we harm one another till we divorce ourselves from it.

I won't pretend that there aren't bad churches out there; there are. I've attended some of them, and if you're at one, it's okay to leave. In fact, you should, lest your good reputation lend credibility to something that has become corrupted. But there are healthy churches, too; press on till you find the (imperfect) good.

Let us not neglect our meeting together, as some people do, but encourage one another, especially now that the day of his return is drawing near.

HEBREWS 10:25, NLT

April 8
GULLY WASHERS

Outdoor spring cleaning is more fun that indoor spring cleaning. I enjoy being out in the fresh air, greeting neighbors who, like me, have been hibernating for the previous months, and seeing all things become new again. Raking is okay, weeding is a necessary evil, and de-mossing is a requirement in my neck of the woods. But one job I really like, even though it includes getting on a ladder, is rinsing out the gutters.

The months of winter bring soggy leaves as well as bits of twigs into my gutters. I bring a hose with the mother of all power-washing heads screwed onto the end of it and blast away. Women like power tools too!

As I stand outside, absorbing vitamin D, the water rinses all the debris away. The bits and pieces of dead material clogging the gutter are washed down and eventually make their way into the street to be raked up and placed into yard waste bags or run into the clean water drains. Once clean, the "arteries" above my house run clear again.

Soaking up the sun, I reflect that the Lord works like a gutter cleaner. By his power, he rinses out the dead and dying material in our lives: the sin, the bad habits, the hurt and the pain, the bitterness, all the detritus from our pasts. By his might, he sends the debris sliding into the garbage or the drain, never to return again.

The beauty, of course, is that we needn't wait till spring cleaning for our hearts to run clean and true again. In Christ, every season, week, and hour can be a time for things to become new.

❧

Wash away all my iniquity
and cleanse me from my sin.

PSALM 51:2

April 9

SOFT SHEETS AND LUMPY PILLOWS

I have always loved the idea of having a guest room in my home, but it hasn't been very many years that we've actually had the space to have one. It was exciting to prepare a room in which my beloved family and friends, visitors to our church, or people the Lord brought our way would be able to comfortably sojourn.

I set about painting it a warm but restful color and decorated with an eye toward France—dried lavender, soft colors, a side-by-side English and French Bible translation. Quiet clock? Check. Little dish of candies? Check. Linens for bathing? Check! The most important element, of course, was the bedding. I piled it on à la *The Princess and the Pea* so our guests would have a restful night's sleep.

After I finished preparing the room, a friend joked that perhaps we should add some lumpy pillows. After all, we didn't want people to become so comfortable that they never wanted to leave . . . right? Her comment reminded me of when our son would not get up on time in the morning, and we finally rolled some marbles under his sheets so that it would be more comfortable to get out of bed than to stay put.

We can become too comfortable in this world, too, which in actuality is not our home. We are just passing through, strangers in the land, as Scripture puts it. Thérèse of Lisieux reminds us, "The world's thy ship and not thy home." God gives us many pleasant, comfortable things to help us see his goodness in the land of the living, but we mustn't become so comfortable that we don't want to depart someday for our true home.

This world is not our permanent home; we are
looking forward to a home yet to come.

HEBREWS 13:14, NLT

April 10

HEALTHY HEARTS

My doctor and I were shocked. I, a seemingly healthy middle-aged woman, had a partially blocked artery. Then there were my blood profiles: both my cholesterol and blood sugar were too high. In my determination to set things right, I spent evenings preparing veggie snacks, and I added salads to each night's downsized dinner. As the knife struck the cutting board, I heard the Holy Spirit murmur, *It takes time and commitment to be healthy, doesn't it?* I knew he wasn't talking about just my body. He was talking about my soul.

I finally understood that my overfed but malnourished body was an outward reflection of an overfed but malnourished soul. While I had many activities that looked good on the outside and garnered praise, they ate up time I might have spent deepening my relationship with God.

When my body and spirit are tuned to recognize only the "sugar high" experiences, the natural sweetness of a quiet relationship between God and me goes unnoticed. Instead of demanding great insights, tangible blessings, or immediate (and positive) answers to prayer, I'm developing a taste for Bible reading that reaffirms what I've learned (even if it doesn't necessarily lead to new insights) and building trust for the long haul (even in the absence of instant answers).

I'm allowing myself to enjoy a slow but steady increase in health and spiritual growth. I used to be on the "lose three pounds a week or I'm switching" diet plan and in the "read through the Bible in sixty days" camp. I now understand that my body will release weight gradually, and my spirit will mature slowly. That's okay. I'm willing to show "long obedience in the same direction," as Eugene Peterson put it. My heart health extends further than a clogged artery. God graciously allowed the physical pain to draw attention to my spiritual need—the heart that, in the end, matters most.

He must increase, but I must decrease.

JOHN 3:30, ESV

April 11

LOCKED IN THE BATHROOM

I was locked in the bathroom, and it wasn't by accident. I had locked myself in there to think, to pray, to worry over what was going on, and even to cry a little. There were only two of us in the house, and both of us were upset. But we remained separated.

It had been a difficult week in a season that was already packed with difficulties. As is so often the case, there was a last straw.

As I prayed in that dark bathroom, I realized that the person I had separated myself from, my husband, was the one ally I had in the situation we were facing. And while he would certainly give me whatever space I needed, our being rooms apart in the house and miles apart in our hearts would not help to move us forward.

I unlocked the door and went to see if we could talk things out. When I took my marriage vows, I promised to be a mate, a companion, and even more than that, one part of a whole. That whole is sometimes broken, because we live in a broken world. Sometimes, though, it can be salvaged, and in our case it was.

It is not good for man to be alone, God tells us. God made a helper that was just right for man, and in our marriage, that helper is me. Although it was okay for me to take time to think and pray, what I really needed to do was to reengage.

Do you ever flee when it would be more helpful to talk things out with a spouse, a child, or a friend? Unlocking that door, to the room and to your heart, might be a good place to start.

The LORD God said, "It is not good for the man to be alone.
I will make a helper who is just right for him."

GENESIS 2:18, NLT

April 12

HOUSE FIRES

I worked a lot of odd jobs to put myself through school, and one of the most difficult but most rewarding jobs was cleaning houses. I really enjoyed that job, and it paid well. Although I'd met with success, I had to quit when I set a house on fire.

I was cleaning in an older home and had pulled out the drawer under the oven in order to wipe it down. I apparently shut it too hard because—I know not how—it broke a gas connection to the wall. Within seconds, that gas found the pilot light and burst into flames, which ignited some towels, and then the wallpaper, and shot up the wall all the way to the dining room, where the drapes caught fire.

It was terrifying.

I called the fire department and looked for the cat—which I could not find—before running to the street and waiting for the fire department. They came and put the fire out (the cat, fortunately, was safe in the basement). The place smelled like smoke and ruined carpets, and I cried. Although the owner was lovely and offered to have me come back, I just couldn't. I was too traumatized.

This is the way gossip works. One comment thoughtlessly let loose upon the world travels more quickly than we could ever have imagined, burning up things in its path and setting relationships, reputations, and hearts on fire within minutes. Even when the fire is eventually put out, it will leave ruin and trauma in its path.

God continually reminds me to be very careful with fire starters, including my tongue.

The tongue is a small member, yet it boasts of great things.
How great a forest is set ablaze by such a small fire!

JAMES 3:5, ESV

SUNSHINE SMUDGES

After a long, dark winter, one of the best things about spring is the sunshine that becomes more plentiful. One room I spend a lot of time in is my kitchen, which has lovely windows that let in that glorious sunlight. I love it for the cheer it brings, but there's something I definitely begin to notice in that bright glow—the beams do more than spread happiness; they also reveal a winter's worth of dust, dirt, smudges, and smears on my cabinet fronts, on my windows, and on my appliances. I hadn't seen the faint smears in the winter gloom.

When the Lord draws near to us and gently whispers or convicts us about something in our lives that is wrong, he's bringing light to an area that he wants us to see afresh. It might be a habit that needs to be cleaned away, like overspending. Perhaps it's a tendency toward thoughtless action that smudges the pure beauty of our hearts, like laziness or being quick to anger. If we are not spiritually mature enough or emotionally strong enough to hear his whisper, he patiently waits till we are ready. When we aren't close enough to hear or feel his quiet direction, he draws us nearer.

In any case, the time to clean things up is as soon as we can see that it needs to be done. His bright light isn't shining on me to condemn; it's to bring that fresh, new feeling I get once I wipe down the cupboard and the fridge, ready for spring days ahead.

Can you, too, feel the Lord shining his light on some dark places in your life? What is he telling you? Quiet yourself—be still. Can you hear him?

I could ask the darkness to hide me
and the light around me to become night—
but even in darkness I cannot hide from you.
To you the night shines as bright as day.
Darkness and light are the same to you.

PSALM 139:11-13, NLT

April 14

SOWING SEEDS

Some of the plants I'd most like to grow, like tomatoes, don't grow easily in my cool corner of the country. I've tried tucking little seeds into tiny, thimble-sized planting pots, hoping and praying they would sprout. Despite my motherly attentions, most of them didn't. When they died, it hurt.

Sometimes the seeds would sprout, only to stop growing at one or two inches. Hope allowed to endure, only to be quickly extinguished, can be more painful than no hope at all. A couple of times, I've planted tomatoes that made it to fruit—unripe fruit. I now understand the previously untested charms of fried-green-tomato sandwiches!

In some ways, allowing ourselves to hope is like planting vegetable seeds. We want something to happen, to come about, to bear goodness in our own life or in the life of someone we love. We work toward it, pray about it, ask God for it, and ask others to pray too. But just as with planting, there is an inherent risk of disappointment in hope. Faithfully planting seeds without guarantee of return makes us vulnerable. It opens us up to the possibility of loss and discouragement when what is wished for fails to sprout, dies young, or bears strange fruit.

Sometimes, though, the plants *do* grow. My neighbor prayed, and then he bought a mini hothouse. Later that summer, in addition to some failed plants, he had baskets of warm, ripe reds!

The apostle Paul tells us that love always hopes. Because of Christ, who first loved us, we can hope in confidence that the seeds that are meant to sprout will. Sow in your heart a variety of hopes—widely, generously, without fear—then combine those hopes with wise actions. Some seeds will sprout, some will not.

If you never plant a seed, you're never disappointed, but you never have the satisfaction of eating your own delicious, homegrown, Big Boy tomato, either.

Remember this—a farmer who plants only a few seeds will get a small crop. But the one who plants generously will get a generous crop.

2 CORINTHIANS 9:6, NLT

BILL PAY

Like most people, I have to take care and pay attention when I'm balancing my budget. There's sometimes a little more money than we planned to spend, sometimes a little less.

I sat down one Saturday morning at my desk, drinking cream-filled coffee to make the onerous task palatable. Like many other people, we keep our budget on the computer and pay most of our bills online.

I set up the bill payments for the month and carefully budgeted everything we'd need cash for. When I reached the end of the budget, I looked at the two remaining categories. "Tithe" came right before "Water." Water was easy. Then I moved back to "Tithe." We always want to tithe. We always try to tithe. We mostly tithe. But if I'm honest, it's often the category I leave to last. If there is money left over, then I pay it. So what is that saying? It's my lowest priority?

Christians around the world and throughout time have argued about whether a tithe is a percentage, if it's flexible, to whom it goes, etc. But it's clear that, in some way, we are to support ministry and those who minister to us. Why had my husband and I gotten into the habit of making this optional?

So we took a step of commitment. We signed up for automatic monthly withdrawals for our tithe. On the last day of each month, a predetermined contribution is sent directly from our bank account to our church. We made it as important as keeping the lights on and our stomachs filled. More important than movie night. After having done it, we did not feel deprived or financially at risk. We felt right.

Thank you, Lord, for all that you've given us. May we continue to learn to trust you for all we'll need in the days ahead, too.

Will man rob God? Yet you are robbing me. But you say, "How have we robbed you?" In your tithes and contributions.

MALACHI 3:8, ESV

TEA FOR TWO

I have a friend who is a good listener. Now, everyone wants the friend who is a good listener, not so much the one who is a good talker. (Note to self: remember this.) My friend has a compassionate heart, she never interrupts, and when it's her turn to speak, she does so with love and grace as well as good advice. Perhaps Solomon had someone like her in mind when he wrote, "A word fitly spoken is like apples of gold in a setting of silver" (Proverbs 25:11, ESV).

The problem is, by the time people are done speaking their piece and receiving her counsel, they feel better, but she feels drained. It's not as often that someone listens to *her* or understands the time alone that she requires in order to dispense those silver-set apples.

One year for her birthday, I bought her two teacups—British, as her reading pleasures lean that way. The idea was that when she sat down with her friends—talking with them, listening and confiding, taking in and offering—she needed to have her cup filled up as much as she needed to fill the cups of others.

Our patterns of communicating are not easy to break, whether we're talker friends or listener friends. A listener friend needs to learn to be brave, vulnerable, and willing to speak up more often: if you want to be heard, you have to say something. And a talker friend needs to learn to sit back and use her mouth for sipping her tea while her ears are engaged.

It's beautiful to be one who pours into others, whether it be a delightful Earl Grey or a word given in season. Just make sure that you let others care for you, too.

Dear friend, I hope all is well with you and that you are
as healthy in body as you are strong in spirit.

3 JOHN 1:2, NLT

PORTION PLATES

Apparently the portion sizes encouraged by all-you-can-eat Sunday brunch and the Old Timey Buffet Café aren't conducive to weight loss. While perusing some health food websites, I came across a product called the Portion Plate. I decided to order one, and when it arrived, it seemed to make a lot of sense.

The plate is divided in half by a line, and on one side is printed "vegetables." Half of the other half—that is, a quarter of the plate—is labeled "protein." The remaining quarter says "carbohydrates." I kept looking for the portion that said "cake," but I didn't see it anywhere. I was tempted to take my Sharpie and write it all across the back. But I didn't.

I used the plate for a few weeks the way a person uses training wheels, as an aid to help me get and keep my balance till I could balance on my own. I learned that it's both *what* I eat and *how much* I eat that matters. What I eat determines whether or not I am getting the required nutrition; how much I eat determines whether I take in more than my body can use, potentially resulting in body fat and physical stress.

I have a portion plate for my non-eating life as well. It's a calendar. In order to achieve balance, I need to choose my servings wisely—saying no to too much work, yes to devotional time and prayer, and yes to fun, leaving an appropriate slice of time for exercise. As with food, it matters both *what* I put on my calendar (ensuring balance) and *how much* I take on (preventing me from taking on more than my mind and soul can handle).

Examine what's laid out before you; select some and not all, and maintain a balance. That will lead to good health.

Hear my words, you wise men, and give ear to me, you who know; for the ear tests words as the palate tastes food. Let us choose what is right; let us know among ourselves what is good.

JOB 34:2-4, ESV

CAT AND MASTER

You've probably heard the joke that dogs have owners and cats have staff. I recently saw a funny picture that showed both a dog and a cat looking out the front window as a car pulled into the driveway. The dog said, "Yay! The master is home!" The cat said, "You're late, slave."

Each animal has its charms, for sure, and there are pet lovers who have one or more of each. But cats, overall, are definitely harder to control. People generally have no trouble herding dogs. They obey. Cats? Herding cats is impossible. And yet taming them is a pleasure, because it can be a challenge to earn their affections.

When a cat begins to show disrespect for its master, it begins to act outside of the boundaries that were laid down for it. It will refuse to use the litter box. It will ignore rules regarding furniture and treats. It will disdain games of Chase the Bird or other previously enjoyable pastimes spent with its master. It pulls away. Discipline is futile. In extreme cases, a cat may not be allowed to remain in the home because it becomes destructive or dangerous to its owners.

Masters need to be masters, enforcing what is good for the pet and for the family. Subordinates (I'm looking at you, kitty) need to fall under the house rules even when they don't want to.

I can hardly blame the poor cat, though. We humans have a hard time coming under authority too. People bad-mouth those in elected office, their pastors, their bosses. It's not that we—or cats—need to accept poor leadership. But we do need to speak honorably of those above us while working for change. And always we must revere our ultimate Master, God, who is worthy of all respect.

Honor everyone. Love the brotherhood. Fear God. Honor the emperor.

1 PETER 2:17, ESV

HOLES IN THE ROOF

There are few ways to spend your money that are more frustrating than repairing a roof. One friend described it, costwise, as paying for a brand-new car, driving it onto the roof of your house, and just leaving it there. A leaky roof is a real problem, though, allowing in not only the elements, but also insects, vermin, and mold, all of which can destroy the house. Roof repairs, though costly, are necessary.

How did Jesus feel when some men punched a big hole in the roof of the home he was teaching in and lowered their friend down through the opening? According to Scripture, he did not seem to be angry. Instead, he commended them for their faith—the faith that prompted them to bring their friend to the Healer—and made no mention of the cost of repairing it. As a result of the men's faith, their friend was healed.

My husband was in the military, and they have a motto: "Leave no man behind." These men did not leave their friend behind, in spite of the potential cost to themselves. But who better than Jesus to understand this? He did not leave us, his brothers and sisters, behind either, despite the ultimate cost to himself.

By comparison, I guess roof repair isn't so spendy after all.

Some men came, bringing to him a paralyzed man, carried by four
of them. Since they could not get him to Jesus because of the crowd,
they made an opening in the roof above Jesus by digging through it
and then lowered the mat the man was lying on. When Jesus saw their
faith, he said to the paralyzed man, "Son, your sins are forgiven."

MARK 2:3-5

LAYER CAKE

It's no secret that I am a cake aficionado. I love cake of all kinds, but my favorite cake—perhaps because it feeds my nostalgia as well as my appetite—is layer cake. The more layers, the better. I've learned that I can bake three layers, then freeze them and, with a long knife, slice them in half to end up with six layers.

My second-favorite cake is angel food cake. It was always a favorite for childhood birthdays, followed closely by cherry chip cake. For the first birthday I celebrated with my husband, he tried to make an angel food cake for me, but he didn't have the right pan. He baked it in a 13-by-9-inch pan, and it came out with the texture of a giant kitchen sponge. We still laugh about that. The reason I love angel food cake? No cloying frosting required—just lots of whipped cream.

I do like a finely wrought frosting, but not too much of it. Too much can detract from the taste of the cake itself. Regular cake without any whipped cream or frosting can be dry, though, and tough to get down without lots of coffee or milk.

That layer cake is like life—the day-to-day part is the cake; the special occasions and mountaintop experiences, the icing. Most of us have layers of each, year after year, throughout our lives. Too much frosting makes us sick and spoiled; too little frosting to hold the monotonous or difficult days together can steal joy. God in his wisdom layers each for us, a bit of both in the same bite, perhaps, or one following the other. He allows blessings and troubles to alternate throughout life, but through them all, he's right there at the table with us.

When times are good, be happy;
but when times are bad, consider this:
God has made the one
as well as the other.

ECCLESIASTES 7:14

April 21

WOULD ANYONE GUESS A CHRISTIAN LIVES HERE?

One afternoon my husband and I walked room to room looking for any light-bulbs and smoke-detector batteries that needed to be replaced.

We walked from the French country–inspired living room, to the library with lots of throw blankets and pillows, to the kitchen with pink-and-black granite, to the powder room with a Marie Antoinette night-light. I sensed more than heard the grumbling. "What?" I asked him.

"Would anyone even know a man lives in this place?" he groused. I laughed and pointed out the man cave, the garage, and the lawn. He nodded, kind of convinced.

He'd made a point, though. Although we're not to judge by appearance, we do look at people and their environs to get a sense of what they are about. Do they treat people in private the same as in public, or are they hypocrites? Do they rail against "sins" that are not forbidden but which may be more a matter of personal taste, and at the same time defend the exercise of free will? What's on their movie list? What kinds of books do they have in their homes? Music on their playlists? Do they never have enough money for church but plenty for travel?

This isn't meant to be a defense for legalism; in fact, by showing that we can enjoy freedom in Christ, we might be showing people a different view of Christianity than they're expecting. Still, we must always be aware that those around us will be learning by observation not only about us but about our faith—and that includes the freedom we enjoy as well. Do your home and your life reflect your heart for Christ?

Whatever you have learned or received or heard from me, or seen in me—put it into practice. And the God of peace will be with you.

PHILIPPIANS 4:9

SPRING CLEANING

One whole bookshelf in my house is devoted to *Little House* books by Laura Ingalls Wilder. Those books—and Laura, Mary, and Carrie—were some of my closest friends in childhood. And who among us didn't crush on Almanzo? I have some new hardbacks, but I also have my old paperbacks, with *Sandy* scribbled inside them in my childish, loopy handwriting.

One of my favorite scenes in the books is when the girls do spring cleaning. I think I appreciate it so much as an adult because I now realize how very few possessions they had. And yet they took the time to replace the mattress ticking, blacken the stove, plump their bed pillows, and beat the dust from the window curtains. All the areas of their home that had been overlooked in the daily living of the months before were attended to. Then all was fresh, clean, and new.

I admit I like spring cleaning my own house for the same reason. During the course of the year, I don't have time to attend to cleaning out closets or wiping down baseboards or throwing away gardening tools that have rusted. But during spring-cleaning weekend, I take care of those tasks. It is also good, I have found, to do an inventory of my habits at the same time. Have I let my thought patterns slip? Am I grumbling and complaining? Have I neglected my friendships? Have I ignored spiritual discipline or companionship? I don't spend time thinking about these things day to day. But once a year, it's good to take stock, search my heart, test my mind—and ask the Lord to do likewise. Sometimes I find things that need to be trashed, but often I just plump up whatever needs attention.

The heart is deceitful above all things
and beyond cure.
Who can understand it?

"I the LORD search the heart
and examine the mind,
to reward each person according to their conduct,
according to what their deeds deserve."

JEREMIAH 17:9-10

PROVIDING OUR DAILY BREAD

One of my favorite *Little House* stories takes place in Laura Ingalls Wilder's book *The Long Winter*. Her town, De Smet, was cut off due to extreme winter weather, and no one was able to acquire food. Eventually, the townspeople turned to grinding wheat in coffee grinders. It was a long, hard process that required persistent effort and commitment. In the end, it provided exactly what was needed.

I thought of this as a batch of bread dough was rising under a dish towel in my warm kitchen. I could just as easily have purchased a loaf at a local bakery or grocery store. Purchasing bread for my family is easy, done almost without thought, and perhaps because of that, without much thanksgiving.

We live in a get-it-in-a-snap world. This makes it difficult to develop an effective prayer life because we find it hard to concentrate for more than a few minutes, and we're disappointed when a positive answer to our prayers doesn't appear within moments of opening our eyes. It isn't a stretch to say that is the store-bought-bread approach to prayer.

Prayer of the crank-the-coffee-grinder variety—hard, persistent, and without an immediate answer in sight—requires discipline and patience. But when the answer comes (and it always does), that kind of prayer provides just what was needed all along, with a slice of character growth, too.

Teaching them more about prayer, [Jesus] used this story: "Suppose you went to a friend's house at midnight, wanting to borrow three loaves of bread. You say to him, 'A friend of mine has just arrived for a visit, and I have nothing for him to eat.' And suppose he calls out from his bedroom, 'Don't bother me. The door is locked for the night, and my family and I are all in bed. I can't help you.' But I tell you this—though he won't do it for friendship's sake, if you keep knocking long enough, he will get up and give you whatever you need because of your shameless persistence."

LUKE 11:5-8, NLT

PIEPLANT

If you'll bear with another Laura Ingalls Wilder example (she's got so many!), I'd like to share about pieplant.

Pieplant is what we call rhubarb, an April favorite of mine and also of my husband. It grows in a great crown, its stalks ruby red, its green-veined leaves like humongous umbrellas. What it's known for, though, is its bitter taste.

Our taste buds sense five basic tastes: salty, sweet, sour, umami, and bitter. Foods taste best when two or more of these tastes are combined. Think lemonade or chocolate-covered pretzels. Rhubarb is like that too; best when combined with plenty of sugar to balance the bitterness.

In the book *The First Four Years*, Laura was a young housewife preparing a meal for the farmhands who had come to help her husband at harvest. Eager to impress, she made a pieplant pie—but forgot the sugar. One of the farmhands graciously proclaimed, "That is the way I like it. If there is no sugar in the pie, then every fellow can sweeten his own as much as he likes without hurting the cook's feelings." When making pieplant pie, sugar is a very important ingredient!

Sometimes when I'm eager to help others see what I've learned the hard way and thus avoid their own pain, I offer a large serving of advice that, even when put kindly, can be bitter if I forget to combine it with love. Is my advice-to-affection balance off with my children? Subordinates? Those I minister to, and with? Unlike that farmhand, most people won't add their own sugar to what we dish out. We need to offer it to them ourselves.

These three remain: faith, hope and love. But the greatest of these is love.

1 CORINTHIANS 13:13

TRIAL BY FIRE

I have already mentioned that I'm not the "ironer" in our family—not for anyone who wishes to have a crisp piece of clothing, anyway. But there is one iron I've grown fairly competent at using: my hair-straightening iron. I need it in this humid climate if I ever want my hair to be beautiful to behold!

I keep the iron in the bathroom drawer of magic tools I call upon to help tame my frizzy hair into a smooth, sleek style. Also in the drawer are hot rollers, brushes with metal cores that heat up, and lotions which, when applied to the hair and then followed by said hot tools, help straighten and smooth the hair. When it comes to crumpled clothes or coarse hair, only heat will smooth out the wrinkles and rough edges.

As much as I wish and pray against difficult times coming into my life and the lives of those I love, when I look back, I can see that those difficult days transformed me in ways that joy and easy living could not. Hard times put character to the test. Can we stand firm in our convictions, either personal or spiritual, when the call goes out to turn up the heat in the furnace? Only by walking through, and then out of, the furnace will we know what we're made of. As for me, the people I most respect and whose counsel I most often seek are those who have come through difficult times with their peace and faith intact. They are beautiful to behold.

When you pass through the waters,
I will be with you;
and when you pass through the rivers,
they will not sweep over you.
When you walk through the fire,
you will not be burned;
the flames will not set you ablaze.

ISAIAH 43:2

WASHING WHITES

I admire homemakers who have sorting baskets in their laundry rooms—one for whites, one for colors, one for delicates. As for me, the greatest thing I discovered on my new washing machine was the setting for "Mixed Loads." Frankly, I'm usually too busy (lazy?) to use anything else.

The problem, of course, is that some garments really do need to be set aside. The sleeves on men's dress shirts can shrink if washed in hot water or dried for too long. (Do not ask me how I know this!) Delicates can be shredded by a too-energetic agitator. And dark colors, especially reds, can bleed.

It's easy to end up with pink whites—T-shirts, towels, or socks—as a result of overlooking a new red something thrown into the wash with them. Then drastic measures are required to avert replacing said garments. Removing the offensive red piece and then rewashing the pinks with bleach usually does the trick. Everything returns to snowy white, as it should be.

God, like a launderer's detergent, comes along when we are too lazy or busy to pay attention and have let some sin bleed into our lives. Sometimes I forget that sin taints everything I do if left unaddressed. God doesn't judge me when I humbly bring my sin-stained efforts to him. He takes them from me, bleaches them with his holiness, and makes me pure again. The cost? Inestimable. But Jesus willingly paid it all.

"Come now, let us settle the matter,"
says the LORD.
"Though your sins are like scarlet,
they shall be as white as snow;
though they are red as crimson,
they shall be like wool."

ISAIAH 1:18

TRADITIONS

"Familiarity breeds contempt," as the saying goes. And it's true that when a ritual becomes familiar, we can fall into a mindless repetition. But of course not all ritual is meaningless.

Having prescribed prayers, holidays, and traditions reminds us to follow through on important occasions. If taking Communion often was not commanded by the Lord, would churches celebrate it as frequently? And if we didn't celebrate it as often, would his death be as regularly recalled?

At the celebration of Jewish Passover, the youngest child in the room poses the question, "Why is this night different from all other nights?" Then the child elaborates on how the night is different:

1. On all other nights we eat bread, but on this night we eat only matzo.
2. On all other nights we eat all kinds of vegetables and herbs, but on this night we have to eat only bitter herbs.
3. On all other nights we don't dip our vegetables in salt water, but on this night we do, and we dip them twice.
4. On all other nights we eat while sitting upright, but on this night we eat reclining.

By calling upon a child, a community of believers passes along stories of faith to every member, including the youngest. A child's voice of faith often softens an older, hardened heart. And rituals help us recall God's good deeds, his faithfulness, and his miraculous provisions. What traditions do you observe that strengthen not only your own faith but that of those around you?

"Obey these instructions as a lasting ordinance for you and your descendants. When you enter the land that the LORD will give you as he promised, observe this ceremony. And when your children ask you, 'What does this ceremony mean to you?' then tell them, 'It is the Passover sacrifice to the LORD, who passed over the houses of the Israelites in Egypt and spared our homes when he struck down the Egyptians.'" Then the people bowed down and worshiped.

EXODUS 12:24-27, ESV

April 28

FATHER BEFORE PHONE

Here are a few things I would never forget to do in the morning: Brush my teeth. Get dressed (even yoga pants count!). Take my medications. Take the dog out. Make and drink several cups of coffee. Check my phone. (Confession: I check my phone before I do any of the other things—but I should get a little bit of a pass since my alarm is on it.)

So why do I find it so hard to make room for God in my day?

All throughout my Christian life I have heard the rational reasons put forth—very often by my own two lips—of why time with the Lord in prayer, in meditation, in Scripture doesn't have to be in the morning, and honestly, it doesn't. But when I prioritize it as a morning activity, I can be sure it will happen. I'm giving God the firstfruits of my day, and the rest of the day is blessed because of it. I enjoy the time I spend reading or praying in the evening, but evening often finds me too tired to give it the best part of my brain.

What could I do to help myself make time with God a part of my morning routine? Maybe I should set an alarm on my phone for my quiet time. Or download an app that will send me a Bible verse or passage each day. Or keep my Bible next to my coffeepot. Or tape my memory verse to the mirror in the bathroom, right above my toothbrush. However I do it, I need to make morning time for the two of us.

In the morning, LORD, you hear my voice;
in the morning I lay my requests before you and wait expectantly.

PSALM 5:3

FOR THE LOVE OF A SPARROW

I went out one late-spring morning to water the geraniums in my window box. As I moved the watering wand inside the box, a bird flew out at me—nearly colliding with my nose. I came closer but saw nothing. Then I spotted it—a little nest with four oval eggs. My geranium box had tenants! I later learned the new residents were juncos, a kind of sparrow.

I had never had this happen and wasn't sure what to do next. I turned to my social media accounts to ask my friends. Do I water? If I do, will the birds or their nest be harmed? But if I don't, will the plants die and expose my young bird family to danger? I knew there were some aggressive blue jays and crows nearby.

Within minutes I had dozens of comments: suggestions on how to water the plant without harming the birds, ways to deadhead the flowers without cutting back the cover, and requests to share the news when the birdies were born.

It was so heartwarming. These were only birds, after all. But people cared, and they were eager to help me attend to them. I could only imagine what wonderful assistance and love these dear people would offer if I had asked for help for a child!

The lesson was not lost on me. I cared deeply for those sparrows; I felt a sense of responsibility to protect them. But my affection for them was nothing compared to my affection for my children, for whom I would lay down my life. God nudged me. I grinned. *Yeah, I get it, God. Thank you—really. Thank you.*

Are not two sparrows sold for a penny? Yet not one of them will fall to the ground outside your Father's care. And even the very hairs of your head are all numbered. So don't be afraid; you are worth more than many sparrows.

MATTHEW 10:29-31

FREE TO FLY

Run, John, run
the law commands,
But gives us neither feet
nor hands.
Far better news
the gospel brings:
It bids us fly
and gives us wings.

ATTRIBUTED TO JOHN BUNYAN

The resident junco family in our geranium flower-box "hotel" this summer made a featherweight straw nest and promptly laid little eggs in it. Within what seemed like a just a few short weeks (wherein I did neither water nor deadhead!), the birds hatched, received food, and were urged out of the nest and into the nearby trees. Mom and Dad were teaching them to fly almost as soon as they emerged from their shells, it seemed. I looked it up: the little chirpers leave the nest about two weeks after hatching.

The birds were not destined to stay flightless within the confines of a nest, no matter how safe and comfortable. Truth is, it wouldn't be very comfortable for six grown birds. They needed the freedom to do what they were created to do—fly.

Likewise, we believers are not meant to be confined to faith by rules, safe as it sometimes may seem. The Old Testament law provided safe boundaries for God's people, but Jesus fulfilled the law for us. We no longer have to worry that we don't measure up; that we haven't followed all the rules; or that our sacrifice, work, and offerings will be rejected. We are right with God and need not perform in order to be acceptable. We can always return to his sheltering wing, but we are also free to fly.

If the old way, which brings condemnation, was glorious, how much
more glorious is the new way, which makes us right with God!

2 CORINTHIANS 3:9, NLT

MAY

May Day Basket

May Day—May 1—is a good excuse to celebrate. Where we live, it's also a good time to come out of winter hibernation, get outside, and reconnect with neighbors. One May Day tradition is delivering little baskets of flowers to neighbors.

WHAT YOU'LL NEED

A small, woven basket (You can get leftovers from Easter on the cheap, or you can use empty strawberry containers.)

Pansies or other small plants (The plants should fit snugly in the basket, but leave enough room to water them.)

DIRECTIONS

Place plants in the basket. If the basket has a handle, hang it on a neighbor's door. Traditionally, givers ring the doorbell and run—but it might be more neighborly to say hello and give the basket in person!

For this month's free printable, go to http://tyndal.es/homeandgarden.

May 1

EMPTY NESTS

So it was time, then, for our little junco family to leave the nest. Mama and Papa bird had taught their young ones to fly, and they were twittering happily in the backyard trees. I looked in my geranium boxes and found that the nest was empty.

It resonated with me. My children have flown away from the nest in the past few years, moving forward into their own lives even while inextricably connected to mine. I was happy for them to be reaching forward into the joyful autonomy of adulthood while feeling, I admit, a little at odds about my new role in their lives and in the world in general. Being a hands-on mom had been such a big part of my daily life for so long. It is no more.

I noticed that the junco parents had completely cleaned out the nest after their young had flown away. And they did not nest in that place again; they, too, had moved on. Perhaps there is a lesson there. Maybe you don't have children, or your children are still young. You may be widowed or divorced, or just lost your job or your house. We each have seasons wherein something we love comes to a close. We move to a different stage of life—maybe willingly, perhaps unwillingly. You might be flailing a little, as I was, struggling to discover a new purpose and direction, wondering if the old fits in somehow, while trying to welcome the new.

I thought that, had the parent birds remained in that empty nest, it would have felt odd. But they'd flown on, too, to other areas, other trees. It is a great big world after all, and there are new things to experience and explore even as seasons march on, fresh things in life to discover and enjoy. The nest may be empty, but life is full for the junco birds and maybe for me, too, in the here and now.

There's an opportune time to do things, a right time for everything on the earth:
. . . a time to hold on and another to let go.

ECCLESIASTES 3:1, 6, MSG

May 2
SINGLENESS

The savvy home decorator knows to group things in odd numbers. An even number of objects, arranged symmetrically, is too predictable to please the eye. But one candle, surrounded by three framed pictures, in a room with five pieces of furniture, creates interest and a natural elegance.

Odd numbers may be fine in decorating, but in real life, it seems like things are designed for two, especially if you are single. Dinner for two at a nice restaurant. Buy-one-get-one-free deals for entertainment options. Driver and passenger. Double beds. It can be very lonely to be single in a world that seems to be designed for couples.

Sometimes the Lord cures that loneliness with the provision of a mate. Sometimes he satisfies it with friends and family or fulfilling activities. For some singles, he simply removes the desire for romantic companionship. But even so, many single people wish that they weren't.

There are no easy answers that aren't simplistic or perhaps even offensive. There is a biblical response, however, and that is that Christ has promised to be the husband to the husbandless. He, too, understands what it is like to be unmarried in a society in which couples are the norm. His calling included singleness, single beds, and loneliness.

He will not call any of us to a place that he will not accompany us to and equip us for. And he will never leave us nor forsake us.

Your Maker is your husband, the LORD of hosts is his name;
and the Holy One of Israel is your Redeemer, the God of the
whole earth he is called. For the LORD has called you.

ISAIAH 54:5-6, ESV

DEMANDING TASTE BUDS

It shouldn't have been a surprise, really, when I got the e-mail from my doctor telling me that my blood sugar was high and I needed to watch my carbohydrate intake. I'd had gestational diabetes twice—two loud warning shots. Now it was time to pay attention to them.

I sighed. Good-bye, lemonade. I'll miss you, chocolate chip cookies. It's been good, mashed potatoes. Maybe I'll see ya around Thanksgiving.

All right, then; it wasn't that bad. While I did have a period of mourning for the foods I'd given up, I didn't feel any regret later for the pounds I'd lost because of the changes I'd made.

I came to a flash of understanding. Why should I favor one part of my body over the others? Were my taste buds the supreme dictators of my life? Did they take precedence over kidney function, vision, and a healthy vascular system? My feet had told me, many times, that they would like to carry fewer pounds, and my knees had joined them in hearty agreement.

Eating only what my taste buds wanted, instead of what the rest of my body needed, was foolish. I couldn't allow my taste buds, like spoiled children, to dictate to the other members of my body. We certainly wouldn't allow that in a healthy family—or in a healthy church family.

Although I cut back, I still indulged in really tasty carbohydrates from time to time. But I added more protein, vegetables, and healthy fats. My feet and knees were happier and so was my blood . . . and my doctor. So am I, and my taste buds have discovered that they like meat and cheese and delicious salads. It's working out all right, all around, and my whole body is happier and healthier now.

No discipline seems pleasant at the time, but painful.
Later on, however, it produces a harvest of righteousness
and peace for those who have been trained by it.

HEBREWS 12:11

SLIPPAGE ZONE

I admit that when I first read the words *slippage zone*, I thought of all the places that phrase might aptly apply to my middle-aged body. Since the words were referring to a plot of land, however, I quickly reoriented myself and took another look.

There had been some landslides in our state that spring—big ones—that had washed away entire neighborhoods and created panic among the residents. We hadn't thought to check into that when we bought our house, but in light of the recent events, we decided we should see what we were dealing with. We were relieved to discover that our house was not built on a slippage zone, nor were most of our neighbors' houses, but one house nearby certainly was. That homeowner needed to take action to rectify the situation lest he and his family go sliding into the Puget Sound. What could be done? Maintaining the trees whose roots stabilize the soil was a place to start.

In Matthew 7, Jesus talks about building our spiritual houses. He teaches that those who hear his words *and put them into practice* are building their houses on solid rock. No matter what storms come against such a home, it will stand. Those who hear and *do not put them into practice*, though, are building on sand. Their houses will collapse with a great crash. The trick, the Lord tells us, is not to simply listen but to act. Just like the homeowner who had to act to save his house, we must take action to save our spiritual homes. Thankfully, the actions we must take are all clearly spelled out. Build only upon the Stone of Zion!

So this is what the Sovereign LORD says: "See, I lay a stone in Zion, a tested stone, a precious cornerstone for a sure foundation; the one who relies on it will never be stricken with panic."

ISAIAH 28:16

DEATH BY CHOCOLATE

Our dog is a little bitty thing, seven pounds dripping wet and after her one meal. She's a picky eater, too, except when it comes to chocolate, which could kill her.

Her first adventure with a few dropped chocolate chips ended up with our having to help her—er—remove them by forcing hydrogen peroxide down her throat to make the offending objects come up. We weren't quite as quick to respond to her second experience, in which she consumed half a chocolate bar left by a houseguest. When we discovered what had happened, we raced her to the vet, who told us that one more incident would kill her.

At first we just tried to keep chocolate out of her reach, but she'd come near the dishwasher when the dishes were dirty, sniffing around for the sweet stuff. When we baked, we worried that a chip could fall off of the counter. Eventually we decided that her life was more important than our taste buds, and we cleared the house of chocolate. If the humans want chocolate, they eat it at a restaurant. It's that serious.

Whatever sin tempts you, you can be sure it is not for your good. You may have indulged in it before, thinking that because you did not die, surely you can continue to indulge. But the sin builds up over time, poisoning your spirit, and perhaps someday you'll reach the point of no return.

For me, the best way to avoid yielding to temptation is to completely clear it from my vicinity. I don't trust my flesh; you see, I'm made of temptable material. It's my responsibility to remove or forestall that which could bring me down. The dog and I have both come to the conclusion that life is better than "chocolate."

Don't let us yield to temptation, but rescue us from the evil one.

MATTHEW 6:13, NLT

CHASING RABBITS

The next street over from ours has a lot of rabbits. The lawns are large and lush, and there are plenty of bushes to hide under, so it seems to be a good place for bunnies. There's also a dog on that street who is a pointer, a hunting dog. The bunnies taunt him when he's running free. Which one should he chase?

One day as I walked up the street, I watched as he first chased after one, then spied another and chased after it. Drawn by a noise, he went back to the first, and then when the second one seemed closer in range, he switched gears again. In the end, he proved the old saying, "People who chase two rabbits at once end up losing both." (It applies to dogs, too!)

It's easy to apply this lesson to simple things: don't date two men at the same time; don't work two jobs if it means you can't do either one well. Less often, we see it applied to our faith. But it should be. The Lord says, "No one can serve two masters. Either you will hate the one and love the other, or you will be devoted to the one and despise the other. You cannot serve both God and money" (Matthew 6:24). I've got to be careful which rabbit I'm chasing, or I'll lose them both!

Fear the LORD and serve him wholeheartedly. Put away forever the idols your ancestors worshiped when they lived beyond the Euphrates River and in Egypt. Serve the LORD alone. But if you refuse to serve the LORD, then choose today whom you will serve. Would you prefer the gods your ancestors served beyond the Euphrates? Or will it be the gods of the Amorites in whose land you now live? But as for me and my family, we will serve the LORD.

JOSHUA 24:14-15, NLT

May 7

I DON'T DO BASKETS

My daughter's mother-in-law told me that the two of them had been plant shopping together when she'd asked my daughter if she wanted a hanging flower basket for spring. My daughter, on a newlywed's budget, said she couldn't afford to buy baskets just yet because they were annuals—they'd die after one year—and she had to invest in plants that would make a return on her investment year after year. She'd spend her money on perennials, not on annuals.

That's my thrifty landscape girl! I thought, wondering just where she'd acquired that trait, because it certainly wasn't from me.

Although eternity is limitless, in this life we have relatively small amounts of time, money, talents, and energy. Each of us desires to be a good steward, to invest in things that last a lifetime and beyond. We want to spend ourselves where it will make a difference, not just for the quick, bright basket of tumbling, short-term, showy blooms but for the slow-growing long-term plant that gives pleasure for generations.

So my stewardly daughter bought a few little plants and planted them. Then she watered and fed them faithfully, knowing that although they would make a puny showing in year one, the next year would bring lush growth and the plants would triple in size. They'd be there for the long haul, and she was willing to wait for that.

What are you investing your time, talent, energy, and money in? The occasional basket of annuals is, of course, more than okay. I love geraniums! But don't be afraid to toil for people and on projects that are perennials; they take some time to show blossoms and come into their own, but then they are, as Psalm 1 reminds us, firmly planted.

Let's not get tired of doing what is good. At just the right time
we will reap a harvest of blessing if we don't give up.

GALATIANS 6:9, NLT

BENCH SITTERS

Some friends and I were out shopping one day for a garden bench. So many of them were beautiful but looked supremely uncomfortable—lots of wrought iron: hot in the summer, cold in the winter, hard in either case—or like they'd fall apart after one season. I liked the cushioned ones, but they were pretty expensive. Finally we came upon one that caused us to laugh. "Look!" I said. "This one's already broken in!"

The bench was rosewood, with beautifully carved arms, but it also had two more carvings, most unusual ones. Carved into the seat itself were two impressions—of backsides. "Perhaps it's for someone who doesn't know what part of the body needs to be placed there?" a friend suggested, and we laughed.

When I was growing up, people were called bench sitters if they joined a team but didn't show up for practice or lacked the skills, desire, or endurance to play. Later that night I thought to myself: *Am I a spiritual bench sitter?*

Do I show up for practice, learning what I need to know to be effective, participating with the team, and contributing my skills? Can I press on, with a smile, through the ninth inning and into overtime? Or am I too tired to get on the field? Am I wearing the wrong uniform so that no one even knows I'm on the team?

Whether you joined the team by your own decision or were drafted, here you are. Show up. Share your skills. Cheer others on and persevere, because you're awesome at both. You have an important role to play!

Everyone who competes in the games goes into strict training. They do it to get a crown that will not last, but we do it to get a crown that will last forever.

1 CORINTHIANS 9:25

May 9

YELLOW ROSE OF TEXAS

I could never plant roses in our front yard because the neighborhood deer looked at them the way you and I might look at a luscious piece of whipped cream–topped pound cake. The roses would be chewed up and gone in an hour. But there was one tiny, empty corner in my fenced backyard, a spot that received lots of sun. Since I had only one small space available for roses, I had to consider carefully which type to plant. It wasn't a difficult decision at all. I'd plant the yellow roses of Texas.

Some years earlier one of my best, dearest friends had passed away from cancer. She'd often talked of the flowers of Texas, the bluebonnets and the roses. When she died, some mutual friends sent a bouquet of yellow roses to me, a touching gesture that I have never forgotten. One of those blossoms is pressed inside my Bible.

As I dug the hole before planting, I thought about my friend. She'd left behind two boys—boys who would not have their mother to guide and comfort them. As a mom, I want to always be around to advise and encourage, as I sometimes feel only a mother can. My friend died knowing that she could no longer mother her kids, but she had firm faith that the Lord himself would guide and guard her children. And he has.

Although I will see her again someday, I am still here on this earth, and I realize that I can hand my ever-present concerns for my children into God's hands right now; death is not required. He is able to care for them when I'm not here, and while I *am* here too. I need not worry. He is faithful.

I am grateful for my dear friend, my Yellow Rose of Texas, who is still teaching me.

Know therefore that the LORD your God is God; he is the faithful God, keeping his covenant of love to a thousand generations of those who love him and keep his commandments.

DEUTERONOMY 7:9

May 10

LEVEL GROUND

One of the most onerous jobs when installing hardscaping—the firm, permanent landscape features such as rock beds, fountains, fences, and such—is leveling the ground. It's not as simple as just scraping the land and eyeballing it. One must carefully consider the slope of the ground, measure precisely, and recruit several sets of eyes, because what looks fine to one person can in actuality be way off. Perspective is needed.

All people are born into a world with unlevel playing fields. Some are born rich, some poor. Some are born into groups of people who suffer unjust discrimination and others into more protected segments of society. Some are born into nations that protect their freedoms; others are persecuted. Some are born into families that nurture and cherish them, some into families that abuse. There is little that is truly fair or just here on earth. Yet our souls cry out for justice, because we are made in God's image and he is perfectly just.

If God is just, why is there so much that is unjust in the here and now? When Jesus came to earth, his people were expecting a Messiah who would be an earthly king, one who would take power and avenge them then and there. Instead, Jesus came gently, on a donkey, which disappointed them but fulfilled prophecy in a way they didn't understand. When Christ returns, he will come in power and strength and set things right. They will remain right for all eternity.

All of us, though born into a variety of circumstances, are equal brothers and sisters in Christ. No one is better, more valuable, more protected, or more cherished. We're each precious in the sight of our Savior. He will put right any inequities in our current situations . . . in his time. Perspective.

There is neither Jew nor Gentile, neither slave nor free, nor is there male and female, for you are all one in Christ Jesus.

GALATIANS 3:28

AFRAID OF HEIGHTS

I'd never considered that I had a fear of heights. I *liked* visiting the top of the Space Needle and the Eiffel Tower! Because I am a short woman, I regularly use a step ladder to reach the top shelf in the pantry, and ladders don't make me nervous either.

Or so I thought.

One summer early in our marriage, in order to save money, we decided to paint our own house. We wanted it brush painted, not spray painted, and every quote was out of our reach. So we bought the paint, and a *very* tall ladder, and began.

Up five steps, seven, ten. I hadn't realized how narrow those treads were. And it's not easy to paint when you're clutching the sides of a shaking ladder. I found that you actually need to have both hands free. Even Hubs, normally unflappable in the face of heights, found it difficult. So we rented a cherry picker.

When the machine arrived, we drove it on the lawn. The kids clapped their hands with glee as they climbed into the small cage and, in the arms of their dad, were lifted upward. We were higher now but felt safe, too. With no more worries about falling, we simply enjoyed the view and confidently went about our work. You can see a lot more from up high, and you have the peace to appreciate the view when you're not afraid of falling.

God has lots of good things to show you along the course of life, and some of them require a seemingly risky climb to get a glimpse of God's perspective. But don't be afraid. No matter how high he takes you, you can be sure that you're not on a shaky ladder. You're in the Lord's hand.

The Lord makes firm the steps
of the one who delights in him;
though he may stumble, he will not fall,
for the Lord upholds him with his hand.

PSALM 37:23-24

May 12

PAY IT FORWARD

I browsed the home-supply store one day, looking for some film that I could apply to windows in our house in rooms that needed a little bit of privacy. I didn't want to block the light entirely (in one room, it was the only window!), and I wanted it to look pretty, too. A cut-to-fit scroll of film designed to look like stained glass fit the bill.

When I got home, my straightedge and I headed upstairs to affix my purchase to the window, which took a speedy fifteen minutes. I laughed at that, recalling the beautiful, breathtaking stained-glass windows I had seen in a thirteenth-century cathedral in France just a few years before. The docent leading the tour told us that the windows were many years in the making; it might take two, three, even four generations of craftsmen to finish a single window. One artisan may have designed the window but never seen it under construction. Another may have begun the work but seen only bits and pieces of the final product. Only the final craftsman would see the project completed. Those who came before him had to trust that the future workers would carry their vision forward. They couldn't have been working for the accolades of the worshipers; they'd never see them. They had to work for the praise of the Worshiped alone.

Many "projects" we undertake will bear fruit that we will never see. Often we do what we feel led to do, but we do not see it succeed. We plant seeds that do not seem to sprout. We pour ourselves into the lives of those who don't turn themselves around. If we keep our eyes on circumstantial affirmation, we're bound to be disappointed. But if we keep our eyes on the Worshiped alone, we work knowing that we'll reap a generous reward.

Whatever you do, work at it with all your heart, as working for the Lord,
not for human masters, since you know that you will receive an inheritance
from the Lord as a reward. It is the Lord Christ you are serving.

COLOSSIANS 3:23-24

ADMONISHMENT AND ENCOURAGEMENT

We'd been working in the yard, and much had turned out right. And yet, not all of it had. The landscape blocks looked odd, and when we watered the plants they bordered, the water ran off onto our stones and into the neighbor's yard, but not onto the plants that needed the water. The running water took the mulch down with it too, which made a woody mess.

A handyman was working next door, a man with many years of experience in the field and whose good work we could plainly see. "You're doing well," he said, pointing toward our blocks. "But you need another layer or this will never work. You've started well. Don't quit before you've finished well."

His advice was a mature blend of admonishment and encouragement: you can do better; don't give up. We were tired. We'd spent a lot of money. What we really wanted was someone to come by and say, "Great job!" But it wasn't a great job. Not yet, although we were on the way.

So we saved up our pennies for thirty more blocks and then laid them, too. The look was just right. The water stayed welled. The mulch stayed in place.

It's not always easy for me to hear, "You're not done yet. You have a ways to go. You might have to redo this. Rethink this. Press on." Maybe it's not easy for you, either. But I'm very grateful for the people God brings into my life to admonish as well as encourage me, because in the end, I want to be proud of my work—whatever it may be—no matter how long it takes to get it right.

*Let the message of Christ dwell among you richly as you
teach and admonish one another with all wisdom.*

COLOSSIANS 3:16

May 14
SEEDLINGS

Spring is a season for planting. While the ground is still hard, we take tools and loosen it up some, breaking big clumps of dirt into soft mounds of black and brown soil. Once it's softened, we place a seed in it, or a tiny plant that needs to take root. We know that even though it doesn't look like much at that point, each has the potential to grow into something beautiful.

Too little water, and the seed or plant dies. Too much rain, and the water rolls away, down into the grass or onto the sidewalk. Or maybe it lifts the plant out of its new bed or washes the seed away, only to dry up and die, so close to home.

Scripture is like water for our souls; our spirits cannot live without it. When we've known Jesus for a while, we want to speak truth with our friends who don't yet know Christ or are new to faith. And that's terrific! But if we try to share too much at once, their minds wander as ours once did, and the good that it might do doesn't really happen; the extra "water" just rolls down the sidewalk. Or maybe the flow of biblical truth is so overwhelming that it lifts them out of the flower bed altogether, and Scripture becomes a lecture, turning them off to the truth.

Your friends are lovely seedlings who are developing into beautiful flowers, and you are an amazing friend to share your water. Just make sure you are watering with measured portions, allowing time for God's truth to be absorbed—slow but steady growth is best. Then watch as, over time, the Gardener grows your friends into sturdy plants too!

*Such things were written in the Scriptures long ago to teach
us. And the Scriptures give us hope and encouragement as
we wait patiently for God's promises to be fulfilled.*

ROMANS 15:4, NLT

May 15

NEW SOIL

The backyard looked, in places, like Jurassic Park: overgrown and weedy, out of control to the point where I couldn't see the ground and was afraid of what might be living underneath the brush. Other parts of the lawn were barren, rock-solid patches that looked like they had been squeezed of every last nutrient. Then there was the pond—slimy and swarming with mosquitoes and, believe it or not, leeches.

"What have we gotten ourselves into?" Hubs muttered.

We dragged out some shovels, the mower, and the yard-waste bins and worked up a lot of elbow grease. Only we're old enough now that our elbows don't have a lot of extra grease! We ripped out what was dead, trimmed back what needed pruning, and purified the pond. Once the land was stripped bare, we amended it with fresh soil—rich, thick, and black as coffee grounds. A season later, new plants flourished there, happy and thriving.

We left a few big rocks, though, for structure and as reminders. The ivy began to grow over them, but they were still visible—memories of what had been there before, reminders of what had been transformed. God, too, is in the transforming business. He takes the rough patches of our lives and clears them of debris. To the barren patches he introduces soft, fertile soil that can encourage new growth. He removes pests. But often he leaves a reminder—perhaps we can call it a scar—to remind us of what came before. It reminds us of how he is in the business of transforming parched lands into springs of water, blessing those he loves with fruitful fields in every endeavor.

He turned the desert into pools of water
And the parched ground into flowing springs;
there he brought the hungry to live,
and they founded a city where they could settle.
They sowed fields and planted vineyards
that yielded a fruitful harvest;
he blessed them, and their numbers greatly increased,
and he did not let their herds diminish.

PSALM 107:35-38

STAGING

A few years back we went to rent a house and phoned the real estate agent who had listed it. We loved the photos of the house we'd seen online. Could she show it to us quickly? We didn't want to let it get away.

Once inside, we realized it bore little resemblance to the online promotion. The walls had been painted different colors, the appliances had been switched out, and there was no furniture. "This looks so . . . different from what we'd come to expect from the photos," I said. "Oh," she replied, dismissing me with a wave of her hand, "those pictures had been staged."

Staging houses is fairly common. All the old furniture, worn and loved by real people who set glasses down on coffee tables without using coasters, is removed. Pristine, unused furniture, perfectly coordinated with accessories, is moved in. As a result, the place looks much more attractive and welcoming than it actually is.

We've all met "staged" people. "Angel in the street, devil in the house" is how one person refers to them. On the outside, they're gracious and kind, pulled together and seemingly superspiritual. But once you get to know them, you can see the mask slip. They gossip and badmouth people without remorse. They judge others by appearances and income. They have no problem stepping on others to reach a higher rung of . . . anything.

Most of us dip into hypocrisy from time to time, only to be caught or to catch ourselves and feel appropriate shame and remorse. But there are others around us, even in the church, who have no higher purpose than self-promotion. It behooves us to be discerning, for our own sakes and for others in our charge.

Woe to you, teachers of the law and Pharisees, you hypocrites! You are like whitewashed tombs, which look beautiful on the outside but on the inside are full of the bones of the dead and everything unclean. In the same way, on the outside you appear to people as righteous but on the inside you are full of hypocrisy and wickedness.

MATTHEW 23:27-28

May 17

THORNS

I spent an afternoon spreading bark dust over the freshly planted beds. Bark dust is a favorite for a few reasons: it keeps the weeds down, it holds the water in, and it looks great. Definitely worth the time and effort.

When I went back to make a little adjustment, though, I forgot to put my gloves back on, and a quiver of slivers pierced my palm, causing immediate and constant pain. Although I used tweezers to remove most of them, some of the splinters just stayed firmly planted, deeply embedded into the skin itself. I wished for them to go away, but they did not.

Scripture recalls a time when Paul asked for the thorn in his flesh to be removed. Although the Lord had miraculously healed many people, he declined to remove whatever this thorn was, and Paul accepted the Lord's decision. I wonder about that sometimes—how God decides whom to heal and whom not to heal. It's easy for us to believe that circumstances, mainly health and wealth, indicate God's pleasure or blessing. But they do not. Solomon was wealthy, as was Joseph of Arimathea. But the widow whom Jesus commended was poor, and Jesus himself was born to poor peasants and was homeless during his ministry years.

Sometimes the thorn remains. Paul later said, "I have learned to be content whatever the circumstances. I know what it is to be in need, and I know what it is to have plenty. I have learned the secret of being content in any and every situation, whether well fed or hungry, whether living in plenty or in want. I can do all this through him who gives me strength" (Philippians 4:11-13).

My grace is sufficient for you.

2 CORINTHIANS 12:9

ROBBED!

One evening we checked our phones, only to find urgent messages from our next-door neighbors. They'd been robbed!

Once they described what had happened, I realized that I'd actually witnessed a part of the robbery in progress. I'd been sitting at my front-facing office window, working, when a small crowd of people I didn't recognize walked in front of our neighbors' house and ours. Some were wearing the jerseys of a college football team playing that evening, so I assumed they were gathering for a game night. Instead, they were stealing jewelry and computer equipment.

When it came time for them to flee, the driver inadvertently backed over a low concrete wall, and the car got stuck. Just rewards, you might think. But one of the thieves approached a neighbor and asked him to help tow them out, and help was rendered. The helpful neighbor did not realize he was an unwitting accessory to a crime; he was simply trying to do a good deed. Later, of course, the brazen nerve of the thieves shocked us all. Rob a house, then request help from a neighbor to escape?

I hope and pray that my friends recover their stolen property, but I wonder about those thieves, too. Are they unredeemable? Or did the kindness they were shown shame them into some kind of self-reflection? Did they continue to live their lives as takers, or did this moment convict them?

The Lord implores us to be kind to our enemies, because it may convict them and cause them to change. And even if our enemies don't change, God promises to reward those who obey him. It's a win-win!

If your enemy is hungry, give him food to eat;
if he is thirsty, give him water to drink.
In doing this, you will heap burning coals on his head,
and the LORD will reward you.

PROVERBS 25:21-22

PADLOCKS, DEADLOCKS

After the neighbors' house was broken into, we decided to reassess our personal security and take a more proactive stance. We hadn't changed any of the locks on our home since we'd purchased it, so who knew how many keys were floating around? We started on the perimeter and purchased some new padlocks to affix to the gates that led to the backyard. Someone could sneak in there and break into the house undetected.

Next we made sure the windows all had locks and sliders. We'd have to be a bit more careful about leaving them open when we left the house, lest they become an easy access point. Finally, we put dead bolts on the doors. The house itself, of course, contained what we loved the most—our people and our pets—so most of our efforts were directed toward protecting them.

Christians, too, are told to safeguard what is most important to us: our reputations, for example. Proverbs 22 reminds us that our good name is of more value to us than gold. We seem to do a lot to protect our financial assets, but what about our reputations? Scripture tells us to guard our mouths, as we all have wounded others and been wounded ourselves by runaway tongues. Above all, we're to guard our hearts, because the heart directs the whole of our lives.

Is my heart filled with thanksgiving or envy? With gratefulness or bitterness? With peace or with anxiety? Is it overflowing with compassion, or is it smoldering and judgmental? Colored with legalism or informed by grace?

I've got to do a checkup pretty much every day. When things go wrong in my life, it's most likely an inside job. I'm going to do a thorough once-over, and then I'm going to sleep well tonight.

Above all else, guard your heart,
for everything you do flows from it.

PROVERBS 4:23

FRESH FLOWERS, LIGHT BREEZES

My good friend was coming to visit, and I was eager for her company. I bought new sheets and pillows for the guest room and placed a new rose in the planter on the dresser. It was a good excuse to wash the windows (a long-neglected task) and then open them to let in a fresh breeze. My friend is precious to me, and I wanted a wonderful place to greet her when she arrived.

The smooth surface of life on earth becomes pockmarked as years go by and we are hit by difficulties large and small. And yet . . . we kind of like it here. It's always been our home. It's comfortable, and for the most part, warm. But when this life is over, don't be afraid to move forward into heaven, into the room Christ has prepared just for you. If you have received Christ as your Savior, heaven awaits you. An unborn baby may believe that living inside her mother's womb is nice—warm, comfortable, quiet—and probably wouldn't choose to be born if given the choice. Birth into this world, like transition into the next, can be a little frightening and even painful for all involved. But once born, would any of us choose to go back? Not a chance.

The Bible talks about heaven more than five hundred times. If God says something once, it's important. If he mentions something five hundred times, he really wants us to pay attention. Jesus himself says he is preparing a place for us to be with him after our lives on this earth are over. I can't wait to see the welcoming, loving place he's prepared for me.

My Father's house has many rooms; if that were not so, would I have told you that I am going there to prepare a place for you? And if I go and prepare a place for you, I will come back and take you to be with me that you also may be where I am.

JOHN 14:2-3

HABITS

I'd planted a flower bed right before some big work and personal deadlines approached. *At least the plants are in*, I reassured myself. *I can leave them alone for a while.*

But when some time had passed and I returned to my garden, I found that my bed had been commandeered by weeds. They'd settled in with the plants, stealing my plants' food. The weeds began to crowd the flowers; they grew tall, shading my own blossoms so they couldn't get the sun that they needed.

It took weeks, really, to get all of those weeds out because they'd become tough and persistent. The flower bed had become dominated by what was wrong instead of what was right. The weeds were beginning to damage the good plants. Had I kept on top of those weeds, I could have stopped them before things had gotten so out of hand.

That's what I did thereafter. I also promised myself to plant fewer flower beds!

If I attend to the things I know are good for me—body, mind, and spirit—I'm rooted and built up in health and strength. But when I get lazy and let my physical health slide to indulge bad habits, or my mental health slide to indulge lazy entertainment, or my spiritual health slide because I'm willing to let other things crowd out what's really valuable, I'm vulnerable to philosophies contrary to my faith.

Plucking out a weed or two when they're small and few in number is so much easier than eradicating them after they have taken over the entire bed.

*Just as you received Christ Jesus as Lord, continue to live your
lives in him, rooted and built up in him, strengthened in the faith
as you were taught, and overflowing with thankfulness.*

*See to it that no one takes you captive through hollow and deceptive
philosophy, which depends on human tradition and the elemental
spiritual forces of this world rather than on Christ.*

COLOSSIANS 2:6-8

SECOND GEAR

The weather was finally nice, and I wanted to get off the elliptical and outside in the (rare) sun for a little exercise. Walking is always good, but in my quest for creative calorie burning, I thought I'd dig out my old bike.

It was propped in a back corner of the garage, and I pulled it out and dusted it off. (Believe me, I checked it over *really* well for spiders and webs.) It looked like it would work, so I swung one leg over and settled into the saddle. You know what they say: once you learn how to ride a bike, you never forget.

One thing I did forget, however, was that the gears on this bike were broken. I could ride in first gear, my legs spinning round and round, and also in second. But I could not shift into third gear, or fourth, or fifth—the gears you should use going downhill. I was stuck in second gear, which made for a tiresome ride. I could ride up the hills with comparative ease, pushing hard, but I didn't really get to enjoy coasting downhill, wind blowing through my hair, because I was scared. The broken bike made me feel out of control.

As I steered the bike back into the garage, it came to me that my gears are sometimes stuck in real life, too. I'm always pushing uphill (perseverance), which builds muscle (character), but how often do I get into high gear and enjoy the ride (confident hope)? Without the high gear of hope, my life-ride feels out of my control, so I'm more inclined to be worried than confident.

A Christian's life is not meant to be one of constant uphill struggles and fearful descents. Even in the toughest times, we don't have to make do with broken gears. God gives us hope—hope that won't disappoint us. Enjoy the ride!

We can rejoice, too, when we run into problems and trials, for we know that they help us develop endurance. And endurance develops strength of character, and character strengthens our confident hope of salvation. And this hope will not lead to disappointment. For we know how dearly God loves us, because he has given us the Holy Spirit to fill our hearts with his love.

ROMANS 5:3-5, NLT

GRAFTED HISTORIES

Although I never minded renting a house, I was eager to buy one so that I could plant a lilac, which would have been too expensive to buy for a temporary dwelling. So after we bought a house, it was with great delight that I went to the autumn sale at my favorite nursery and selected two lilac bushes, one to grace each side of my front door.

I chose a variety of dwarf lilacs created by grafting one lilac onto another. For grafting, one plant is selected for its sturdy, healthy base and stem (the root) and another for the lovely flowers, leaves, or fruit that the planter hopes to grow. The flowering plant is called a *scion*, which is a word that also means "family descendants."

In the case of my lilacs, the scions were a fluffy, little pink variety called "Tinkerbelle," just like the fairy. They bloomed the very first year after having been grafted onto the sturdy stock plant, perfuming all who passed between them. Although it didn't get the looks of admiration, it was the stock plant—the root—that sustained the whole operation.

Our Christian faith has a deep history, going back thousands of years before our Lord's incarnation. That history is the Jewish background from which Jesus and Christianity were born. Judaism gives our faith the strong stock it needs in order to blossom into all that Christ means it to be. He made it clear that he did not come to do away with the faith and heritage that came before, but to fulfill it. It's good to honor that which came before as well as that which is now. Both are required for descendants, physical and spiritual.

You, though a wild olive shoot, have been grafted in among the others and now share in the nourishing sap from the olive root. . . . You do not support the root, but the root supports you.

ROMANS 11:17-18

WELCOME BROWNIES

I scrolled through the list of houses online, page by page, looking for the one that might be my family's next home. Among the callouts of kitchen upgrades and lovely views, a single line on a listing caught my eye and made me stop clicking ahead.

"One of the neighbors is known to deliver homemade brownies."

It seemed quaint, somehow, a memory of a bygone welcome-wagon era. A neighbor who did not wait in an idling car, windows up, till he could pull in the garage and close the door behind him. Someone who baked with a purpose, to feed and treat not only his own family but those he shared a street, and in some respects, a life with. The fact that the listing mentioned it pointed to the fact that it was recognized as both unusual and desirable.

"Maybe this really is the one," I said to my husband.

"Because of the brownies?"

I nodded.

We did indeed buy that house, and the neighbor came over with flowers one week, brownies a month later. Another neighbor shared fresh cherry tomatoes from the bounty of her greenhouse. I reciprocated with jam the following summer.

We hear a lot about *random* acts of kindness—buying coffee for the person in the car behind you, for example. Not spoken of as frequently, but perhaps even more important, are *deliberate* acts of kindness. When we choose people to be the focus of our good intentions, sharing our bounty, thinking of them ahead of ourselves, it speaks to them of how we value them. For those of us in the house of God, it shares insight into our true home.

Let your light shine before others, that they may see your
good deeds and glorify your Father in heaven.

MATTHEW 5:16

May 25

STUFFED ARMOIRES

I'd made a really good friend online; we bonded over our shared love of reading and our newly launched writing careers. Soon we were e-mailing every day, sharing more than our writing. We shared our prayer requests, our financial concerns, our health issues, our worries about our families. We confessed our sins to each other and held each other accountable.

One spring she and I were both freshening up our homes and decided to send pictures to each other via e-mail, since we didn't live close enough to visit. After cleaning up my house, I went from room to room, snapping photos from the best angles. Then I sent them to her. Within a day or so, she responded.

"Beautiful house," she said. "But it's so . . . neat. Where's all your stuff?"

I laughed at that. I knew what she meant. Magazines, dog-grooming brushes, socks taken off before a nap the day before, TV remotes, etc. I had discovered the magic of armoires and placed one in almost every room. When I wanted the room to look pulled together and neat, without anything out of place, I'd pile all the clutter in the armoire. It wasn't long before it all migrated out again, though.

Do you pile all of your "stuff" in armoires, hidden from everyone and anyone who can help? It was great to have that comment come from a friend with whom I could be honest, one who trusted me with honesty about the details of her life in return. With those I trust, I can let it all hang out, confess my faults, and ask for help. It's good to have friends who don't mind your stuff.

Confess your sins to each other and pray for each other so that you may
be healed. The prayer of a righteous person is powerful and effective.

JAMES 5:16

CUTTINGS AND TRANSPLANTS

A recent addition to my gardening arsenal is rooting hormone. This is a neat little liquid that helps plants transplant more easily; it gives the roots a healthy boost. You can use it two ways: if you want to replicate a plant you already have, especially vines like ivy, take a healthy cutting and then dip the end into the rooting hormone before planting. Second, if you buy a plant from a nursery or are gifted one from a friend, a little of this added to the initial watering will help it transition into its new home—in your yard!

As I dipped a few cuttings into the rooting hormone, it seemed to me that this is very much like introducing our friends to our faith. Christianity is an evangelizing faith; we're called to share the Good News with others. We're not to duplicate ourselves, of course, but to be agents through whom the Holy Spirit works.

Sometimes when people are fresh in their faith, the new "territory" can seem a bit bewildering, and we don't want them to wither and die. Here's where the second use can come in handy. We've got to come alongside and make the ground hospitable! Cultivate the soil with love so there's a soft landing for those who stumble. Water with kindness and attention; offer a hand, an ear, a prayer till they're rooted and beyond. It can be overwhelming to be transplanted from one kingdom to the next—we've all experienced it, haven't we? But what a pleasure and a privilege to come alongside the Gardener as he works.

Restore us, God Almighty;
make your face shine on us,
that we may be saved.

You transplanted a vine from Egypt;
you drove out the nations and planted it.
You cleared the ground for it,
and it took root and filled the land.

PSALM 80:7-9

IN MEMORIAL

Not long ago we needed to retire our flag, as its exposure to the elements had left it a frayed and worn. While exploring how to honorably do just that, I came across a newspaper article featuring a Florida woman who took in well-loved flags, cut the stars out of them, and sent those stars, one each, to active servicemen and servicewomen. She wanted to let them know that they weren't forgotten and to remind them of what and why they were serving. One recipient sewed his star onto a T-shirt so that it was next to his heart.

Don't take that story as license to cut up and repurpose your American flag, though; it's often illegal! Why?

The flag is not just a piece of fabric; it's representative of the nation, of the people, and of all those who came before and will come after us. It reminds us of the sacrifices made on our behalf and the responsibility we have to steward the nation for those who will follow. The courage of those who serve and protect is summed up in the phrase, "These colors don't run." So we honor those who serve, because it is their blood that bought and maintains our freedom. And we honor the flag that represents them—and us.

To serve to the point of risking death is the greatest expression of love. We see this in Christ's sacrifice too. Our ultimate freedom, of course, was bought with his blood and is maintained by his affections and power. When faced with a situation so daunting it brought blood from his pores, he did not run. He stood and served, fulfilling his calling.

May we always remember those who have laid down their lives for our freedom. Hurrah!

Greater love has no one than this: to lay down one's life for one's friends.

JOHN 15:13

DRIP LINES

After weeding, watering is the most onerous garden chore, because you have to do it every day, or at least every other day. Once perennials are established you can slack off a little . . . but not for long, unless you want stuff to die.

One year we got smart—or lazy—and decided to install drip lines. It takes a little work up front—the preparation part—but then once it's all established, all you have to do is turn on the faucet and the plants get watered! If you're even lazier—er, smarter, like us—you can install a timer so you don't even have to remember to turn the water on. The plants get just what they need, constantly, a little drop at a time, so they are never dry nor flooded. They thrive. And we sit nearby and drink iced tea!

One day, while sipping said tea, it came to me that those drip lines are like regular Bible study. It's best to get a little bit, every day—not a flood, but enough to keep me hydrated. When I'm well watered in the Word, I can withstand a day or two of scorching heat. I can grow in spite of the circumstances. I'm healthy enough to deal with things that bedevil and pester me. The trick, of course, is to do the "setup work" in advance.

Do you have a time set aside each day in which you can read a few verses? How about listening to Scripture on audio, during a walk or a commute? I've found, in gardening and in my spiritual disciplines, that the easier I make it to follow through, the more likely I am to grow strong and thrive. God's Word never fails.

The LORD will guide you always; he will satisfy your needs in a sun-scorched land and will strengthen your frame. You will be like a well-watered garden, like a spring whose waters never fail.

ISAIAH 58:11

LITTLE YAPPY DOGS

We have a wonderful little Gary Larson cartoon posted in our kitchen. It shows a small dog (like mine) on a step stool (like mine) making espresso. The caption says, "While their owners sleep, nervous little dogs start their day." Caffeine fuels yapping.

My dog lives in a comfortable home where no serious crime has ever been committed, but she barks night and day like she's the appointed town crier. She barks:

1. at nothing,
2. at leaves,
3. at neighbors,
4. at cars driving up,
5. and once in a long while at something that kind of deserves it, like a new UPS man.

For some reason, that nonstop yapping reminds me of my own anxious thoughts, barking all day long inside my head. Bad things happen to all of us, but I've found that the bad that has come my way has rarely been something I'd been worrying about; instead, that worry just drained my reserves so they were weak when the actual situation arose. Fear fuels yapping.

The answer? A muzzle. No, not for the dog, bless her heart, but for my anxiety. I invite God into my heart and mind, and I ask him to show me if I am worrying needlessly over imagined things. And then I ask him to show me when there *is* something to be concerned about. I can set the other concerns aside, trusting that he will move in when the time comes.

My dog isn't giving up barking, and I'm not giving up espresso, but we can both probably let go of those harrying worries.

Cast your cares on the LORD
and he will sustain you;
he will never let
the righteous be shaken.

PSALM 55:22

MARIGOLDS AND BUGBANE

I was browsing garden forums online for advice about some plants I was considering purchasing, when I came across a thread entitled "Plants you can't stand the smell of!" Who could pass up reading that?

Various plants were described as smelling like melted plastic, baby diapers (clean), garbage, onions, and rotting leaves. Bugbane can smell awful, like cat urine, which isn't surprising since its Latin name, *Cimicifuga,* means "bedbug repeller." I hope that is something I shall never have to find out for myself.

A plant I have decided not to grow, but which is very common, is marigold. I know its flowers are beautiful and long lasting, but to me, they stink. I don't like bending over to weed them, and I don't like walking by them on the path to my house. But they have that scent for the very same reason as bugbane—they repel pests. Once marigolds are in the garden, pests remove themselves from that area. The companion plants stay relatively untouched because of that. I admit: If I had pests in my garden, I'd plant marigold. If I had bedbugs, I'd plant bugbane, too. No wise person turns away help!

We, too, have pests in our lives; some of them are minor irritants, and one is a major enemy. We have a Companion, though, who is much stronger than any of them, and he promises to keep us from evil. He's "planted" right next to us, wherever we are, watching over us. Yes, pests may circle, and they may land. They may even take a nibble or two, which hurts, certainly. But they will never ultimately destroy us, because we're protected from evil.

The LORD will keep you from all evil;
he will keep your life.
The LORD will keep
your going out and your coming in
from this time forth and forevermore.

PSALM 121:7-8, ESV

WHAT AM I HUNGRY FOR?

There's a ritual at our house. Somebody (we seem to take turns) meanders into the kitchen, opens the refrigerator door, and—after staring for some time at the food choices inside—says aloud, "What am I hungry for?" Despite (or perhaps because of) the dazzling array of food choices available, it is apparently a difficult question to answer. Usually another family member will pipe up with suggestions, trying to be helpful. But really, how can any of us know what another is truly hungry for?

Truth is, if you're standing in front of a cornucopia and have to ask what you're hungry for, you're not hungry.

Most of us, even those who have experienced lean times, have not gone hungry and would rarely choose to. Satiety makes our senses dull and our desires ambiguous, and it tempers our ability to discern needs from wants. We have no drive to eat, really. Instead, we merely graze, and as a consequence we never experience real hunger nor complete satisfaction. If a person is truly hungry, she desires food above all else, unable to focus on anything till her hunger is satisfied.

I'm afraid sometimes that my spiritual appetite has become dull too. The Lord calls us blessed when we hunger for righteousness—that is, moral uprightness, goodness, blamelessness—not just when we pick here and there, grazing, but when we really *hunger* for it. I want to have the courage to hunger for a deeper faith, to challenge myself to go after that next level of goodness, righteousness, and godliness. Psalm 145 tells us that God is righteous; Psalm 34 urges us to taste and see that the Lord is good.

Am I hungry enough?

Blessed are those who hunger and thirst for righteousness, for they will be filled.

MATTHEW 5:6

JUNE

Gorgeous Garden Pots

I love to use flower pots in my garden. They can bring a spot of color into an area that doesn't have enough room for a flower bed, and they create a lovely collection in a sparsely planted area. They're easy to tend, cheap to plant, can be changed with the seasons, and give a lovely, rustic feel to any corner.

My pots always looked a little one dimensional till a friend shared a trick for deciding what to plant. She suggested choosing a thriller, a filler, and a spiller.

Choose the thriller first. This will be the tallest plant in the pot. It goes in the middle of the planter and will be the first thing to catch the eye. Around it, you'll alternate the fillers—plants that will grow to about half the height of the thriller and generally bloom continuously and profusely—and the spillers—plants that will tumble over the side of the planter.

Fill your pot halfway with fresh soil before starting. You'll want to use soil that already contains added plant food. Plants in pots need more food and regular watering than plants in the ground. Add the thriller plant, and pack it in a little. Add the spillers and fillers, alternating them. The plants should not be crowded—they'll grow, remember. If the plants are root-bound when you buy them, break up the roots a little when you pull them out of the container.

Once your plants are settled in, water them till the water runs out of the bottom of the pot.

Don't forget to buy either all sun-loving plants or all shade-tolerant plants. As long as all the plants have the same sun and water requirements, they'll become good neighbors and friends.

For this month's free printable, go to http://tyndal.es/homeandgarden.

June 1

CRACKED POTS

"How much did you pay for that?" My husband gestured toward the terra-cotta pot I'd just scored from a yard sale.

"Ten dollars."

"It's cracked! And it has green stuff growing up the side!" Hubs looked at me as if he were revealing new and potentially distressing information.

"I know," I replied, grinning. "Isn't it great? Patina!"

Now, we'd watched enough episodes of *Antiques Roadshow* together that I knew he understood the concept. Patina is the wear and tear on objects that comes from age and use. Some novice collectors attempt to remove the patina from their antique finds. Bad idea. Removing the patina actually removes some, if not most, of the value of the piece. Patina verifies character and individuality; it speaks of the object's history and can even offer protection from the elements. Hubs walked away, muttering something about putting a "patina" sign on all of his broken tools and holding a garage sale, but I was satisfied. I liked the character my new pot lent to my front porch, and I went on a hunt in the backyard for a plant to pot in it.

By some "random coincidence" I had that very week been considering the gray streak in my dark hair. Did it add character? Or make me look, prematurely, like someone's Italian grandmother? Some other signs of age—crow's-feet, laugh lines, or a less-even skin tone—aren't as simple to cover up. And yet . . . when I have a problem in life, those are the very signs on a mentor that mark, for me, the wisdom that informs her suggestions, guidance, and prayer. The patina of wisdom offers protection from the harsh realities of life, reflecting triumph over trials endured and storms weathered. It grows with experience and becomes ever more lovely—and valuable—with the passage of time.

In a youth-obsessed culture, there's something freeing about saying no to some cosmetic redirections. Even in terra-cotta.

Gray hair is a crown of glory;
it is gained by living a godly life.

PROVERBS 16:31, NLT

CINDERELLA, CINDERELLA

The other day I saw the funniest photo of a woman declaring, "My daughter wanted a Cinderella party, so I invited all her friends over and made them clean my house." If only!

Girls have dreamed of being princesses for hundreds of years. But not many of us dream of being servants, which is how Cinderella starts out, after all. The word *servant* conjures up thoughts of scrubbing clothes on a wooden board, slopping a wet mop against a dusty stone floor, or ironing someone else's beautiful ball gown. In other words—real life! But the truth is, in the real world of royalty, those who are chosen to serve actually have a lot of honor and power.

Even today, a queen chooses her ladies-in-waiting from among her very best friends. They are closest to her, after all, so they have to be trustworthy. And because they are friends, those servants get royal household benefits. They share the best food, go to the best parties, do the most important jobs, and receive the best gifts. Even if you're very rich, you can't buy your way into royal service; you have to be invited.

In royal service, value isn't based on what your job is; it's based on the status of the person you serve. That's what it's like to serve God, too. Because we are his servants, we will get to go places we never dreamed of. Because we are trustworthy and he knows we are his friends, he will give us jobs and adventures that others won't get. Our value isn't based on what we do—it's based on whom we serve. He has invited you to serve him right now, and he will bless you when you do.

Mary responded, "Oh, how my soul praises the Lord. How my spirit rejoices in God my Savior! For he took notice of his lowly servant girl, and from now on all generations will call me blessed."

LUKE 1:46-48, NLT

WIFE LOCATOR APP

We had decided to divide and conquer the grocery list—I'd take the cart and the big list; Hubs would go through the store looking for some specialty items. A memory of finding him wandering, looking up and down the rows for me, flashed through my mind. "Will you be able to find me?" I asked. He pulled out his phone. "Yes. I have now installed the Wife Locator App. In other words, I'll just call and you'll answer, and I'll find you in no time."

Simple!

So often I want to take the long, hard route. Well, I don't want to, but I end up doing so, mainly because I have an inherent belief that tells me, *It can't be as easy as that.* And yet, it often is.

The Lord is right by us, night and day. He says he will never leave nor forsake us. He intercedes for us. He is an ever-present help in times of trouble. So why do I wait so long to simply ask for help?

Maybe it's a matter of pride, or of busyness, or of thinking he's not concerned with the small stuff. Or perhaps it's unbelief. But to take him at his word is to simply ask. There's that old saying, "God always answers; sometimes he says yes, sometimes he says no." But for me, I've found that sometimes he says yes, and sometimes he says, "Here, let's try this instead." And it's always better.

I know how to use the God Locator App. I'll bet you do too.

I say to you: Ask and it will be given to you; seek and you will find; knock and the door will be opened to you. For everyone who asks receives; the one who seeks finds; and to the one who knocks, the door will be opened.

LUKE 11:9-10

June 4
BREATH OF LIFE

I had a long stretch of land, south facing, hot with sandy soil, and I knew just what to do with it: plant a hedge of lavender. Soon, I thought, my front yard would be scented with the heavenly perfume of French Provence.

I rototilled the ground and then, for protection, laid down black landscape fabric. This, I hoped, would keep the weeds down, making my life a little easier. *Better to stop the problems before they start,* I thought. I cut holes in the fabric and planted the lavender in them.

Twenty-five lavender plants.

Spring came around, and the plants were not looking so good. In fact, instead of shooting out wands of blooms, they were turning brown. Then they began to wilt, and finally, over the course of several weeks, they began to die. I consulted an expert, who told me that the landscape fabric had not only stopped weeds from growing, it had stopped my plants from growing as well, trapping water beneath the fabric that had caused the roots to rot and die.

That week I had been struggling with a decision made by a loved one. I did not think it was the right decision and was firmly convinced that it would lead to problems down the road. Although my advice was cordially considered, it was not taken. Worried now that doom lay ahead, I thought about offering it again. Then the Lord brought my lavender to mind. I did not want to lay down black fabric on our relationship. In my desire to help prevent "weeds," I might end up smothering our relationship or my family's joy.

I want the freedom to live and make choices by which I gain benefits—or, if necessary, suffer consequences. We were created as autonomous beings, making our own choices, living life as we feel led. I've been so grateful for those who gave me the room to breathe. I now realize how much I want to go and do likewise.

Do to others as you would like them to do to you.

LUKE 6:31, NLT

June 5

VIPER IS ARMED

A few years ago we lived down the street from someone who really loved his car. Because he had a small garage and several family cars, he always parked his car on the street. Each night when he locked it, we heard the threatening warning of the alarm system: a few short beeps followed by "Viper is armed!" We walked a wide path around his car to be sure we didn't trip that alarm.

Hubs brought that memory to mind last month when I was showing him my new app, which tracks a woman's monthly cycle. "Can I get a copy of that?" he asked. I cocked my head, uncertain why he'd be asking, as he clearly didn't need one. "Of yours," he said. "So I'll know when to tiptoe through the minefields. You know, the days when 'Viper is armed!'"

Ha. Although I appreciated the humor in that, the truth is there are times and places in life when we really do feel that we are tiptoeing through minefields of one sort or another. In particular, when you're involved in ministry, you can expect opposition; often the more good your ministry is doing, the more people won to Christ or freed from addiction or fed, the stronger the pushback. That doesn't mean you should back off or take a detour; just walk wisely and bring reinforcements. Loving others in the name of Christ. Give financially above and beyond for the sake of the gospel.

"Viper" may think it's armed, but its fangs have been removed, and the venom is powerless. Even though we become targets when we're doing good, those are indeed the good works created in advance for us to do, so we can't back off! Instead, we must press on, knowing that we're making the best use of time and that Someone always has our back.

Be careful how you live; be mindful of your steps. Don't run around like idiots as the rest of the world does. Instead, walk as the wise! Make the most of every living and breathing moment because these are evil times. So understand and be confident in God's will, and don't live thoughtlessly.

EPHESIANS 5:15-17, VOICE

PLAYLISTS

There's one thing that makes my housework go more quickly and enjoyably (other than contracting it out!), and that's listening to music while I work.

When I turn on some tunes and put my earbuds in, I enter another world. I love eighties cardio (this dates me!) and classical music. I like something with a little spice to give me some attitude. No matter what is coming through those earbuds, it's just between me and the music.

Or is it?

Music that is cheerful makes you smile more often, even after the song is over. Downer, depressing music makes the whole day feel like rain. Praise music brings God to your mind as you face challenges throughout the day. It's true—what you listen to becomes a part of you and how you act.

What I listen to even more often than music are my thoughts. What are they saying? That I'm fat, ugly, or dumb? That anyone could do my job better than I? That I can't get it together? That I deserve to be left out? Unliked? Unasked? Thoughts like those will affect how I view every situation and face every challenge.

I've got to clean up more than the countertops; I've got to clean up my mind. We are pearls without price, treasures worth seeking, and beautiful in God's (and others') eyes. I need to remind myself of those truths. No one but me and God hears what comes out of my earbuds—or what's going on between my ears. But what I'm playing or replaying matters because *I* matter, and what I listen to adds to or subtracts from the woman I view myself to be.

Do you like what you're listening to, or is it time to consider a new playlist?

May the words of my mouth
and the meditation of my heart
be pleasing to you,
O LORD, my rock and my redeemer.

PSALM 19:14, NLT

June 7

DOUGHNUTS IN SHRIMP GREASE

We don't fry food very often, but my son had tried coconut-battered shrimp dipped in chili sauce and wanted the rest of the family to try it too. So we bought the shrimp, the sauce, and some oil, and got busy.

I admit—with a high-quality fryer, the shrimp was tasty and not greasy. It got me to thinking: maybe we should make some doughnuts. I whipped up some dough and then turned the fryer back on. A smell emanated from the warming oil. Shrimp. I wrinkled my nose. I was pretty sure I didn't want to eat doughnuts fried in shrimpy oil, even if they were covered with cinnamon and sugar. I turned off the fryer and replaced the oil before beginning the great doughnut adventure.

Think of your life as a series of recipes. Are you frying doughnuts in shrimpy oil? It's not that the earlier "recipes" were bad; experiences we have undergone and undertaken in the past have shaped us into the people we are now. Perhaps they strengthened us, or if they were difficult or sinful, taught us things that helped us to grow. We are stronger now, and as a result we can operate out of a maturity, a gravitas, we did not have before.

But sometimes we have to change the oil. When faced with a challenge or an opportunity, consider not returning to the way you've always done things. Is a new approach called for? Is a fresh start at hand? Perhaps you've read a passage of Scripture and now see things in a new light. Maybe a friend has illuminated a situation with her wisdom, pointing you in a different direction. We grow and change every day; don't be afraid to risk and do something new. No sense cooking doughnuts in shrimpy grease, no matter how great the shrimp tasted.

No one puts new wine into old wineskins. For the old skins would burst from the pressure, spilling the wine and ruining the skins. New wine is stored in new wineskins so that both are preserved.

MATTHEW 9:17, NLT

DRY RIVERBEDS

When we were making plans to redo our landscaping, we would walk by other people's houses, picking up ideas that we liked and noting features that might work on our lawn too. We saw quite a few properties nearby with dry riverbeds, ribbons of rock and stone coursing through or around the properties.

"I like those," I said to my husband.

"There's no water," Hubs answered. "What's the purpose of a riverbed if there's no water? It looks abandoned and unused. Expired. A dry river is an oxymoron."

While I still like the look of dry riverbeds, it's true that we are often disappointed when things aren't as we expected. When we anticipate something—for example, lemon meringue pie—eyebrows are raised when something clearly made with pumpkin is set in front of us instead.

Most people have assumptions and—dare I say it?—hopes about how a Christian will act and respond. It's why a pastor caught embezzling makes the headlines more often than a mechanic accused of doing the same thing. A pastor—or any Christian, for that matter—is named after his Master, and the expectation is that he or she will reflect Christ. Like waterless riverbeds, Christians who don't fulfill their purpose may look fine. But they are merely decorative landscaping.

I want to live up to the life I was created for by the God whose name and image I bear. *Sandra, Christlike.* I don't want to be an oxymoron, dry ahead of my time.

Don't copy the behavior and customs of this world, but let God transform you into a new person by changing the way you think. Then you will learn to know God's will for you, which is good and pleasing and perfect.

ROMANS 12:12, NLT

June 9
THE "WRONG" SIZE

Some women arrange the clothing in their closet by color. Others arrange theirs according to season. Some don't arrange theirs at all—reaching into a virtual grab bag each morning for a wardrobe surprise. Me? I arrange mine by size.

The sizes in my closet go like this:

- Fit.
- Don't quite fit, and I hope they will soon.
- Someday I hope to be back to this size, but I doubt it.
- I'm never getting back to this size again, but I can't bring myself to get rid of them.

Most of the time, the clothes I most wish I could wear fall into the last category, even if the styles are hopelessly out of date. Instead, I take an outfit from category *Fit*, and leave the closet, sighing.

But why, I ask myself now, the deep sigh? It's true that I may never fit into those old clothes again, but the body I have now has carried me faithfully through many years and adventures. It works hard day and night to keep me alive, working, and loving. God loves me as I am, as I've become.

I decided to rearrange my clothes into new categories:

- These work for now, and I'm glad to have them.
- I'm hoping to be even healthier soon; I believe that I will be. I'll hold on to these.
- I might get to this size again someday, but someone else could use these now, so why don't I give them away?
- These fit before I had children, before I lived and gave of myself for decades, before I knew how to cook. Wouldn't want to go back to that time, no matter what! Out they go!

I'm not sighing anymore. I'm praising instead.

I praise you because I am fearfully and wonderfully made.

PSALM 139:14

June 10

WATERING DEEPLY

My husband and I have an agreed-upon division of labor for household projects. Inside the house, both of us are brawn and brain or the project doesn't get done. We have an agreed-upon division of labor in the garage: Hubs decides what goes where, and I agree. We have an agreed-upon division of labor in the garden: I'm the brains, he's the brawn. We're both happy. It works!

One day I asked Hubs to transplant a few shrubs while I pruned others. Later, I was shocked to see him sprinkling water on the leaves of the new transplants for about, oh, ten seconds each.

"What are you doing?"

He looked at me as if I had been in the sun too long. "Er . . . watering the transplanted shrubs?" We switched places: he pruned and I watered.

Plants that are watered by the "sprinkling" method are often harmed rather than helped, because their leaves remain damp and susceptible to fungal infections. Plus—the water never reaches the roots. In order to survive and thrive during the hot, dry days, most plants need to be deeply watered at the roots rather than just sprinkled lightly.

As I stood there, hose in hand, I thought that we Christians are much like plants. Deep watering prepares us for the long haul, the dry days of unrelenting heat that come into all our lives. We need to dive deeply into faith, trusting when we're afraid, reading Scripture every day, listening to music that nourishes our faith, being an active part of a body that sustains us. Sometimes "watering" at the surface level tricks us into thinking we're okay when, really, our roots are withering away.

They delight in the law of the LORD,
meditating on it day and night.
They are like trees planted along the riverbank,
bearing fruit each season.
Their leaves never wither;
and they prosper in all they do.

PSALM 1:2-3, NLT

BAROMETER CHANGES

One year my son bought a weather station for me as a birthday gift. Colored liquid in the old-style barometer would go up or down with the air pressure, sometimes alerting us that a storm was on the horizon and that we should take cover.

Because we have people with bad backs and sinus issues in our family, we pretty much know when the barometric pressure is changing, even without the meter readings. The changes are subtle, but they affect us in ways we have come to recognize, and we then take appropriate actions for the sake of our health and safety.

People are sensitive to other kinds of subtle signals too. We can tell when our work isn't appreciated or a new friend just isn't that into us. We find groups at home, at school, and at church where we are welcomed, and we sense a subtle snub when we're not—a good hint to move on. Paying attention to those gut feelings can prevent heartache down the road.

Genesis tells us that Laban, the father of Leah and Rachel, first welcomed Jacob to his family, his lands, and his home. But along the way, Jacob noticed a change in the way Laban and his sons felt about him. The Lord then validated Jacob's hunch and told him to move on, reassuring Jacob of his presence.

I think the Lord reveals subtle clues to us, too, when a job or relationship is about to change, so we are not taken by surprise. He then reassures us that it's okay to move on, because he will always be with us. Do you feel something new afoot? Don't be afraid to move on. Bounty and blessing lie ahead.

Jacob soon learned that Laban's sons were grumbling about him. "Jacob has robbed our father of everything!" they said. "He has gained all his wealth at our father's expense." And Jacob began to notice a change in Laban's attitude toward him. Then the LORD said to Jacob, "Return to the land of your father and grandfather and to your relatives there, and I will be with you."

GENESIS 31:1-3, NLT

June 12

LOVE COVERS A MULTITUDE OF SINS

In a house I lived in as a child, the bathroom wallpaper had been hung upside down. The pattern was intricate, so it was not easily evident unless you were sitting there for some time with nothing to do but stare at the walls. Once you noticed it, however, it was easy to see that all of the little birds woven throughout the pattern were actually flying toward the ground, dive-bombing toward death, so it seemed. The bathroom decor was a constant source of amusement after that discovery.

I've hung some wallpaper in my own homes over the years, and while it isn't easy to do, I've found that it can be well worth the effort. Not only does the paper add texture, color, and design, it quickly and efficiently covers any defects on the wall. Perhaps there are dings or dents that a coat of paint simply can't conceal; wallpaper can. And hey, besides adding value and beauty to the room, the right paper can give you or your visitors something to stare at while sitting there for a time, doing nothing.

In my early Christian life, I'd always heard the verse "Love covers a multitude of sins" used wrongly, as in, "I've sinned against you, but I don't feel like owning it, and because you're a Christian and supposed to love me, that love should cover any sin I've committed against you, or else you're unforgiving." Um, no. Here's what it does mean. We are humans, and we err, and we have bad days in which we make bad calls. We sin against others. But if *we* ask for *their* forgiveness and show them by our subsequent actions that we mean it, well, our sin is usually papered right over by our sincere desire to make things right. In a healthy relationship, love always has the dents and dings covered. So love, and love well!

*Most important of all, continue to show deep love for
each other, for love covers a multitude of sins.*

1 PETER 4:8, NLT

WRITTEN DEEP WITHIN

I have seen Scripture written in a lot of neat places in people's homes—framed and hung on the walls, cross-stitched into pillows, or scrawled on dishes and place mats. Some of the best places I've seen it written, however, are not readily visible.

Once during a research trip, we climbed into the attic of a very old home to examine the structure and found a verse written—or burned?—into the wood on one of the beams supporting the house: "Unless the Lord builds a house, the work of the builders is wasted" (Psalm 127:1, NLT). I've seen Psalm 18:36 written on the floorboards before carpet was installed: "You have made a wide path for my feet to keep them from slipping" (NLT). One lovely home had a rock garden feature in their backyard. On one of the rocks someone had written Psalm 31:3—"You are my rock and my fortress; and for your name's sake you lead me and guide me" (ESV).

Some of us wear crosses around our necks, and some of us don't. Some have Scripture displayed on our cars or in our homes, and others do not. What is most important is that Scripture is hidden in our hearts, minds, and spirits, embedded in the foundation of who we are as believers, informing our decisions and attitudes.

I love the thought that God's Word is hidden deep within me.

I will put my instructions deep within them, and I will write them
on their hearts. I will be their God, and they will be my people.

JEREMIAH 31:33, NLT

IVY IN THE WALLS

Ever since reading the children's book *Madeline*, I have been enchanted by the look of vines growing on a house. Vines make a house look sophisticated and beautiful, aristocratic somehow. When we moved into a new house with a broad face, I knew just how to accentuate that. Vines! I did some research and found the name of a vine I loved, one that was green in the summer and copper in autumn. Then I asked some friends, "Does anyone know anything about growing Virginia creeper?"

"Don't do it!" most of them told me. "Yes, yes, beautiful—all right, we'll give you that. But it is so invasive that you will never get it out, once started. It not only grows along the face of your house, but in the cracks, under the siding (which loosens it up), and into the window casements (which makes them leak). You may pull, and you may spray, but once it's there, it's the owner and you're the tenant."

So we changed our plans. No Virginia creeper. I knew that it was strong—that a simple ivy could, over time, strangle a tree. But I did not think that it was strong enough to rip my home apart. But it is.

Sin, it seems to me, works like that in our lives. It presents itself as something desirable and beautiful—or at the very least, harmless. So I invite it in, welcoming whatever excitement it seems to bring my way—till it starts to wreak the havoc it always does. If I catch it in time, I can rip it out before it does harm. But that's not always possible. The best thing is just not to plant it at all and avoid the pain it will most surely bring.

The wise woman builds her house,
but with her own hands the foolish one tears hers down.

PROVERBS 14:1

June 15

GUARDIAN ANGELS

A friend needed to baby proof her house, and among her biggest concerns were her second- and third-floor windows. The windows needed to open in order to allow for air circulation in the house. But an energetic toddler could push a screen right out, tumbling with it in the long drop to the ground. Together we searched the Internet and ultimately came upon a product called Guardian Angel Window Guards.

These nifty products screw into the sides of windows, barring the window with rods about three or four inches apart. The bars provide plenty of space for air to circulate, but not enough room for a kid to squeeze through. Once we installed them, everyone was happy—life could go on comfortably in all seasons without the risk of a child being harmed. The window guards could be quickly installed and then forgotten, one less thing to worry about.

Many of us are enchanted by the idea of angels, especially a guardian angel or someone sent specifically to watch over us. Christ himself watches over us, of course, but Scripture tells us that there are also heavenly beings God has commissioned to care for his people. Daniel had firsthand experience of this when he was in the lions' den. "My God sent his angel, and he shut the mouths of the lions," Daniel reported (Daniel 6:22). Perhaps you've heard modern-day stories of cars being lifted and assailants being repelled. As with anything in the spiritual realm, we do not completely understand how and when and why angels work. But they do—and that's part of the mystery of faith.

A good parent anticipates the difficulties and dangers that might befall her children and takes precautions to keep them safe. Isn't it comforting to know that your heavenly Father has also prepared others to serve and protect *you*?

Angels are only servants—spirits sent to care for
people who will inherit salvation.

HEBREWS 1:14, NLT

GOOD NEIGHBORS, GOOD FENCES

He is all pine and I am apple orchard.
My apple trees will never get across
And eat the cones under his pines, I tell him.
He only says, "Good fences make good neighbors."
ROBERT FROST

Although there are times when neighbors share chores—mowing a lawn for someone on vacation, for example—for the most part, we each care for our own yards. So a friend was surprised to see her neighbor pulling weeds on her property. The neighbor apparently did not like weeds next to her driveway. Generally, we consider doing something "nice" for a neighbor without permission to be a no-no, a form of trespassing. Would you go onto another family's property and blow their leaves without asking? Walk into the garage of an elderly person and take his garbage to the curb without permission? Each piece of land, each person, has his or her own boundaries to be respected.

None of us would think of planting a tree on another person's property. But we know there is little we can say when the neighbors plant one on theirs—even though it may spoil our view. Property lines clearly, legally delineate land ownership. I can do what I want on my own property, but I must respect your autonomy on yours. Keeping yourself to your own interests and not interfering with those of another without permission—that makes for good neighbors.

This is true with people as well as with land. The Bible tells us to have self-control; it never tells us to control others. We may advise (when asked) and we may assist (when asked), but ultimately, free choice is given to adult men and women. It's okay to help; but ask if your help is wanted, and be okay with being told no. No, in a way, is a boundary too. You can use that yourself if someone steps over the line.

Stay calm; mind your own business; do your own job. . . . We want
you living in a way that will command the respect of outsiders.

1 THESSALONIANS 4:11-12, MSG

MONEY-BACK GUARANTEES

One of my favorite online retailers offers a "money-back guarantee." They promise that if customers don't like the product, they can get their money back. Because of that, I'm willing to risk ordering things I might not have ordered otherwise. I take chances and try new things because there is nothing to lose. The companies offering these guarantees have never let me down. Every time I have had a problem, they have solved it, consistently keeping their word.

When we come to faith, we're asked to trust God implicitly. We give our lives over to his will, and that can seem a bit frightening early on . . . and even sometimes later, when we're pulled to new challenges. Our trust needs to be built on his character, which we come to know better and better over time.

When God made us, he made us to be his friends as well as to serve him. To be in awe of him, yes, but also to love him. And we can't love him if we're not honest with him about the heavy things on our hearts and minds. It's okay to share your deepest fears and worries with him, even if that feels odd. He already knows what we're thinking!

The Lord makes a lot of promises to us: to love us, to never leave us, to repay those who wrong us, to care for us, to forgive us. He will never abandon us. Sometimes, when circumstances look iffy, it's easy to wonder, *Will he really do everything he said he would?*

The answer is—yes. He is always good, always just, and he always does what he says. His promises are backed up with something better than a money-back guarantee: the honor of his name.

I praise your name for your unfailing love and faithfulness;
for your promises are backed
by all the honor of your name.

PSALM 138:2, NLT

TOPIARIES

Because I love all things French, I desperately wanted to have a topiary inside my house. There were a number of pretty silk ones, but I wanted to try growing a live one.

There are any number of plants you can use for topiary—as long as they have long, winding shoots. Whichever you choose, you must plant it in the pot when it's small and young. After that, you nestle in the frame. Choosing the frame is perhaps the most fun part of doing topiary. I saw all kinds of classic frames—a ball, two balls, a cone, a tower—as well as some fun ones—a chicken, a dachshund, a Loch Ness monster. I settled on one that looked kind of like the Eiffel Tower and placed it into my pot.

Over the months as the plant grew, I would take its long, leafy tendrils and weave them through the iron frame. The shoots would grow longer; I'd weave them further in. With sunlight, water, and plant food, I managed to grow a work of art. My topiary was the exact shape of the frame inside it, even though in the end the frame could no longer be seen.

What kind of framework am I growing around? To what and whom do I shape my life? And can I do that and still remain . . . me? There are many potential frames we can choose from—though I'm guessing none of us wants to look like the Loch Ness monster—but choose we must. The beauty for Christian women is that we can be both delightfully different, unique, with a style all our own, and still, to others, look like Christ.

Those God foreknew he also predestined to be conformed to the image of his Son, that he might be the firstborn among many brothers and sisters.

ROMANS 8:29

June 19

SOMEONE ELSE'S MONEY

My in-laws lived with us for a time, and throughout their stay I took care of ordering a few of their necessities. To make things easier, my mother-in-law gave me her credit card number, and I added it to my accounts so that I could simply bill their items to them.

After they left, I forgot to take the card off one of the online retail accounts that I use quite a bit. I'd ordered a bunch of household goods, and for some reason the card defaulted to my mother-in-law's number. I realized it just before I clicked *pay*.

God talks about this in Haggai, although in that case the misuse of funds was not accidental. For those laboring under the misconception that God is never angry, this passage proves otherwise. The Lord is angry because the people are building beautiful houses for themselves, complete with rich paneling, but they are not setting aside any money to rebuild his house as they had been commanded. They are, in effect, using his money for their own households.

I would not be happy to find out that a friend or a child had used my credit card without permission. But I can sometimes find reasons why I "can't" give to the Lord in a certain month. Can I expect that he won't be unhappy about that? He has given us an answer.

The word of the LORD came through the prophet Haggai: "Is it a time for you yourselves to be living in your paneled houses, while this house remains a ruin?"

Now this is what the LORD Almighty says: "Give careful thought to your ways. You have planted much, but harvested little. You eat, but never have enough. You drink, but never have your fill. You put on clothes, but are not warm. You earn wages, only to put them in a purse with holes in it."

HAGGAI 1:3-6

June 20

HOLD MY PURSE FOR A SECOND, WILL YOU?

I have a friend who carries around a suitcase. All right, not quite, but her bag is really large. She's got everything you can imagine in it, including a portable hair straightener, books to share, snacks, and an EpiPen in case someone has an allergic reaction. I love being her friend, because she has a generous heart. But I cringe a little when we're out and she's looking for something and asks me, "Hey—can you hold my purse for a second?" That second has often turned into many minutes—and the purse is not equipped with wheels! Once in a while, as she is walking from rack to rack oohing and aahing, I might have to remind her: "Can I give you your purse back?" She always takes it right back.

At home we have installed superstrong pegs on our coatrack just to accommodate her. But I can't always accommodate her elsewhere, because I've got my own purse, and *my* arms get tired too. Ultimately, she's got to take some stuff out. Or carry it on her own.

This is how it is in life sometimes too. Clearly, we are expected to share the burdens of our friends and fellow Christians. And yet they are also called to make wise decisions about the choices they make—so their purses, and lives, aren't too heavy to bear.

The Lord doesn't expect anyone to buckle under the weight of someone else's choices. Help others, but don't feel bad when you've done all you can. Do you have a friend who relies on you too much, a loved but untenable burden? Do you pass off your own "purse" too often or have you got stuff packed in it that's weighing you down? Sometimes we need to clean out our own purses and to know when to lovingly say no when others expect just a little too much.

Carry each other's burdens, and in this way you will fulfill the law of Christ. . . . Each one should carry their own load.

GALATIANS 6:2, 5

UPGRADES

Our elderly neighbors were trying to sell their home. It was a lovely place, and they had lived in it for quite a while but decided the time had come to move to a retirement community. They were shocked when the real estate agent told them that their house, as beautiful and well cared for as it was, needed to be updated to have a "wow" factor. Their agent advised them to replace their perfectly fine refrigerator with stainless steel and redo their countertops with granite. And the floors? The old linoleum had to go—only tile or wood floors would sell.

About that same time, some churches in our town were sending missions teams to Mexico. One pastor shared how shocked he was to find that most of the children in that town suffered from breathing problems that resulted from cooking over open fires within their houses. Same year, same world. Very different circumstances.

I'm not here to blessing-shame. There's nothing wrong with having nice things and enjoying the fruits of our labors. I enjoy my home and my yard, but I also need to make sure that I share. I have been thinking about how I might do that in a meaningful way. Perhaps set aside enough money each month to buy a stove for someone in Mexico? Pledge a monthly contribution to a furniture bank? Give $25 to pack baggies with warm socks and water for the homeless? Sponsor a child who shares my birthday?

I make mental lists of things I'd like to do for my home, goals to work toward. I think it might be a good idea to work toward goals on behalf of others, too. Will you join me?

All of you should be of one mind. Sympathize with each other. Love each other as brothers and sisters. Be tenderhearted, and keep a humble attitude.

1 PETER 3:8, NLT

June 22

WEEDS HIDING

My new pink fountain plant had taken off, and I was thrilled. It was the third plant I'd placed in that exact spot, but it was the only one to thrive there. It was time to trim back its lush loveliness, though, and when I did, I found something unexpected. A large weed, hiding behind it, had completely entangled itself in the roots of the fountain plant. The weed had taken refuge within the foliage of the desirable plant but was sucking up its nutrients, and that back section of the plant had started to die. I carefully pulled it all out: the large weed, the weed suckers, and all the roots I could find.

Most of us mean well, have good intentions, and do good deeds. And yet . . . we still sin. The places I'm most vulnerable are where I've been meeting with some success—where pride can sprout right alongside godly accomplishments—or places where I haven't taken root at all—where envy or bitterness grow. Eventually, if I let them, my sins choke out the pleasure, joy, and good that my wholesome works produce. In the plant world and in life, weeds take root faster, grow stronger, and spread more easily than desirable plants. However, they also pull out easier when I finally get around to weeding.

I love this section of Psalm 139 because it indicates that the psalmist's anxious thoughts spring from the concern that he may have offended God. He asks God to search his heart, to have a look and see if there is anything offensive, and if so, to show him how to uproot it. He's not anxious about things he doesn't have or things he may lose, but rather, his anxiety stems from his desire to keep himself righteous before God. I feel certain this is a prayer that is always answered.

Search me, God, and know my heart;
test me and know my anxious thoughts.
See if there is any offensive way in me,
and lead me in the way everlasting.

PSALM 139:23-24

June 23
FELINE AFFECTION

Cats are circumspect in their emotions. Simply not leaving the room when a person enters is a display of, well, acceptance if not affection. But even that acceptance isn't guaranteed. A friend of mine who got too busy to give her cat regular attention began to arrive home to find her cat stationed by a back window, no longer willing to come to greet her at the front door.

My friend kicked off her shoes and went in search of her resentful kitty. Sometimes cats need to be reminded that they *like* being loved. If the owner gets busy and cares only for the cat's physical needs but not her emotional needs, the cat will learn to care for herself. By the time her owner remembers, kitty will feel convinced she doesn't *need* love anymore. Once scooped up in the arms of her loved one, though, kitty will eventually relax and remember: *Yes, I do love being loved. I like and miss this attention.* She lets her guard down again, recalling anew just how good it feels to be loved.

Our Master never pulls away from us, but in our busyness we sometimes withdraw for a time from him. Sometimes we're angry with him due to circumstances; sometimes we just let our earthly concerns distract us and we forget to invite him into our day-to-day lives or meet him for time apart. But once drawn back into his presence, we remember. *Ahh. Yes. I was meant to be loved like this, meant for companionship, designed to be loved, and to love.*

Set aside time to love and be loved by the Master. After a few minutes in his arms, you'll relax again and recall just how good that companionship feels. Run to greet him. He has never left you, and he never will.

I [the LORD] appeared to them from far away and said:
"I have loved you with an everlasting love—
out of faithfulness I have drawn you close."

JEREMIAH 31:3, VOICE

THE THREE SISTERS

The Iroquois people describe squash, beans, and corn as three sisters who can't be separated if they are to grow and thrive. When planted side by side in the same mound, the three plants help one another out. Bean plants are vines—they need something sturdy to wrap around. The corn provides a tall pole for the beans to grow on. Once they do, they act kind of like a rope, helping to anchor the cornstalks against the wind. Beans also put nutrients into the soil that the squash needs to thrive. Squash plants have prickly leaves and stems that repel animals who would otherwise nibble on the growing plants, and so they provide protection for the beans and corn as well. Working together, all three plants can flourish and grow into an abundance of good eating.

There are three "sisters" in our Christian lives that work together too—in fact, where you find one, you're likely to find the others. Why? They help each other grow strong. Scripture tells us that these three things—faith, hope, and love—will last forever.

Each of us has a little more of one or two of these than the other. For me, faith and love come more easily than hope. But if I carefully water and weed my heart, I find that the third sister can grow tall and strong too. They need one another to thrive.

Do you have more faith, more hope, or more love? How can you feed and water the one or two that need a little boost to grow? What can you do to stake up the one that needs a little help?

Three things will last forever—faith, hope, and
love—and the greatest of these is love.

1 CORINTHIANS 13:13, NLT

June 25

A GOOD FRIEND,
A BAD ENEMY

Hubs got a new toy: a gas blowtorch that kills weeds. Oh, he dressed it up in environmentally friendly language—good for the earth, no chemicals leaching into the stream that leads to the Sound, yada yada. But I saw the gleam in his eye when he headed out to burn the weeds. Our son, for the first time ever, jockeyed to do yard work.

Hubs went up and down the driveway, the sides of which were lined with plants we wanted, not ones we wanted to get rid of. Although he was careful, he singed a few of the keepers. It took time, practice, and control to get rid of the weeds that were choking the desirable plants. What was left, finally, were the keepers: the plants that brought life and health and beauty.

Our tongues are like blowtorches—good friends, bad enemies. We can use them to do good or we can use them to work evil, and sometimes we use them to do both. James admonishes, "Out of the same mouth come praise and cursing. My brothers and sisters, this should not be" (3:10). A little gossip can poison a pleasant conversation among friends. A tacked-on criticism can completely undermine a compliment. A lie can decimate, perhaps forever, a previously good reputation. The desire to destroy another through words will, in fact, burn up one's own life.

Each time I open my mouth and "turn on the gas," I have the potential to hurt or to help. Whom can I speak life to today?

The tongue is a small thing that makes grand speeches.
But a tiny spark can set a great forest on fire.

JAMES 3:5, NLT

June 26

GREEN GRASS

You've heard the saying "The grass is always greener on the other side of the fence." It's a cliché, I know, but when I look around my neighborhood, it really does seem that the rest of the houses have lusher, greener lawns.

Some of my friends seem to have greener-grass lives. They have no financial problems. If they're married, their husbands are perfect, and their bumper stickers refer to perfect honor-student children. They lead Bible studies. They're naturally thin. Martha Stewart calls them for decorating advice. Okay, I'm kidding, but when I get in a funk about not measuring up, I can let myself get into this tailspin, and once I begin to spiral, it's hard to pull out.

Grass looks greener at a distance because you can't see the dirt—you see only the green grass tops. Up close, in my own yard, I can see the dirt intermingled with the grass, weeds, and moss. But my neighbor across the street tells me that from *her* perspective, my grass actually looks greener than *hers*. (You can't see my weeds from that distance either.)

Whatever I focus on seems to be bigger in my life—which is why my problems often seem bigger than my blessings. I see the dirt close up, and honestly, I've developed a bad habit of looking for it instead of for the patch of tender, new grass.

When I focus on what I have, whom I love, what I enjoy, and do it without comparing myself with anyone else, I live a contented life. It has been said that comparison is the thief of joy. How true that is.

Jealousy and selfishness are not God's kind of wisdom. . . . For wherever there is jealousy and selfish ambition, there you will find disorder and evil of every kind.

JAMES 3:15-16, NLT

June 27

I DON'T WANT TO BE THAT WOMAN, BUT . . .

Like many women, I periodically serve on one committee or another. If only it could be a committee made up of people who act, think, believe, and talk just like me, all would be well. Right?

Somehow, though, it doesn't end up that way. I know that iron sharpens iron, but sometimes all that clinking up against one another hurts a little too. And yet, the whole idea of a committee is to bring together a variety of experiences, talents, insights, and—yes—personalities. I think it's a little bit like cooking.

I wonder who the first person was who said, "Hey, I know. Let's eat what comes out of that hen, before it hatches." Or, "Drinking milk squeezed from a cow seems to be good for baby cows. I think I'll try it too!" And yet, as odd as those two ingredients may seem, they work beautifully together with another favorite, vanilla, to make some of our favorite treats.

That delightful scent that perfumes our houses while treats are baking comes mostly from vanilla. Have you ever tasted vanilla on its own? It's bitter and not tasty at all. Vanilla needs to be blended with all of the other ingredients to bring out its best—eggs from chickens, butter from cows, flour from wheat. The Lord made us that way too.

When we work together, each one making her own unique contribution to the whole, the result—like cake—can be absolutely delightful. In the end, this cooperation will make our projects better, richer, and more successful than they would have been if they had come from only one perspective—even mine.

He makes the whole body fit together perfectly. As each part
does its own special work, it helps the other parts grow, so that
the whole body is healthy and growing and full of love.

EPHESIANS 4:16, NLT

BEEPING FRIDGES AND SQUEAKY HINGES

When our son was a teenager in the I-can-eat-anything-and-everything-all-day-and-night stage, we finally had to tell him to limit his grazing. Once in a while after meals was fine, but we weren't willing to take on second or third jobs, nor sell plasma, to indulge his nonstop noshing.

He agreed, promising to limit his snacking after dinner.

At the time, we lived in a house that had a refrigerator with a clever, helpful feature. If the door was open longer than ten seconds, it would beep loudly as a reminder to close it. This does not work in the favor of teenagers. Unless he could open the door, reach in, and grab something quickly without looking, we would know our son was snacking. The doors on the pantry had squeaky hinges, too. We declined to oil them.

There was still a fair amount of nighttime noise till we renegotiated what he needed.

This wasn't about denying a hungry young man basic sustenance (although he may have claimed that was the case) as much as it was about his keeping his word. The Lord tells us to let our yes be yes and our no be no. We are known by our word, and trust is difficult to earn and easy to lose. How helpful it would be for me if a little beep would go off right when I am ready to break a promise, or stretch the truth, or make excuses. But, in fact, I do have an alarm deep within: the voice of the Lord gently urging me to be truthful and follow through on what I promise.

His voice is softer and gentler than beeps and squeaks, but so much more powerful.

"This is the covenant I will make with them after that time," says the Lord.
"I will put my laws in their hearts, and I will write them on their minds."

HEBREWS 10:16

WOUNDED BIRDS

My daughter had always wanted a pet. But budgets and allergies would not allow our family to care for a cat or a dog for some years, so she had to content herself with fish. One day, God sent something special her way.

She came running into the kitchen from the backyard, where she'd been playing with her brother and his friend, gasping for breath. "A bird is on the ground! Its wing is broken." She tugged me by the hand to the soft grass carpet under a large tree. Sure enough, a bird lay there, healthy, it seemed, except for what looked like a broken wing. We cleared the area and then watched from a window to see if other birds would come to its aid, but none did. So we gently scooped the injured bird into a shoe box and drove to a wildlife rescue clinic about an hour away.

There, the vet tech assured us that the bird could be cared for and then returned to the wild. Although she couldn't keep her "pet," my daughter was satisfied that she had taken care of a beloved being that could not, for the moment, care for itself.

Sometimes we might wonder why the Lord has entrusted a certain person to us, someone who may have unexpected challenges. Perhaps it's a child facing a serious illness, or a friend wrestling with mental or emotional health issues. Maybe it's a coworker struggling with a difficult relationship. Realize that God sends wounded birds, his beloveds, to those with tender hearts, who will notice and care and help them to deal with their challenges.

Are not two sparrows sold for a penny? And not one of them will fall to the ground apart from your Father. But even the hairs of your head are all numbered. Fear not, therefore; you are of more value than many sparrows.

MATTHEW 10:29-31, ESV

June 30

PETER RABBIT

This year my husband finally got to plant his vegetable garden. In addition to cherry tomatoes (they can ripen here in the Pacific Northwest without a greenhouse!), he put in zucchini, cucumbers, beets, and squash. The plants put out luscious green leaves and began to produce tiny, tender vegetables. They began to look good to eat . . . and the neighborhood rabbits thought so too.

My husband, transformed suddenly into Farmer McGregor, chased the rabbits out of the backyard. They followed the lead rabbit, perhaps the mother, and scampered under the fence to safety. The next morning, I went out to the backyard to have my coffee and saw a baby bunny sitting on the lawn as still as a statue, unsure which way to run in order to escape me, Mrs. Farmer McGregor. Her mother soon appeared from under a large rhubarb leaf and scooted under the fence; baby followed.

When frightening, unexpected circumstances startle us, we want to move, to act, to do! Anything to get ourselves and our loved ones to safety. Like that little bunny, we're not entirely sure what's going on around us. It's smart to get more information before scampering forth, or to wait for guidance so we don't move in the wrong direction.

Next time you don't know what to do, stay still and do nothing except ask God to lead the way. It's okay to wait for him to guide you, and when he does, you know you'll be moving in the right direction.

We all encounter trouble, trauma, and even just garden-variety anxiety when we don't know what to do or say. Do you believe that if you wait quietly, God will act or tell you to act? Trust him. He will make the first move and show you the way out.

Be still in the presence of the LORD,
and wait patiently for him to act.

PSALM 37:7, NLT

JULY

Paint-Sample Sheets

Summer is an ideal time to paint inside your house or apartment. It's easy to have the windows open (this lets out fumes, and the fresh air helps to dry the paint), and the bright sunlight allows you to see exactly what your chosen color will look like in brightest light.

I've always found it difficult to figure out if a color was going to work in a big room with just those tiny squares they give you at the paint counter. But I didn't really want to paint big swatches on my wall either. Here's what I do instead: I purchase a sample-sized can of the paint I'm considering. I then apply the paint color to laminating sheets (the kind used to laminate documents) and use poster putty to attach the sheets to the walls.

Laminating sheets, which you can buy at an office-supply store or online, have a rough side and a smooth side; you'll want to paint on the rough side. Coat the sheet once, and let it dry. It will look crackly, but that's okay. Paint a second coat.

When it's dry, you can hang it on the wall and get a good idea of what the color will look like in your room. The painted sheet will bend around corners, and you can do three or four of them and hang them at the same time to see what the paint will look like in different areas and in different light!

For this month's free printable, go to http://tyndal.es/homeandgarden.

OF FRUIT AND FLOWERS

For most plants, the right time to prune is just after they have flowered. It's lovely to enjoy the display of their floral glory, but if you wait too long to prune, you risk clipping off next year's blooms. For many plants, those blooms and the tips of the branches some of them grow on are not visible to the eye till the following season. But the plants begin to set their buds within a short period of time, so you can't procrastinate with pruning.

In one sense, it's fantastic to know that there will be another showy season to enjoy the next year. In another sense, it's actually hard to bring yourself to cut a plant back when a few vibrant blooms are still clinging to it. The willingness to make careful, timely cuts, though, is what allows the new display.

After we have come through a period of success—whether in ministry or our careers, with our families or friends—we're often tentative, waiting, as it were, for something bad to happen. And it always does, eventually, because life on earth is not one sustained high experience after the next. There are always valleys; there are always seasons of pruning. Perhaps the error lies in the perspective. It's not the end of a good run. To prepare us for another season, the Lord is clipping back that which has already been productive and fruitful but is now spent.

Most gardeners know that in order to provoke more blossoms, more fruit in the coming seasons, a good pruning is required. Our Master Gardener can be trusted to clip gently, carefully—but clip he will. And we desire to blossom, to bear fruit, right? So it can be no other way.

He cuts off every branch in me that bears no fruit, while every branch that does bear fruit he prunes so that it will be even more fruitful.

JOHN 15:2

FORECASTS

I have an app on the computer in my office that will tell me not only what today's weather holds but what's ahead for the next ten days—even the next month! How does it know? I've noticed that sometimes the forecast proves true, and sometimes it's truly off. The meteorologists update the app frequently, changing the forecast as they do. But isn't that contrary to the idea of a forecast? I want to know what the weather is going to be like today, tomorrow, next month, and in ten years so I can plan appropriately! Will it be sunny? I will prepare to enjoy. Stormy? I will hunker down and pack in the provisions.

This is what we often want in life, too, aside from weather forecasting. I want to know, well in advance, any trouble that is going to come down the pike for me or my loved ones. I tell myself that if I know it's coming, then I can find a way to avert disaster. And while there's nothing wrong with preparing for possibilities, none of us can foreknow the future. Instead, we are to be wise, watch the sky, and enjoy each day as it comes.

Our faith is not tested and our resilience is not shown on sunny days. When the hurricane batters and we huddle with neighbors, when the earthquake shatters and we pray for protection, when a simple rain shower ruins the plans for a picnic and we take it inside and play board games, we show our ability to ride out whatever storms come.

Maybe we each struggle with the desire to know what lies ahead before it happens: a job loss, a child born with medical challenges, the rejection of a friend, the collapse of a church. But none of us knows exactly what lies ahead, so we can't always avoid the bad, nor can we predict the good. We do have control over how we respond, though, and faith in the one who will see us through.

Indeed, how can people avoid what they don't know is going to happen?

ECCLESIASTES 8:7, NLT

THE RIGHT TOOL FOR THE JOB

My husband tells of when he, as a young boy, went into his father's garage to find tools for a woodworking project. He found the tools, all right. His dad had arranged them all very neatly on a pegboard in front of his work area. It was clear how well he cared for and valued them: they were arranged by size and sorted by type along the pegs, ready whenever he needed them. Toward the edge of the board was hung an expensive new crescent wrench with a heavy head. My husband wanted to pound a nail into a board, and he thought that heavy head would be just the tool to do the job.

After several metal-dinging pounds, he felt a hand, strong as a bear's paw, grab and hold his forearm. Another hand reached around, took the battered crescent wrench from his hand, and slipped a hammer in its place. "It helps to use the right tool for the job," his dad said with a long-suffering sigh.

Our God is a father of love, long suffering and patient, but also equipping. He does not call us to a task that we cannot fulfill, and not only fulfill, but do to his satisfaction and ours. The problem occurs when we either

1. use the wrong tool for the job, damaging it and making poor progress because of it; or
2. undertake tasks that were not assigned to us in the first place.

Have you ever felt the hand of God reach down and stop you, midswing, before you could do damage or take on a project intended for someone else? I have. And when I've resisted, I've felt pain akin to that which comes with a hammered thumb. I'm so grateful the Lord has created good works for me to do in my home, in my family, and with my friends and that he desires me to be a tool in his hand. What role do you play in his handiwork?

We are God's handiwork, created in Christ Jesus to do good works, which God prepared in advance for us to do.

EPHESIANS 2:10

RED, WHITE, AND BLUE CARNATIONS

The floral display was irresistible. (My family will tell you that the floral display is always irresistible to me!) The day before the Fourth of July, the store offered bunches and bunches of red, white, and blue carnations. Some even had sprays of fiber-optic lights threaded in them, mimicking the fireworks that would be fired off the very next night. How could I resist them? I couldn't. And they were inexpensive! I bought a clutch for the kitchen vase.

A young friend later asked me how to grow the blue buds, and I had to explain that they weren't naturally blue. The florist made the flowers blue by cutting the stems and soaking them in dyed-blue water. I pulled one out of the vase to show her the traces of blue along the stem, the telltale sign of a dyed flower.

These flowers became blue because they had drunk blue water. Day after day, the water traveled up their stems, eventually reaching the petals but discoloring both the stems and the leaves a little bit along the way. They had become what they consumed. It's a beautiful result when you want a festive bouquet, but it provided a clear illustration for me to muse on later that day. What kind of "water" am I taking into my heart and mind every day? Is it pure, clean, and good? Do my petals reflect that purity, or do they display a tint of the worldliness I sometimes absorb? Does a faith discoloration show? Likely, yes.

Sadly, you can't make a dyed flower white again; once it has soaked up tinted water, it remains tinted. God, however, has no such limitations for his people. Once we turn from that which stains us and return to drinking in the pure water of his Word, he creates our hearts anew: fresh, pure, and lovely.

Create in me a clean heart, O God.

PSALM 51:10, NLT

A HOME OF OUR OWN

For much of my life, I have lived in homes in which I was a tenant, not an owner. But actually, Scripture tells us that none of us really are owners. We are God's tenants, as Leviticus 25:23 instructs: "The land is mine and you are but aliens and my tenants." We are to be good caretakers of that which God entrusts to us.

We tried to leave each house in better condition than we had found it. We planted perennials that would bless those who came after us. We tightened light fixtures and deep cleaned tile that hadn't been cleaned for a while. We did misstep sometimes—one landlord was a little distressed to arrive and find I'd painted the front door red. I didn't realize I should have asked him first. He was gracious.

Then we finally owned a house. Then we lost that house. The Lord gives, and the Lord takes away. And then sometimes he gives again.

Eventually, the Lord restored the years that the locusts had eaten, and we bought a new house, the house we hope will be the last home we live in. We are redoing the landscaping and interior with zest and enthusiasm, using the skills we gained while fixing up other people's homes. God has encouraged us all along to be good stewards.

This applies not only to homes, of course. Many of us are entrusted with other people's finances, careers, or even children. We're all entrusted with the care of the earth. The way in which we care for others' property helps us build character so we can be entrusted with more. If I returned to a rental, I would be at peace because that would be the home the Lord wanted me to care for—for the landlord, but especially for the Lord himself. I'm glad he finds me trustworthy.

If you are not faithful with other people's things, why
should you be trusted with things of your own?

LUKE 16:12, NLT

NOT ON MY WATCH

Some nights we're lazy and don't feel like eating at the kitchen table. We'd rather sink into the couch with a good movie or TV show. A lot of times Hubs and I choose a nature show, but I have two rules:

1. No shows with animals mating
2. No shows with animals killing other animals

After all, we're eating!

I've learned a lot from nature shows, though. You'll see that many animals travel in packs, and they have good reasons:

- They help one another find food.
- They help one another keep warm.
- They take care of one another and the babies.
- They are safer in a pack than alone when enemies threaten to attack.

If the pack of animals is on the move, sometimes one that is sick or young or tired drops farther and farther behind. If you watch carefully, you'll notice that the laggard is the one the predator starts to track. He works hard to separate that member from the rest of the pack so he can pick her off when she's alone. A predator knows he can't take on the whole pack, but if he can separate one member, he can attack that one pretty easily.

Consider this: the devil has a whole pack of evil tricks, but one of the ways he works to hurt Christians is to separate us from other believers. We're members of a "pack" too; Christians are all members of one body. We need to move together, stick together, care for one another, and keep one another safe when the enemy is trying to attack. We must stay in church, stick close to our believing buddies as well as those who don't yet know God, and make sure we don't fall away from the tribe. The pack needs us, and we need the pack!

Stay alert! Watch out for your great enemy, the devil. He prowls around like a roaring lion, looking for someone to devour.

1 PETER 5:8, NLT

DINNER GUESTS

Have you ever found out that a group of friends or family had dined together, but without you? That can hurt. You feel excluded from a group of people that you thought were your own.

In Numbers 28, we read that the Lord reminded the Israelites about the food offerings he expected them to present. Sometimes those food offering passages in the Old Testament can be confusing, but as you read this chapter, it becomes clear. The Lord asked for those offerings to be presented to him each day in the morning and at twilight—when his family was eating. He asked them to present the same kinds of foods to him that they were serving to themselves. He wanted to sit down with his family and enjoy an intimate meal.

When Jesus came to earth, he continued to show us that he wanted to share intimacy with his people through meals. He ate roasted fish with his disciples. He dined with tax collectors. He shared the Last Supper with his closest friends, a meal we continue to celebrate with and for him.

I say in jest that I have offered many burnt offerings to my family over the years, but all kidding aside, it's important to me to ask the Lord, the provider of everything that ever appears on my table, to join us in the feast. He's my most welcome, most honored dinner guest, and I'll make the extra effort to ensure he's never overlooked.

The LORD said to Moses, "Give this command to the Israelites and say to them: 'Make sure that you present to me at the appointed time my food offerings, as an aroma pleasing to me.' Say to them: 'This is the food offering you are to present to the LORD: two lambs a year old without defect, as a regular burnt offering each day.'"

NUMBERS 28:1-3

July 8
COWBOY MAGIC

My daughter's hair had twisted into a terrible tangle. She'd been experimenting with different colors and techniques (just like I did at her age), and her hair had become damaged and weak. We wanted to comb through but not break it. None of the products we found at the drugstore helped, till someone asked us, "Have you tried products for horse manes?" She told us the name of the product that had worked wonders for her horses—and for her own hair.

We giggled and drove out to the local tack store. Once there, I flagged down a clerk and said, "Excuse me. We're looking for Cowboy Magic." With a smile she responded, "Aren't we all, honey?"

My daughter turned two shades redder than her newly dyed hair, but we found the product, paid for it, and took it home. For an hour we massaged it into her hair while we watched a chick flick, and then, just as the product had promised, her tangled hair combed right out. A comb went straight and smoothly through. The product had prepared her hair.

The Bible does talk of making paths straight, of clearing a way for easy access and ready understanding. Isaiah helped clear the way when he foretold about the Savior so we'd recognize him when he arrived; John the Baptist came ahead of Jesus, telling what would need to be done to receive Jesus and salvation. By speaking truth and pointing out need, he smoothed the rough paths for the Lord to walk upon as he calls us to him. Because of that we have a way out of tangles and jams of much more consequence than those nesting in our hair.

He went into all the country around the Jordan, preaching
a baptism of repentance for the forgiveness of sins. As it is
written in the book of the words of Isaiah the prophet:

"A voice of one calling in the wilderness,
'Prepare the way for the Lord,
make straight paths for him. . . .
The crooked roads shall become straight,
the rough ways smooth.'"

LUKE 3:3-5

DIY DAMAGE

While installing a new window screen in our daughter and son-in-law's home, my husband pierced his thumb on a jagged aluminum edge. I saw the grimace that instantly came over his face and knew what had happened. We located a bandage, and after we cleaned and wrapped the cut, he went back to work.

While digging a hole for a new plant, I hit an underground rock, er, boulder, with the shovel and felt it resonate all the way to my shoulder, which felt displaced. I took a few days off, then went back to the task.

An arm burned by a steam cleaner. A foot smashed by a new cabinet as it was being installed. A hand pierced by a nail that had not been hammered flush. A toe smacked against the foot of the bed.

Anything that requires work entails some risk, and the longer you work at it the more likely that some kind of injury is going to occur. Thankfully, whenever my husband or I have gotten hurt, a loved one has been around to help us stanch the bleeding, clean the wound, and wrap and protect it. Most of the injuries we've incurred while working around the house haven't done permanent damage, but they sure were painful.

And yet, we never wanted to quit the work. The results were so satisfying that they were well worth any risk undertaken. So it is with the work in the Kingdom of God. Don't go into it thinking that there will be no pain, no injuries incurred. There will be. And the injuries that hurt the most and persist the longest will be those that break the heart, not the toe. The best news? There will be others at the ready to bind your wounds, the chief of whom is the Master Craftsman who is building the house.

He heals the brokenhearted
and binds up their wounds.

PSALM 147:3

RATS AND COCKROACHES

So here's something I'll bet you didn't know: rats can live longer without water than camels can. They have a remarkable ability to outlast almost every circumstance thrown their way, and they multiply more quickly than rabbits do. They're responsible for spreading pestilence like the bubonic plague. They also scare grown women.

No one likes cockroaches. They . . . scurry. And carry disease. And they are not only bug-bomb proof, they are real-bomb proof. They've developed over time to be able to survive almost everything set out to kill them. They hide in dark places and come out at night; if light shines on them, they flee as if they somehow know their very lives depend on it. When we find pests in our houses, and we all do, we must get rid of them.

We have an enemy who is every bit as real, present, and sinister as either of these creatures, and he has a horde working with him. Like cockroaches, they persist over time, their tactics have evolved over the years, and they do their deeds in the dark, afraid of the light that exposes who they are. Like rats, our enemy and his minions spread pestilence and whisper gossip, doubt, fear, and rumor into ears willing to entertain them.

It's no fun to expose evil or its agents; the people pushing bad things are often intimidating, punitive, and manipulative. They threaten, overtly or subtly, that they'll make you pay for speaking up. But that's how they spread and multiply their sin in the dark. Prayerfully speak up if you see something looking amiss. One courageous voice starts a chorus that can overcome evil. Another's well-being may depend upon it!

Take no part in the worthless deeds of evil and darkness; instead, expose them.

EPHESIANS 5:11, NLT

July 11
NOT TONIGHT, DEER

When we first moved into our current house, we discovered that one of its immediate charms was the number of deer in the neighborhood. Whole deer families lived nearby, and they walked up and down the streets, unafraid of humans. They had no reason to be afraid, actually; people would stop their cars for the deer, throw apples in gullies for their snacking pleasure, and hold their dogs back. In a very real way, they were common pets.

And they were also common pests. They did not care how much I had just spent at the nursery for the flowers planted in a porch urn. They ate them. Plants that were supposed to be deer resistant were apparently irresistible to the deer in my town. I told my husband that the deer had just nibbled my new plants down to nubs and sticks. "They're supposed to be deer resistant!" I insisted. "Apparently, no one told the deer," he said.

I didn't often see them actually eating the plants. Instead, I found evidence that they'd been there—damaged plants, incriminating hoof prints, buck scat. Sometimes they allowed their friends, the cute bunnies, to eat the low branches while they nibbled the high ones!

How could something that seemed so innocent do so much harm? Why, we'd welcomed them in and taken care of them. But they had an agenda and didn't care if they stole or destroyed my hard work.

So I sprayed deer repellant. I planted tougher flowers. And I let my dog bark at them.

Sin so often sneaks into our lives that way. It doesn't look harmful at first, and a lot of other people seem to have invited it in too. We let our guards down, get distracted, or lose faith. Only when we see the damage left in sin's wake are we alerted. Fortunately, there's a remedy, and it's 100 percent effective. Submit to God. Resist the devil, and he will flee. It's a promise!

My plants look good and healthy now too!

The thief comes only to steal and kill and destroy; I have come that they may have life, and have it to the full.

JOHN 10:10

DIVINE SANDWICH LOAVES

When I was growing up, I had an aunt who made the most divine sandwich loaves. In case you had a deprived childhood, let me explain. The loaf is like a layer cake made in a loaf pan, except made with layers of white bread where the cake would be and layers of creamy, savory filling where the icing would be. The filling might be egg salad, tuna salad, whipped cream cheese, shrimp salad, olive-nut spread, or my all-time favorite, deviled ham salad.

A while ago, I had a craving for a sandwich loaf and decided to make one on my own. This procedure is not for the fainthearted, I discovered. Sharing the delight with my family in a backyard picnic made it all the better. It was fun not only to eat it together but to reflect back on a tiny bit of my culinary heritage and the woman who had made the loaves when I was a girl.

We think of our heritage as something major, well thought through, and of great consequence. It's good to plan some things along those lines, but most of the heritage we leave to our friends, relatives, children, nieces, and nephews comes through our everyday interactions. When I eat the sandwich loaf, I think not only of its deliciousness but of my aunt's willingness to prepare something difficult that others might enjoy. Another aunt would wear a funny-colored wig to make us laugh when we were feeling down; this is a heritage. The way we stop to hand a bottle of water to a homeless person or take our children or nieces and nephews shopping for a needy child is the heritage we pass on. What you do regularly is the testimony you pass down forever.

I will sing of the LORD's great love forever;
with my mouth I will make your faithfulness known
through all generations.

PSALM 89:1

REBUILDING

It is possible that there really are more natural disasters happening in our world right now—tsunamis, earthquakes, hurricanes, and the like—or it may be that the 24-7 availability of global news just makes it seem as if there are. But either way, it is true that these disasters have devastating consequences.

Afterward, people sometimes wonder, *Well, why do the victims build there again? They should simply move.* And sometimes—for example, if you've built right on top of a steam vent or within a tidal area that erodes year by year—that is pretty good advice. However, simply relocating people from large swaths of land is neither feasible nor necessary. Perhaps tornado victims in Oklahoma could move to Washington state, for example, but then they'd have to worry about earthquakes. There is some potential for disaster everywhere.

Relationships are like this too. Some, truly, are complete disasters. We like to believe that there is redemptive potential in every relationship. But if the history of a plot of land shows no real change and tornadoes come down that alley regularly, perhaps it's better to move on rather than to continually seek shelter.

For most relationships, though, there will always be some fault lines or seasons of stormy weather. Rather than flee, how can we fortify? Get some good counseling? Consider how we may be contributing to the situation and ask for help to address it? Own what *we've* done, not adding "but you . . ."?

The beautiful thing is that—in the absence of any kind of abuse—relationships, like homes, can usually be rebuilt. And keeping the past in mind when rebuilding, we can fortify them so they are stronger than the originals. Our God is a God of restoration.

I will bring my exiled people of Israel
back from distant lands,
and they will rebuild their ruined cities
and live in them again.
They will plant vineyards and gardens;
they will eat their crops and drink their wine.

AMOS 9:14, NLT

July 14

TELLTALE CRUMBS

I've always loved fairy tales, maybe because in the end there's always a happily ever after. I was thinking about Hansel and Gretel this week as I cleaned my office. It would be very easy for anyone to discern where to find me if they went looking. They'd just have to follow the crumbs . . . right to my office.

Crumbs were under my chair (where is my dog?), and crumbs were scattered on top of the desk. Worst of all, crumbs had fallen into my keyboard, and no matter what I did, they would not come out.

Why was my kitchen clean but not my office? Why was my living room—you know, the room I'm supposed to be living in—tidy, but my office was not? I had spent too much time working. Too many meals had been taken at my desk instead of my dining room table.

Of course I have a lot to do, and I'm guessing you do too. But I don't have more to do than the apostles did. When Jesus' followers returned to tell him everything they had done in his name, he knew exactly what they needed. They needed to come away from that very important work—work he had commissioned them to do—and rest.

I sat in my office the other day, looking out through the slats of the French blinds at some neighbors talking and preparing to drive off together. For a moment I was jealous of their leisure, and then I realized I am mostly in charge of my own schedule. If I want to follow the Lord's advice and ensure I have time to come away, I'm the only one who can do it. And I can!

The apostles gathered around Jesus and reported to him all they had done and taught. Then, because so many people were coming and going that they did not even have a chance to eat, he said to them, "Come with me by yourselves to a quiet place and get some rest."

MARK 6:30-31

July 15

POUND CAKE AND COOKIES

When my husband and I were seriously dating, I hoped to score some points with his mother by making her a birthday cake. Let's just say my husband didn't have a lot of good baking equipment, and I was not a very good baker. The first cake ended up completely burnt. Acrid smoke filled the apartment, and the smell lingered no matter how many windows we opened. We ran out and bought a cake, which worked, till my future sister-in-law found the burnt cake hidden in a kitchen cupboard. What gave it away? I'm guessing the smell of death.

I went on to make more cakes, learning as I went, and today there is nothing that says "home" to me quite as much as a pound cake. Vanilla, butter, sugar, warmth—all of it spreading from kitchen to house to heart. I read recently that in order to sell houses more quickly, some real estate agents suggest baking cookies just before an open house. People smell that fragrance and think, *I want to live there!*

The apostle Paul's second letter to the Corinthians explains that believers are fragrant, too, and that fragrance extends everywhere. To those who are perishing, we bring an aroma of death with us. Not because we're bad, and hopefully not because we're critical or judgmental, but perhaps because when we come into a situation, we bring the Spirit with us, and he convicts. To our fellow Christians, we bring that same Spirit, and he reaches between us to bond, build fellowship, and remind us of our common heritage and future.

I believe with all my heart that heaven will be perfect, and therefore there must be pound cake and chocolate chip cookies waiting for us. I'm truly excited to have eternity to indulge in them (calorie free?) with my sisters.

We are to God the pleasing aroma of Christ among those who are being saved and those who are perishing. To the one we are an aroma that brings death; to the other, an aroma that brings life. And who is equal to such a task?

2 CORINTHIANS 2:15-16

SOUR GRAPES

My daughter has always loved fruit, especially grapes. Her favorite grapes are Concord because they're so sweet. One week I brought home a batch of grapes that were the first of the season. She eagerly washed a bunch and then stuffed a few in her mouth. Her face screwed up. Her eyes squinted closed. She chewed as quickly as she could and swallowed.

"What's wrong?" I asked.

"Sour grapes!" she replied.

Scripture uses sour grapes as a metaphor for sin. Several times, the Bible says that when the parents eat sour grapes (sin), their children's teeth are set on edge (the children suffer the consequences). But in Ezekiel, the Lord clarifies. He says that we are each responsible for what we do and say. This is a great comfort for parents whose children wander, even if for a season, or for a teacher who pours everything into a student who never rises to his or her potential. Was that time well spent, rightly stewarded?

Yes, so press on! You do not know whether a seed you plant will flourish, whether it will lie dormant past your time on earth, or whether it will die. You are not held accountable for the fruit, only for the planting. That is definitely within our reach!

The word of the LORD came to me: "What do you people mean
by quoting this proverb about the land of Israel:

"'The parents eat sour grapes,
and the children's teeth are set on edge'?

"As surely as I live, declares the Sovereign LORD, you will no longer quote
this proverb in Israel. For everyone belongs to me, the parent as well as the
child—both alike belong to me. The one who sins is the one who will die."

EZEKIEL 18:1-4

July 17

ROOTED

I have a childhood memory of seeing an avocado pit suspended by toothpicks, halfway submerged in a glass of water. Would an avocado really grow from that? I had no idea. Although I saw roots dangling down from said pit, drinking up the water below, I never saw one grow to successfully bear fruit.

It's hard to know how well someone is rooted in faith, because unlike those avocado pits, human roots are mostly unseen. All we can do is look at how healthy the plant itself is. Is it thriving, even when the sun is hot? Can it persist through a little drought? Does it flower or fruit, and are its leaves green, bringing pleasure and pride to the Gardener and his guests?

We recently moved a healthy plant from the full-sun front yard, where it was getting a little sunburned, to the back, where I thought it would thrive in more shade. We had to cut a wide arc around the plant so as not to damage the roots. Conventional wisdom says that plants' roots extend below ground as far as the longest branch extends above ground. We pulled the plant, which had been in the ground only a year, and shook it. Sand and dirt tumbled from it, exposing an intricate, strong, and healthy root system. It had "taken," and I knew it would move successfully too.

One thing is certain. You, my friend, are deeply planted and grounded in love. Your roots are healthy and will remain so no matter where you are transplanted. The Gardener tends to you fondly, and your blooms are lovely and unique, bringing him pleasure.

I pray that you, being rooted and established in love, may have power, together with all the Lord's holy people, to grasp how wide and long and high and deep is the love of Christ, and to know this love that surpasses knowledge—that you may be filled to the measure of all the fullness of God.

EPHESIANS 3:17-19

DANDELIONS AND DAISY BOUQUETS

One midsummer day, our family piled into the car for a drive. We rounded a corner and saw a little boy, about six, at a makeshift stand. He wasn't selling lemonade. He was selling the wild daisies we could see growing in his yard. His stuffed animal was on the table with the flowers, and we couldn't resist him.

I dug through my purse looking for cash, and my daughter urged me to give him more than he was asking for, so we did. In return, the little lad handed us not one but two of those bouquets, which we brought home and put in a vase.

Now in case you didn't know, daisies do not smell good at all. In fact, the reason they're planted in vegetable gardens is to ward off pests. But these were so beautiful, as was the innocence of that little boy. It reminded me of a time when my children were young and picked a large bouquet of dandelions for me. (Good thing I hadn't been weeding.) My kids thought the dandelions were beautiful and offered them from the depths of their hearts, so excited to see my reaction. It was their idea to look for them, to pick them, to offer them. It didn't matter to me what the value of the gift was; it mattered why and from whom it was given. We then spent sweet time together arranging them in a jelly-jar vase.

There is nothing we can offer the Lord that will make him richer, but we can offer our love, our affection, our will, our time, and our companionship freely and willingly. From the perspective of a parent, what better gift could there be?

Each of you should give what you have decided in your heart to give,
not reluctantly or under compulsion, for God loves a cheerful giver.

2 CORINTHIANS 9:7

MESSY-HOUSE FRIENDS

The first time a friend comes to visit my home, I make sure everything is in order. I plan our food and drink with care—not so much to impress as to make sure my guest's visit is comfortable and enjoyable. As our friendship grows in time and depth, my standards relax—not because I care about her less, but mainly because we've become more like family, living life together, in her house or in mine.

Conversations, e-mails, and texts are like this too. At the beginning of a friendship, we are more formal, writing "Dear XX" and signing off with "Till later!" or however you sign e-mails. Eventually, you can send one-liners. "Please pray! Water heater is broken!" Or "Do you know any way to get a pesky neighbor to fit the lid on his garbage can?" Or "How can I pray for you today to keep myself from focusing on my own problems?" Such casualness implies even deeper love and concern as well as a level of comfort in the relationship.

I've come to think of my friends as either "messy-house friends" who can drop by any time, or "clean-house friends" whom I normally know in advance are coming. I welcome both, and I know I'm a welcome visitor as both kinds too. But the messy-house friends are the ones who can ask me, "Want me to help clean the kitchen?" when I'm feeling unwell or "Let me come over and help you pack" when I'm moving—again. They're the ones who can quietly point out my inner messes, too, and offer to help or pray for those as well. I'm so grateful for my messy-house friends. I hope I'm a good messy-house friend too.

Two are better than one,
because they have a good return for their labor:
If either of them falls down,
one can help the other up.
But pity anyone who falls
and has no one to help them up.

ECCLESIASTES 4:9-10

ALLERGIES

As a young girl, I developed an allergy to raspberries, a fruit that I loved. I'd spent many days plucking the ruby fruit off the thorny bushes in my great-aunt's yard before I had to call it quits. Imagine my happiness, years later as an adult, when I discovered that I was no longer allergic to them—or so I thought.

Living in the berry capital of the world (okay, at least *we* think so!), I had plenty of opportunities to eat berries, but I didn't overindulge in raspberries till last summer. I looked at them and they at me, and we fell in love again as I spent time picking them near my house. They appeared night after night in my dessert repertoire, and then we had a falling out.

The first rash appeared on my chest, and although I had changed laundry detergent and thought about whether I'd been taking any new medications, it soon became clear that the raspberry revenge was back. I didn't want it to be so—how could I get along without raspberry pavlova? Raspberry jam? Raspberry lemonade? But wishing it wasn't so didn't make the symptoms go away. Instead, they got worse as I persisted in eating the berries. Ignoring what was harming me only made it worse. My body, wanting to protect me, kept sending increasingly alarming signals . . . on my skin.

Maybe, like me, you're reluctant to let go of a habit, a relationship, or a way of interacting that isn't good for you. It might be a sin, or it might simply be unhealthy. It could be something physical or emotional or spiritual. But your body and spirit and mind keep sending you signals to let go. Let go; there are other fruits, habits, relationships, ways of living. Ones that help and don't hurt you.

Hate what is evil; cling to what is good.

ROMANS 12:9

GOING IN CIRCLES

My dog isn't always a tail chaser, but sometimes she is. She circles around and around, and although some people say that dogs do that for fun, I do think that the first few times, at least, she really didn't realize it was a part of herself that she was chasing.

She also circles around and around before doing her duty when she is let outside. What exactly is she looking for that makes this spot of grass different from the others? And before lying down on her bed, she circles like an airplane waiting to land.

What's with the circling?

I laugh at her, but I realized one afternoon, as I hand-washed dishes to buy myself some quiet time to think through a problem, that I go in circles too. I ruminate on a problem, running mental circles to find an explanation or solution other than the one I already know is the right one. I circle back to bad habits that I know I need to drop. I walk all the way around a problem, looking for an answer that doesn't include distressing actions or uncomfortable consequences. No matter how much time the circling buys me, though, I eventually have to address the problem head-on. As Robert Frost said, the best way out is always through—in my case, *straight* through.

Thankfully, we have a resource, a Father who is ready to offer a quick hand and a loving heart when we need to address our troubles. He doesn't promise a pain-free solution, but he does promise eventual deliverance. No circling required!

Call on me in the day of trouble;
I will deliver you, and you will honor me.

PSALM 50:15

July 22

BELOVED LITTLE BIRDS

It's so easy for me to judge others by what they look like. Are they buttoned up and therefore unlikely to be open minded? Richly attired and therefore unlikely to be generous? How about heavily tattooed and therefore unlikely to be Christians? Most of us have, at one time or another, made some snap decisions about someone's morals, occupation, or faith based solely upon how the person was dressed. Yet Scripture tells us that the Lord doesn't look at the outward person, as we do, but rather he looks at the inner person. And it's clear that he has called some from every group on earth.

One day while looking at the barn at the back of my friend's property, I was reminded of the Sunday-school story of the swallow who flew into a burning barn. There was only a tiny, swallow-sized hole under the eaves from which the birds inside could escape. They couldn't go the way of the pigs, or the cows, or the horses; they could not see below them because of the smoke. They could escape only through the hole near the roof, and another swallow—who looked just like them—entered through the hole and guided them safely out.

The story illustrates Jesus coming in the flesh to show us "the way out." But it is also culturally relevant today and offers insight into the way we view others. Perhaps the Lord sends "missionaries" into each culture and ethnic group, sharing their interests and values and showing them the exact manner by which to flee the burning barn and find life.

And who am I to judge God's missionaries by how they look?

Go into all the world and preach the gospel to all creation.

MARK 16:15

ONE-DAY WONDERS

At the plant nursery, I looked at the haul in my wagon. It added up to just a little more than I had budgeted, but I went ahead and bought everything anyway, fully understanding the no-return policy. I drove home, unsettled that I had broken the financial promise I'd made to myself.

I had fallen back into an old, bad pattern. I'd succumbed to a temptation I thought I had overcome—spending "just a little more" than I'd planned on because I could justify it. The project would be done right! It would add value to our home! You know the drill, I'm sure.

Later that day we planted the rock roses, which I'd coveted because they are the only "roses" that deer don't like to nibble on around here. After reading up on rock roses, I had a sinking feeling. They are rose-like, yes, but each bloom lasts only *one day*!

Each morning, really early, before the sun was up, that day's blooms opened, unfurling five pink petals, each marked by a mauve spot that looked like a drop of blood. No matter how much rain or wind came down that day, the blooms hung tough. At the end of the day, right as it was turning dark, the five petals let go of the shrub and quietly fluttered to the ground. So, yes, each flower lasted but one day. However, the bush was ripe with dozens of buds, and each day, without fail, several blooms opened up, so that over the course of the growing season there were always fresh flowers to enjoy.

I felt the Spirit touch me as I stared at the plant I shouldn't have bought. *I'm sorry, Lord. I overspent. Again. I'm so glad you exhorted your disciples to forgive a truly repentant spirit seventy times seven, because I find myself in need of that from you.* He drew my eyes to the buds that would bloom tomorrow, then to the blossoms that were new just this morning, then to the spent petals of yesterday lying on the ground. I lifted my eyes, knowing what he was saying to me, and I responded. *Thank you. I'll try again.*

Because of the LORD's great love we are not consumed, for his compassions never fail. They are new every morning; great is your faithfulness.

LAMENTATIONS 3:22-23

July 24
HOARDERS

One of the shows I enjoy watching on TV is about two men who travel across the country looking for junk. Really, junk. They pay money for it, then turn around and sell it for more money.

It is astounding to me to see just how much *stuff*—er, trinkets and treasures—some people on the show have accumulated. For the most part, the dealers are generous; just because they have a lot of stuff doesn't mean they don't share a lot of stuff too.

It's possible to collect too much, though, even in the average person's life. We might not have time to sort through everything and clean out a closet, a task none of us wants to spend a Saturday doing. Many times we hold on to things because they have sentimental value, and that's okay. But often we hold on to things because we *might need it someday*. Sometimes, we even hold on to our financial resources because we *might need them someday*.

It is not wrong to be a prudent planner; in fact, Scripture speaks highly of it. But at what point does our desire to plan prudently for the future become hoarding things that we could share instead with people who have needs right now? There is no simple formula, except perhaps to pray and trust. Keep enough to be wise. Give enough to show that you trust God will provide for whatever needs may someday come.

He told them this parable: "The ground of a certain rich man yielded an abundant harvest. He thought to himself, 'What shall I do? I have no place to store my crops.'

"Then he said, 'This is what I'll do. I will tear down my barns and build bigger ones, and there I will store my surplus grain. And I'll say to myself, "You have plenty of grain laid up for many years. Take life easy; eat, drink and be merry."'

"But God said to him, 'You fool! This very night your life will be demanded from you. Then who will get what you have prepared for yourself?'"

LUKE 12:16-20

WHOLLY ORGANIC

At one time, we lived next door to a man who insisted upon organic garden-ing. He frowned on anyone who was "caught" using synthetic weed killers or plant food other than fish emulsion. Lengthy lectures about mulching versus mowing would ensue if he saw you emptying your mower bag into the yard waste bin. Doing it his way might take longer, he said, but it was the right way.

One morning I was out early, and although it was from a distance, I could clearly read the label on the bottle he was spraying from. Roundup. Synthetic weed killer!

What a hypocrite, I thought. Lecturing everyone else on how to live the right way—his way—while in public, but privately relying on the same old things the rest of us do.

A few hours later I went to Bible study; we had been studying living by faith. I admit that although my faith is strong, there are too many times when I am so worried about a problem that I give God about ten minutes to solve it his way, and when he doesn't, I wrest control back from him to do it myself.

Is that really living by faith? The Scriptures I hold in such esteem teach that we are to live by faith, and that is truly my goal every day. Was I telling myself I was living by faith and encouraging others to do likewise, but actually relying on my own efforts when I got worried or fearful? Did I lean into God for the long haul, or panic and choose to solve things myself?

I asked forgiveness for my self-righteous attitude toward my neighbor, thankful that the Lord used that to show me that if I truly want to be the per-son inside that I claim to be on the outside, I need to rely on him all the time, even when it takes him more time to resolve things than I am comfortable with.

Trust in the LORD with all your heart;
do not depend on your own understanding.

PROVERBS 3:5, NLT

July 26
LIGHT AND EASY

Our son was home for the summer, and being the good man that he is, he offered to help us do some work around the house. We have a large, cobbled patio in our backyard, and it had been neglected for a time. I asked him to tidy up the patio and the little walkway that led up to it.

I didn't give it much thought till a few days later when I went out back to find about a hundred stones all stacked and the entire area ripped up, roped off with thin yellow ribbon. "What's going on?" I asked, shocked.

"I'm fixing this, like you asked," he replied. "It's going to take another week or so. I'm not going to be able to tidy the walkway to it, I don't think. This is a lot of work."

I had envisioned him perhaps power washing the area, but he had taken up every stone and purchased sand in order to make the area completely level. He told me later that it had been a more trying and difficult project than he had imagined. I smiled, not daring to tell him after the fact that I had intended only a quick, couple-hour cleanup. The finished project looked wonderful, but perhaps not too much more wonderful than the power washing alone would have wrought. I appreciated his heart toward doing things right, but I hadn't meant to place a heavy burden on him, or on his time, that summer.

Keeping God's commandments can be as simple as seeking out knowledge through Scripture, prayer, and good teaching and then moving into action as the Holy Spirit nudges. He will always ask us to do a little, to do our part, for him and the family. It is my own misinterpretations, I think, that sometimes burden me with well-intentioned but over-the-top labors.

Loving God means keeping his commandments, and
his commandments are not burdensome.

1 JOHN 5:3, NLT

July 27

DISTRESSED

The men in my house have found great amusement in the decorating concept of distressing furniture. "So you take a perfectly fine piece of furniture, then you drag nails across it or scuff it up with sandpaper, and then paint it?" they asked me. "Then you remove some of that paint to see the raw wood underneath?" "Yes!" I enthusiastically replied. "Great, right?"

Once on a trip to England, we met a man who had lived in the area for a long time. He told us of a family who had moved into a storied estate many centuries old. However, the furnishings had not come with the property. Upon visiting the home, one of the neighbors was heard to say, "But the furniture is all . . . bought!"

It may seem like snobbishness on one level to place a higher value on inherited furniture than on that which has been newly purchased. But what I took it to mean is that there is value in something that has been around for a while. A saggy chair has proved its value and worth. A sofa that has been sat upon for centuries has stories to tell. A family bed has tradition. Perhaps that's what we're after when we make nouveau furniture look distressed. Life includes distress, over time, but what is wrought by distress is beautiful.

My son, Samuel, is named after the one in Scripture. I, like Hannah, cried bitterly for a time when I was unable to conceive a child. In the end, the Lord did allow me to conceive my children, and the wait for them and the fear of not having them makes their lives even sweeter to me. I have not forgotten the distress that preceded their birth. What has been hard won in your life? Does the distress that preceded it make the final gift even sweeter?

*In her deep anguish Hannah prayed to the L**ORD**, weeping bitterly. . . .*
In the course of time Hannah became pregnant and gave birth to a son.
*She named him Samuel, saying, "Because I asked the L**ORD** for him."*

1 SAMUEL 1:10, 20

July 28

SIN RESISTANT

I'm amused by the picture on some of the plant picks at my nursery. They show a doe with a "deer in the headlights" look on her face and a big red circle with a strike drawn through it. The language on the back of the pick is careful to note, though, that the plant is deer "resistant" and not deer "proof." No plant is fully deer proof, no matter how much we'd wish it to be so. So we plant carefully and build an environment that at least makes our garden less desirable to those who would damage or destroy.

As we grow as people, as Christians, the sins that so easily ensnared us early in our walk with the Lord seem distant and much less of a temptation now. We've replaced their dark and dangerous false pleasures with wholesome, righteous ones. And yet, we still inhabit our bodies of clay, our very human flesh, and none of us will stop sinning till the day we die. The book of 1 John tells us that to think otherwise would be to deceive ourselves and make us liars. None of us is sin proof yet!

Since that is true, we can try, instead, to make a good environment for ourselves and others, planting our gardens and theirs with habits that make us resistant, at least, to sin. Surrounding myself with good books; spending time with people who love God and love others; listening to and sharing music that is uplifting and upbeat; and sharing entertainment, pleasure, and fellowship with like-minded sisters and brothers builds me up rather than tempts me toward that which tears down.

It's more fun this way too. Everything to gain, nothing to lose.

Well, my brothers and sisters, let's summarize. When you meet together,
one will sing, another will teach, another will tell some special revelation
God has given, one will speak in tongues, and another will interpret
what is said. But everything that is done must strengthen all of you.

1 CORINTHIANS 14:26, NLT

July 29

BESETTING SINS

Everyone I know has some kind of persistent medical irritation. One friend has a bad back—no matter how much she tries to baby it, it goes out from time to time. Some people suffer sinus issues or on-again, off-again depression or anxiety. I have had nearly constant dental issues since reaching adulthood. They plague me every year, and every year I have to take steps to get out of pain and be healed.

Spiritual weaknesses, it seems, are very much like physical ones. They're part and parcel of living in an imperfect world in imperfect bodies. Back in the day, people referred to "besetting sins," particular sins that regularly tempt you, in spite of your best intentions. Besetting sins are like an old enemy, like the kid in middle school who taunts and teases you and just won't give up. They're also like spider webs—you walk right into them and then have to pick your way out. I like the word *besetting*, because when I fall into an old sin pattern, that's just what it feels like: a trap was set, and I stepped into it. It reminds me of the time I tried to leap out of bed not realizing the sheets were entangling my legs and fell right onto the floor.

The good news is that just as paying good attention to your physical health allows you to avoid some negative consequences, and time and doctoring help you work your way out, you can move past any sin, besetting or otherwise. Learn where the traps are, and step around them. Wipe the house free of webs. If you do set a foot wrong—and sometimes we all do—the Doctor is in to fix you; you don't need to stay entangled. Repent, turn around, keep a sharp eye out, and carry on!

Since we are surrounded by such a great cloud of witnesses, let us throw off everything that hinders and the sin that so easily entangles. And let us run with perseverance the race marked out for us, fixing our eyes on Jesus, the pioneer and perfecter of faith.

HEBREWS 12:1-2

WEEDING

These are the fun things about gardening:

- planning a garden
- buying plants
- getting them in the ground
- cutting flowers
- enjoying the view

These are the not-so-fun things:

- watering
- weeding

If history comes full circle and heaven really does have a garden, I hope someone else is doing the weeding. My elderly neighbors, who have a lovely garden, tried to find someone to come and weed their yard, as they are unable to do the required bending and pulling anymore. Finding someone to employ was not easy, and the service cost as much as a minor surgical procedure. Because weeding is such an onerous chore, every gardener usually must do it herself.

Without weeding, though, the noxious sneaks would overtake my garden, destroying the beautiful plants I want to flourish. For some reason, weeds are stronger than many desired plants. So out I go, month after month, to pluck the weeds. I'm not happy to do it, because it's hot work and hard, but when I'm done, I have a garden I am proud for others to see as well as to enjoy myself. My spiritual life, too, requires tending. As the Spirit or others make me aware that weeds have suddenly shown up in my garden (and Scripture tells us who sows when the gardener isn't watching), those weeds must be removed. Thankfully, we don't have to weed our own lives by ourselves. Jesus stands ready to pull the weeds out of our hearts and minds. It's hard and unlovely work, but when I'm done, I have a life I'm pleased to present and enjoy.

*Dear friends, let us purify ourselves from everything that contaminates
body and spirit, perfecting holiness out of reverence for God.*

2 CORINTHIANS 7:1

DON'T LOOK BACK

Down through the ages, Lot's wife has been regarded with condescension and perhaps judgment. When told to flee her town, which was without a doubt a literal den of iniquity, she raced out of town and then, in disobedience, turned around for one last look. For her sin, she was turned into a pillar of salt.

She did wrong, no doubt about it. She disobeyed. Of course, we do not know her complete story. But who among us cannot understand a woman who, when called to leave her home, glanced back? What she was asked to do was in her best interest, and that of her family, yet what lay ahead was unknown. Likewise, the Israelites, once in the desert, began to grumble about wanting to be back in Egypt because where they were at the moment did not meet their high expectations.

Perhaps the most compelling argument against the Exodus Israelites and Lot's wife is that they did not fully consider what they were fleeing from. Death. Evil. Slavery. Yes, what lay ahead was unknown, and the life was not guaranteed to be easy. It's easy to be wistful for what you once knew when you don't remember the whole picture. I do that sometimes too.

Jesus calls us to a life apart, one that looks different from before and goes places we don't expect. When he says, "Follow me," the implication is that we must leave something behind. Something comfortable, like my old couch; it's true that the springs poked through and scratched me, but it was familiar. What's ahead will be hard work, but it will be good and right. And, best of all, Jesus will be leading.

I want to be worthy; I do. It's time to throw out the old. No more looking back.

Jesus replied, "No one who puts a hand to the plow and looks back is fit for service in the kingdom of God."

LUKE 9:62

AUGUST

Porcelain and Pumice

I've long known that pumice stones were good for removing tough skin from the heel of my foot, but a friend who has worked as a housekeeper shared another trick with me: a pumice stone will remove the dark spots and circles that sometimes appear around the drains in porcelain sinks, tubs, and toilets.

Wet the sink or tub, then wet the pumice stone. Very gently, but persistently, rub against the stain. A little pressure is enough to remove the ring but not scratch or damage the porcelain. Rinse with water.

This will also remove hard-water rings in your toilets but, well, you'll probably want to use a stone you've dedicated for toilet use only!

I haven't yet tried this on porcelain cookware, but it might be worth investigating.

For this month's free printable, go to http://tyndal.es/homeandgarden.

THE DESTROYER

As we sat out on the patio in late summer, a couple of very large insects flew by. I didn't recognize them, so I asked my husband, and he told me they were flying termites. Termites!

Most likely they came from some fallen logs in a wooded area nearby, but to be on the safe side we hired a pest inspector to come and look over the house. This kind of inspection happens before the sale of a home, too, and for good reason. Once termites infest a home, they can damage it from within to the point that all the structural beams holding up the home are destroyed, ruining the house. We often see pictures of homes destroyed by fire, hurricane, or earthquake. But the infestation that carries on quietly, till collapse occurs, happens more frequently and is often as deadly.

Scripture tells us that a house divided cannot stand, that one cannot be working in the interests of God and of Satan at the same time. Just as a house can appear solid from the outside when in fact it is being destroyed by pests from the inside, a person can appear clean on the outside but be eaten up inside with sin that will eventually become evident and lead to that person's destruction. The antidote? Inspection and termination when sin is found. It requires, as twelve-step programs say, a fearless and sweeping moral inventory of ourselves and a ridding of sins and habits that are tearing us down.

Termites are fine in fallen, dead logs, but they can wreak awful damage inside the temple of the living God.

We must not indulge in sexual immorality as some of them did, and twenty-three thousand fell in a single day. We must not put Christ to the test, as some of them did and were destroyed by serpents, nor grumble, as some of them did and were destroyed by the Destroyer. . . . Therefore let anyone who thinks that he stands take heed lest he fall.

1 CORINTHIANS 10:8-10,12, ESV

August 2

OVER AND OVER AND OVER AGAIN

I wish I'd raised my children in the era of the smartphone. I'm sure I'd have had a lot of cute pictures to share; mainly, though, I would have used it to record and replay phrases like these:

- Didn't I tell you to clean your room? Do it now or you're not going.
- Do you have your homework? Do you have your lunch?
- Pick your stuff up off the floor before someone trips and gets hurt.

These are the kinds of things I said over and over and over again. I'm sure the repetition was as irritating for my kids as it was for me, but I had to keep saying things over and over because unless I did, they didn't get it—and there was a whole bunch of stuff I thought was really important for them to get. I can hardly complain about it, though, because I'm guessing God might want to record a few things to say to me:

- Did you read your Bible? No? How can you say I'm not talking to you, then?
- Are you sure you want to do that? Remember last time . . .
- Do not worry. Instead, pray about everything.

I think this is why, maybe, the phrase "by faith" is used twenty times in Hebrews 11. I've read it before, and after the repetition goes on and on, I'm thinking, *Okay! I get it!* And the still, small voice says, *Do you?* And I wonder, *Do I?* And then, yeah. I do.

I'm glad good parents say things over and over and over again till we get it!

Faith is confidence in what we hope for and assurance about what we do not see. This is what the ancients were commended for.

HEBREWS 11:1-2

PRUNED

We have two giant Chocolate Cherry tomato plants in our backyard. They are like babies to my husband. He's up checking them first thing in the morning and counting blossoms and fruit after work. He sprays them with organic spray and stakes them where they need it.

Over the course of a month, the bushes grew so large that they spilled over their cages onto the landscape stones, crowding the rest of the garden. There were many branches and leaves on each plant. As the summer wore on, though, it was clear that some branches were loaded with fruit, but some had no fruit at all.

The fruitless branches were plenty green, to be sure. But because they were not bearing, they were hoarding resources that the fruit-bearing branches needed in order for the green tomatoes to mature to red. And the big leaves of the fruitless branches were blocking the sun from other productive branches.

"They have to go," Hubs said. I agreed.

With a sharp trimmer, he cut back enough branches to completely fill our yard-waste container, shaping and snipping with great care. When he was finished, what was left were the fruit-bearing branches, those with promising yellow blossoms as well as those with budding fruit. If we had kept the non-productive branches, the productive branches would continue to be robbed of the resources they needed to ripen the fruit. One doesn't grow a tomato plant, after all, for beautiful foliage. One grows it for fruit, and the conscientious gardener prunes with that in mind. Our Master Gardener can be trusted to know what and where to cut.

I am the vine; you are the branches. If you remain in me and I in you,
you will bear much fruit; apart from me you can do nothing.

JOHN 15:5

August 4

THE NARROW GATE

When we walk the nature trails in our town, we come upon many forks in the trail. We might take the path that leads to the Sound with its beautiful view, or the one that leads deeper into the forest, where we might spot deer. Some days we choose a wide trail that is covered with gravel; other days we might be daring enough to choose the narrow trail that we can barely see. Each time we come to a fork in the trail, we have a decision to make.

We have learned that regardless of the trail's appeal, it's best to make our decision based on where we want to end up. No sense taking the way through the woods if you want to get to the Sound, deer or no deer. Often the path that seems like it might be the hardest or least used eventually leads to the most beautiful view.

THE ROAD NOT TAKEN
Two roads diverged in a yellow wood,
And sorry I could not travel both
And be one traveler, long I stood
And looked down one as far as I could . . .
Two roads diverged in a wood, and I—
I took the one less traveled by,
And that has made all the difference.
—ROBERT FROST

The Bible teaches that those who confess that Jesus is Lord and believe in their hearts that God raised him from the dead will be saved. It also tells us that we have a choice: to believe or not to believe. Make sure you pick the trail that leads where you want to end up!

Which path do you choose?

You can enter God's Kingdom only through the narrow gate. The highway
to hell is broad, and its gate is wide for the many who choose that way.

MATTHEW 7:13, NLT

August 5
PESTS

I had a phone call to make. A call I didn't feel like making because it would be awkward, uncomfortable, and apologetic. *I'll just take a little nap first,* I thought. *To get my strength up and feel more calm.* I lay down on my bed.

Within a few restless minutes I heard buzzing. It got louder and louder, and no amount of swatting would get rid of the fly harassing me. In a rather large room he had chosen to fly about a two-foot circumference right around my head. *All right! I surrender. I'll get up and make the call.*

I like to believe that most of the time I can be wooed by the promise of reward or just the satisfaction of doing the right thing. But sometimes I need the motivation of negative consequences, too. Maybe I'm supposed to make a call, leave a job, or end an unhealthy relationship. Perhaps I know I should volunteer for or give more money to a cause, and I don't really want to. Wooing often works. So does pestering.

When the Egyptians would not let the Israelites leave, God motivated them with negative consequences. It's not surprising to me that one of the plagues he sent was flies! In the end, God's method worked. The circumstances became so uncomfortable that Pharaoh finally said, "Enough!"

Next time you're pestered or plagued, don't look on it as an absolute negative. Perhaps God is nudging you, through unpleasantness, to do exactly what will bring wholeness, freedom, and peace!

The LORD said to Moses, "Get up early in the morning and confront Pharaoh as he goes to the river and say to him, 'This is what the LORD says: Let my people go, so that they may worship me. If you do not let my people go, I will send swarms of flies on you and your officials, on your people and into your houses. The houses of the Egyptians will be full of flies; even the ground will be covered with them. . . .'"

And the LORD did this. Dense swarms of flies poured into Pharaoh's palace and into the houses of his officials; throughout Egypt the land was ruined by the flies. Then Pharaoh summoned Moses and Aaron and said, "Go, sacrifice to your God here in the land."

EXODUS 8:20-21, 24-25

LEFTOVERS

Have you ever bitten into an apple or eaten most of the way through it, only to discover a worm at the center? It will kill your appetite for a few days. A friend of mine bought a prepared salad and, after eating most of it, discovered a dead bug at the bottom. Salad was off her menu for some time.

When God led the Israelites out of Egypt and into the desert, he provided food for them day by day. The food was called manna, which he provided through miraculous means. By description it was sweet, savory, and crispy, so it covered a lot of taste preferences. God instructed Moses that the people were not to save manna from one day to the next, with the exception of the Sabbath. Some of them ignored the instructions, though, and when they went to eat their hoarded manna, they found it loaded with maggots. Ick!

God tells us in the New Testament to ask for our daily bread—not our weekly bread, or our monthly bread—instead, to trust him to provide what we need day by day. Hoarding resources shows a lack of trust that what we need next Wednesday will be there—maybe not by Tuesday night, but by Wednesday. And as we shall not live by bread alone, I think I'm to spend time in the Word day by day too. The word of encouragement I needed last week is likely not the instruction I'll need next, but the right word in the right season is guaranteed to be there!

Moses said to them, "It is the bread the LORD has given you to eat. This is what the LORD has commanded: 'Everyone is to gather as much as they need. . . .'"

Then Moses said to them, "No one is to keep any of it until morning."

However, some of them paid no attention to Moses; they kept part of it until morning, but it was full of maggots and began to smell.

EXODUS 16:15-16, 19-20

HECKLERS

I sat in my backyard one morning, closing my eyes and hoping for a few minutes of peace and quiet before returning to the housework. My eyelids had barely touched when I was rudely shocked out of my comfort by the loud chattering of a flock of crows. I opened my eyes and watched them strut across the lawn, staring me down with their beady black eyes and refusing to scatter until I threw a stone. They flew into the treetops, still watching.

Then some small sparrows flitted down to the ground. One seemed to signal to the others that there were good pickings in the area behind our squash plant, and the rest floated down to join him in a bug-hunting expedition. Before long the crows started up again, heckling.

It reminded me of being at a football game. Without fail, one or more fans in the stands (who perhaps have imbibed one too many) shout insults toward the players to throw them off their game. One heckler questions the defensive players' abilities, another the ref's capacity to see, a third the parentage of another player. It detracts from the enjoyment of the day, but it also forces the players to purposefully shut out those voices in order to win. The quarterback has a headset inside his helmet that transmits instructions and, I hope, encouragement from his coach. By concentrating on his coach's voice and shutting out the hecklers, he can focus on the task at hand.

Back in my yard, I closed my eyes again and turned my heart to prayer, so my Coach could transmit instruction and encouragement. When I opened them again, the crows had disappeared.

Whether you turn to the right or to the left, your ears will hear
a voice behind you, saying, "This is the way; walk in it."

ISAIAH 30:21

August 8

HANDICAP ACCESSIBLE

A friend shared with me that during a recent trip to the store, he had parked his car in a slot set aside for people with disabilities, and when he returned to his car, seemingly able bodied, he was met by a man with a mission: to prove my friend to be a liar.

My friend pulled his disabled-driver paperwork out of his wallet and showed it to the self-appointed vigilante, who immediately fell silent and then apologized. He had seen my friend walk into the store, and when he could not discern any obvious handicap, he made his judgment. Although my friend's disability isn't always visible, it's still there, making life a challenge sometimes. What he needed was an assist, not an ill-informed lecture.

Disability has been defined as a physical or mental disadvantage that can make living life more difficult than it might be otherwise. It doesn't mark people as lesser; it might even mark them as stronger, having more to overcome. It does often mark people as needing help—like a more convenient parking spot or a home arranged to accommodate special needs and provide assistance.

Spiritually, we are all handicapped from birth. Sin places us at a spiritual disadvantage. Thankfully, we have a Healer—one who forgives us and heals us. Because of Christ's death and resurrection, heaven is handicap accessible, no permit needed.

What are you struggling with? What sins tie you up and make living the life you want to live more difficult than it could be? Your struggles don't mark you as inferior; you may be stronger for recognizing your need. God is there not to lecture but to offer an assist. Take him up on it!

Praise the LORD, my soul,
and forget not all his benefits—
who forgives all your sins
and heals all your diseases,
who redeems your life from the pit
and crowns you with love and compassion.

PSALM 103:2-4

FOOD POISONING

My son was home for the summer, and my food bill skyrocketed. Not only do young men eat quite a lot but they also have odd eating habits. Late-night snacking is for old-timers; he has late-night meals. I didn't usually see what he was eating, but from my bedroom upstairs I could often smell midnight fried chicken or three-in-the-morning salmon.

One morning, I went into the freezer and found a plastic bag of pink . . . something. "What's this?" I asked.

"I started to cook the frozen salmon, but I got tired of waiting, so I took it out of the oven partway through and then refroze it."

I looked at him, horrified. "Is this how you eat at school?" He nodded. "How do you thaw chicken?" I asked, afraid to hear the answer.

"On the counter, or sometimes under hot water."

Oy.

I affixed my best patient, motherly smile and launched into a discourse on the dangers of food poisoning. "It smelled okay!" he insisted. "But did you taste it?" I asked. He hadn't.

Most of us can tell at a glance when food is thoroughly bad, a science experiment in a plastic serving dish. But just-turned-the-corner hamburger? Maybe. Listeria in soft cheese . . . maybe. Once you've visited the bathroom with a sick stomach a few times, you learn to discern the more subtle clues. The older you get, the more run-ins you've had and the more you know what to avoid.

Scripture speaks of the value of wisdom, and wisdom is gained through experience melded with the insight given from God. Once given, discernment has to be used to remain sharp. The more often you apply it to sort right from wrong, good from evil, the sharper your detection senses become and the less often you become "sick." And it doesn't hurt to learn from someone who's lived a few years longer than you. Like Mom!

Solid food is for the mature, who by constant use have
trained themselves to distinguish good from evil.

HEBREWS 5:14

JUST RIGHT

There is nothing more soothing to my soul than taking a long lavender branch between my finger and thumb and crushing it till the quieting essence of the flower perfumes the air. I like to throw dried buds on the floor and then vacuum them up, releasing that sweet French goodness that says "welcome home" to me. In order to afford that luxury, I have to grow my own.

If you give lavender plants sun and poor soil (now *that* I can do!), they are happy. But watering is a tricky thing. I feel a little like I am growing my own Goldilocks plants—sometimes I give them too much, and the bases of the plants begin to turn black with rot. Sometimes I give them too little, and their heads nod sleepily toward the ground till I give them a drink. Once I figure out the perfect balance, they thrive!

Over the course of my life, I have had much and I have had little—but mostly what I've had is just right. I would love to win the lottery and prove that I could do good with the money, but I realize that I am made of flesh, and perhaps God knows—better than I do—that I wouldn't be up to the challenge. The lean times have taught me to lean in . . . to God. I wouldn't miss that intimacy for anything, although I'm not in a hurry to return to months of want. Mainly, I've learned to be content with "just right." Just right, right in the middle, is where I've learned to blossom most regularly in the places I've been planted.

Two things I ask of you, LORD;
do not refuse me before I die:
Keep falsehood and lies far from me;
give me neither poverty nor riches,
but give me only my daily bread.
Otherwise, I may have too much
and disown you and say, "Who is the LORD?"
Or I may become poor and steal,
and so dishonor the name of my God.

PROVERBS 30:7-9

August 11

WAR AND PEACE

Who really wants to put down a big chunk of change for a new roof? You pay for it, you insure it, but you really take no pleasure in it. And then there's the noise.

We learned this firsthand when we replaced our roof. There was the ripping off of the old tiles—using power machinery—and tossing them into an echoing Dumpster. The noise expanded to fill every room, assaulting our eardrums and triggering headaches. Within just a few minutes, the dog was hiding under my desk in fear. Within an hour the kids were arguing because they couldn't hear the TV, each other, or *me*, transforming our usually tranquil house into a place of irritability. On day two, we begged a friend, "Can we come and stay with you?"

When we returned to the finished house, it looked beautiful. The new roof gave our house a classier appearance, and in addition, it gave me a sense of security. Best of all, with the work completed, the interior was serene and inviting.

We've all wondered about the seeming madness of our own lives and in the world around us. People experience difficult—sometimes terrible—circumstances, and most of us are under constant stress. No one escapes the sculpting—sometimes with a sharp tool—and the resulting pain that is a part of becoming mature in Christ. Perhaps the Lord, too, wants his home to be one of peace and camaraderie; maybe not completely quiet (there is singing, after all), but without constant construction cacophony. While we are here on earth, we are being built and molded and shaped so that when we are all home with Christ, we will more deeply appreciate the peace, security, companionship, and joy of heaven.

The stones used in the construction of the Temple were finished at the quarry, so there was no sound of hammer, ax, or any other iron tool at the building site.

1 KINGS 6:7, NLT

HERE, KITTY

One night Hubs and I were slumped on the couch watching TV when an unusual advertisement caught my attention. A woman in her nightdress, squinting to see clearly, walked out onto the patio outside her bedroom to call for her cat. "Here, kitty," she called, and shortly, a big, gray raccoon padded past her. "Oh, there you are. Come snuggle with Mama," she said, not realizing that it was not her pet but a mean old predator making its way into her house and onto her bed. The commercial was for eyewear; if you can't see clearly, bad things happen. You can unwittingly let trouble into your home and perhaps even into your bed.

We've had our share of run-ins with raccoons: They make a mess of your garbage if your lid isn't tight. They're happy to eat your pet's food—or even your pets—if you don't keep an eye on them. They spread disease. You don't want them in or around your house.

Sin can work its way into our homes in the same way when we're not seeing clearly. Sometimes we don't actually know that we're not seeing well. Sometimes we deliberately leave the glasses off because we don't *want* to see better. The patio doors that give sin entrance are our apps, television, the Internet, music, and social media. It can enter through the books and magazines we read, or the thoughts and friends we entertain when we know it would be better if we didn't. Sin slips in looking like something welcome and then wreaks havoc once inside. Put on your glasses, and lock the patio door.

My child, don't lose sight of common sense and discernment.
Hang on to them,
for they will refresh your soul.
They are like jewels on a necklace.
They keep you safe on your way,
and your feet will not stumble.
You can go to bed without fear;
you will lie down and sleep soundly.

PROVERBS 3:21-24, NLT

RUNNING AWAY FROM HOME

We have all wanted to run away from home at one time or another, haven't we? When did you last have that impulse? As a child? Last week?

I remember the first time I wanted to run away from home; I was about six years old. I took a brown paper sack into my bedroom, filled it up with . . . something . . . and likely topped it off with my Mrs. Beasley doll. I opened the front door to find that it was raining out. I really didn't want to walk down the street in the rain, and where would I go, anyway? So I stood wedged between the screen and the door long enough, I hoped, to make everyone worried, and then came back into the house. I don't remember making a grand announcement, and I probably just quietly unpacked my brown sack.

There are times as an adult when I want to run away from home too. I feel overwhelmed by my circumstances. I don't see a good solution no matter how many options I consider. Things have not turned out as I expected or hoped, and I feel real despair drilling into my soul. I'm angry with God. Didn't he say the faithful prayers of a righteous person would avail much? Was I not righteous? Faithful? What had gone wrong?

Then when I stop between the door and the screen and look at my rainy options without God, I think, *Where would I even go?* I don't really *want* to go; I just feel defeated. I open the door and walk back toward him, and he helps me unpack my bag and holds me for a while, and I feel soothed and cared for. I don't always know right then how things will work out. But he's there with me, cherishing me. He's my home.

I am always with you;
you hold me by my right hand.
You guide me with your counsel,
and afterward you will take me into glory.
Whom have I in heaven but you?

PSALM 73:23-25

PARADISE FROM MY UPSTAIRS WINDOW

One afternoon I was running around madly, trying to get the chores done before company arrived. I stripped the bed in the guest room, and as I did, I took a moment to peek out the window.

It was a rare clear day, and off in the distance I could see Mount Rainier. Everyone around here simply calls it The Mountain, and not just because its near relative, Mount St. Helens, lost her head a few years back and is now much harder to see. No, it's called The Mountain because it's the tallest and most majestic. The best part of Mount Rainier is the area called Paradise.

Paradise is often dotted with purple and red alpine flowers, bathed in sunlight and soothed by cool breezes. To walk its gentle slope is to have a preview of heaven. I don't get to visit Paradise often, but nearly every week or so I catch a glimpse of it from my home.

The Lord has told us that this world is not our home. Although there are many wonderful things here, and God desires for us to be filled with peace and joy in our present lives, something much better lies ahead for those who believe. The Bible offers few clues as to what heaven will be like, but Jesus has promised that it's a place he has prepared for us, where he'll be with us and we'll be with our brothers and sisters throughout eternity.

In my day-to-day life, when I listen to a baby's laughter, when I receive the gift of a hug or a card in the mail from a friend, when I share a meal with new friends or worship with old ones, I catch a little glimpse of paradise from my earthbound window. When do you glimpse paradise?

He said, "Jesus, remember me when you come into your kingdom."
Jesus answered him, "Truly I tell you, today you will be with me in paradise."

LUKE 23:42-43

DON'T TOUCH MY SUNBURN

I married a man whose skin is so fair he's often teasingly referred to as Vanilla Ice or Mighty Whitey. Accordingly, I have a daughter whose skin is so fair she has a hard time finding foundation that is light enough for her. But as a young teen, she always wanted to have a tan. In pursuit of that which was not to be, she suffered a few angry sunburns.

After the last one, we were unable to touch her skin long enough even to smooth aloe vera gel on it, so I ran to the store and bought spray gel. That way, she could still get some soothing relief. When I went to tuck her in that night, one light sheet gently draped over her, she recoiled just a little. "Don't touch my sunburn!" she implored.

I didn't, of course, brushing her cheek with my lips. As I got ready for bed myself, I thought about how often we encounter things in this world that burn us. People who have betrayed us in one way or another. Thieves who steal from us. Employers who do not follow through. Friends who turn their backs. Churches that prove untrue to Christ. It's easy to walk through life feeling hurt by these things and withdrawing from others. *Don't touch my sunburn!*

And yet the touch that could bring hurt could also bring healing. The embrace that could bring pain might just as well bring the comfort, love, and affection we desperately need.

When we meet the Lord in our forever home, there will be no tears or pain; emotional burns and sunburns will be things of the past. But don't retreat from those who love you in the here and now. Some have a gentle, faithful touch.

He will wipe every tear from their eyes, and there will be no more death or sorrow or crying or pain. All these things are gone forever.

REVELATION 21:4, NLT

MIDNIGHT IS NEVER COMING

I was an avid reader as a child, and I also loved to listen to records (remember them?) of dramatized stories while I fell asleep at night. Fairy tales were always my favorite because although the heroine had to walk through dark and questioning times, she always ended up living happily ever after. And there was usually a twist in the story that I could not have anticipated.

I was shopping a few months ago when I saw a small wire carriage made in the shape of a pumpkin. It stood on a plaque that read, "Live like there's no midnight." I thought about that for a long while. So often, even when something good is happening, we're worried that just around the corner all of the good things are going to go away, darkness will fall, and happiness will be but a fleeting memory.

Jesus came, he said, to give us abundant life in the here and now. That's good news number one. Good news number two is that when we've put our trust in him, abundant life continues infinitely. Death has lost its sting. It has been defanged for our benefit.

Yes, we, like our fairy tale heroines, may find ourselves washing too many dishes, or waiting to become a swan, or fearing Prince Charming may have escaped or will never arrive at all. But take heart! No matter what your life looks like midway through the story, you can be assured that you have a happily *forever* after just ahead—with some story twists along the way.

I have said these things to you, that in me you may have peace. In the world you will have tribulation. But take heart; I have overcome the world.

JOHN 16:33, ESV

August 17
FACING FORWARD

Hubs and I have taken to walking around our neighborhood for health, for companionship, and just to get out into the great outdoors after sitting on our behinds inside all day. As a treat, we sometimes stop along the way and pick blackberries for the journey. I start scouting for them as soon as we hit the street they line. I know something good awaits just ahead!

Another street next to ours has a very steep hill, and someone told me that if I walked up the hill backward I could tighten my glute muscles. Well, it worked. I could hardly sit on my backside all the next day! But that's not the reason I'm going to stop walking backward.

I'm stopping because it's scary. I have no idea if a car is coming, or if a dog is loose, or if the road is dangerously buckled from a tree root. But also, when I walk backward, I spend so much time concentrating on safety that I miss the scenery: the beautiful lawns, the families watering plants together, the distant snowcapped mountain, the Sound. And ripe blackberries! Also, I look downright silly. It's true—you can't move confidently or enjoyably ahead if you're always looking back.

I'm applying that to my day-to-day life, too. Instead of rehashing the past all the time, tormenting myself by second-guessing what I might have done or said, what I should have acted upon or left undone, I'm choosing to remember that everyone makes mistakes; I want to leave those mistakes by the side of the road and move on. God tells us that he has a wonderful future planned for each of us. Isn't that delightful? But how will I be able to see it, look forward to it, plan for it, and enjoy it if I'm always looking backwards?

I'm looking *forward* to what's coming next!

*I focus on this one thing: Forgetting the past and
looking forward to what lies ahead.*

PHILIPPIANS 3:13, NLT

THE POWER OF DEEP ROOTS

One of my favorite flowers is lily of the valley. I think it all started when I was a girl, and one of my first bottles of perfume was Tinkerbell's Lily of the Valley. I love that the blooms are delicate, parchment-thin bells that clump and perfume an entire area, sometimes even hiding under trees or shrubs. They aren't easy to start growing, but once started, they're tough little plants that hang on, because their roots grow sideways. If you cut the plant off, or even dig it up and move it, you likely will still have lily of the valley nearby the next year. Once established, they are persistent and strong.

Faith is sometimes like that, isn't it? When we're new believers, we're excited, but we've just begun to sprout from the seed of our faith, and Scripture tells us we can go wrong in several ways. A joyful embracing of faith can be short-lived when followed by trouble and persecution. Perhaps the worries (the omnipresent weeds) of this life or the deceitfulness of wealth chokes it off. Maybe, on the other hand, the seed of faith settles into fertile soil, becomes established, and grows to maturity.

But once it is established, our faith can resist those other troubles. We may face trauma (I once ran over my lily of the valley with a lawn mower!) and yet be able to spring back, a little damaged but stronger than ever. I don't know what troubles and worries and difficulties you face, but I do know that your roots can be strong and sturdy and persistent. You are rooted and established in love and firmly planted; you're unmovable, unshakable; you can't be mowed down, because you understand how strong the love that sustains you is. It's long and high and deep, and it's all yours.

I pray that you, being rooted and established in love, may have
power, together with all the Lord's holy people, to grasp how
wide and long and high and deep is the love of Christ.

EPHESIANS 3:17-18

August 19
FRIGHTENING NOISES

For some reason, my dog is truly afraid of beeping noises. The only time she refuses a treat is when something is beeping. Instead, she'll run for high ground, literally. She races upstairs and then jumps onto the guest bed, the highest bed in the house. Meat thermometer plugged in? *Beep.* Waffle iron? *Beep.* I've even taken her places in the car to get her out of the house while someone else changes the batteries in the smoke detectors—seven beeps in a row. But I regularly subject her to the beeps of the washer and dryer. I have to do laundry. There will be some beeps in life.

I have sympathy for her, though. When things go wrong in my life, I want to run for the high ground too. When our last earthquake hit, I ran outside. I don't know why; I just ran. It reminds me of the children of good parents. When something goes wrong, they go running, shouting, "Mom!" or "Dad!" Once they locate their parents, they head straight into protecting arms.

Once we're adults, we don't have Mom or Dad to run to anymore, at least not most of us. But we still have earth-shattering, beeping occasions that we can't face alone. The Lord is always with us, he tells us, an ever-present help in times of trouble. God is in your house. He is in your room. He is behind you, beside you, and walking ahead of you to clear the path. The reason for running to Mom or Dad is that they are big enough to face, and face down, whatever scares us. That's our reason for running to God, too.

He never turns us away when we run to him as things go bump—or beep—in the night.

God is our refuge and strength,
an ever-present help in trouble.
Therefore we will not fear, though the earth give way
and the mountains fall into the heart of the sea,
though its waters roar and foam
and the mountains quake with their surging.

PSALM 46:1-3

FIFTY HANGERS

My friend signed up for a new service that assigned her a personal shopper. She looked through pictures of clothing online, filled out a style profile, and sent in her measurements. Then once a month she received a box of clothing and accessories chosen exactly for her. It's like getting birthday gifts once a month instead of once a year! A few months (and boxes) down the road, another friend reminded her of the "fifty-hanger rule," which says that every woman gets fifty hangers in her closet, and no one should go beyond that.

Does that include overstuffed dresser drawers, too? I have quite a few of those, some that haven't been sorted in a while!

The principle is sound. There are only thirty days in a month, and even if we keep clothes from season to season, they do get worn, grow out of style, or simply don't beckon to us anymore. Does anyone remember Imelda Marcos and her collection of three thousand pairs of shoes? Her items were damaged in a monsoon, and they became waterlogged and moldy. Imelda is dead now, no one wants moldy shoes, and that collection is worth exactly . . . zilch.

I comfort myself by remembering that I don't own even thirty pairs of shoes, and certainly not three thousand, and I remind myself that there's nothing wrong with liking good things to wear, to eat, or to decorate with. But why keep all those good things for myself? There's no magic to the number fifty, either. Could I limit it to thirty hangers and four drawers? That will work too. Keep some, give some away. Buy some, give some money away. Find one little black dress and wear it well—no need for lots of dresses. Yoga pants feel better at home anyway.

Let it be said of me, and you, too: she wears that (generosity) well!

Anyone who has two shirts should share with the one who has
none, and anyone who has food should do the same.

LUKE 3:11

RIPE AND RIPENING

My daughter has a cascade of thorny blackberry bushes growing behind her house, and I love to sit out there with her, picking them and then eating them. The bushes are on my daughter's private property, which means we get the whole haul to ourselves. We head out with little cups and each pop one berry into the container and one into the mouth! The hardest part, though, is waiting till the fruit is ripe.

For some reason, the fruit does not ripen all at the same time but rather over the course of several months. You can find a luscious, dark berry that pops with sweetness growing alongside a slightly lighter berry that has a blend of tang and sugar. Everyone knows not to pluck the red berries unless they want an hour-long pucker and maybe a sick stomach. That fruit is not bad; it's simply not ripe.

In our lives, too, we have potential that has not yet had time to ripen. So often we look toward the red berries on our branches, embarrassed that we are not further along in our faith or ashamed that we have made mistakes—usually, in my case, publicly! But we are works in progress; God is working on and in us. Someday our red berries will darken to black; they will be sweet and lovely and ready to be harvested for the good of God's Kingdom.

Be patient and loving with yourself. You were created to bear fruit over time, which means that you'll always have some red berries waiting to ripen.

A good tree cannot bear bad fruit, and a bad tree cannot bear
good fruit. . . . Thus, by their fruit you will recognize them.

MATTHEW 7:18, 20

A DISH CALLED PATIENCE

I've heard that revenge is a dish best served cold. I can't attest to that, having never served it, to the best of my knowledge. I do serve up a lot of patience, though, every Easter. I have twelve servings of Patience—or, I should say, twelve place settings.

When I was a young woman, I took a job in a department store. I do not advise doing this: for every dollar I earned there, I spent two—even with my employee discount. One thing I set my heart on early in my employment was a set of fine Noritake china in a pattern called Patience. I wanted Noritake because it was the brand my grandmother had; I wanted Patience because I had little of my own.

In those years, I wanted everything "right now." I wanted an answer to a prayer, the right boyfriend, the perfect job, a great car. I had little time to sit around while others did things that I thought I could do more quickly. Even as I grew older, I often rushed in to do it "right," which led to hurt feelings and damaged relationships. After a few of these chipped plates, so to speak, I learned to slow down. Plates may be replaced; relationships often cannot be.

Showing love for others is understanding that they operate differently than I do; their comfort levels might not be the same as mine. I am a planner; they may be spontaneous. I may like to speak up and solve problems quickly; they may like to think things through first. I came to understand that love for others meant holding my peace till they felt ready to move forward. Patience is waiting—peacefully, quietly, expectantly—on those we love: God and others. Patience can't be bought. It has to be cultivated, one circumstance at a time.

Love is patient, love is kind. It does not envy, it does not boast,
it is not proud. It does not dishonor others, it is not self-seeking,
it is not easily angered, it keeps no record of wrongs.

1 CORINTHIANS 13:4-5

August 23

THE RIGHT SPOT

It can be difficult to find the perfect spot for a new plant. Usually I take the garden pot and set it in one area for a day or two to see if I like the look of it. Will it get the right amount of sunlight? Water? Will it encourage rabbit nibbles?

I imagine after a few days of this, plants would say, "Come on, Sandra! Pick a place and put us in already. It's getting a little tight inside this pot." So I do. I bring them to what I feel is the place where they'll do best, where they'll get what they need, and then I spade the ground and plant them. Soon, they thrive.

I wonder if I'm as persistent in inviting and bringing my friends to the right places: retreats, concerts, book clubs, and church—the places where they can get love and health and healing, where they can grow and thrive despite the often troublesome world we live in. I work hard to find the right spots for my plants; how much more valuable are my friends? It's something to think on and take seriously. I want them to get all the Sonlight they need to thrive.

Send me your light and your faithful care,
let them lead me;
let them bring me to your holy mountain,
to the place where you dwell.
Then I will go to the altar of God,
to God, my joy and my delight.
I will praise you with the lyre,
O God, my God.

PSALM 43:3-4

August 24

A VERY FORGIVING FABRIC

We recently went to pick out some new furniture. The family room is a place where we exercise and snack while we watch movies; we fold laundry there, and the dog sits with us. So it was important that the furniture not be fussy or hard to care for. The saleswoman patted the upholstery. "It's a very forgiving fabric," she said, which sounded perfect to me.

As Christians, we spend a lot of time thinking about forgiveness because it's central to our beliefs. Without God's forgiveness of us through Christ, we would not be saved, born again, or able to experience intimacy with him. We still sin, though, and it damages all involved, which is why we are required to forgive one another as Christ forgave us.

How did Christ forgive us? Extravagantly. Repeatedly. Sacrificially. In this he reflects the Father: "The Father . . . has qualified you to share in the inheritance of his holy people in the kingdom of light. For he has rescued us from the dominion of darkness and brought us into the kingdom of the Son he loves, in whom we have redemption, the forgiveness of sins" (Colossians 1:12-14).

We have a very forgiving Father, and we are to be forgiving, just as he is.

Bear with each other and forgive one another if any of you has a grievance against someone. Forgive as the Lord forgave you.

COLOSSIANS 3:13

August 25

GARBAGE RISING

We had decided to lay down mulch to retain water and keep the weeds down. We wanted to be respectful of the environment, so we ordered up some mulch that had a mix of wood chips and composted yard waste. That's all that was supposed to be in there: wood chips and yard waste.

It looked good at first—nice and brown and clean. Then the rains came, and the mulch settled, and odd bits and pieces began to rise to the top. Pieces of paper. Bits of glass. Band-Aids. Medical waste! At that point, I called the people who had delivered it, and they sent someone out. He didn't make it past the driveway before glancing over and reassuring me, "We'll remove and replace this."

Someone had mixed trash in with the organics, perhaps thinking he could get away with not having to pay for trash removal. As I watched it scraped and cleaned from my land, a verse came to me: "Be sure that your sin will find you out."

I hope in my own life I don't have to wait till the garbage floats to the surface in order to clear it out. But when it does, Jesus is there to help remove and replace. And when others sin against us—and it seems like they are getting away with it—don't worry. The Lord will ensure their sins are found and addressed too!

You may be sure that your sin will find you out.

NUMBERS 32:23

BIRD SCARERS

We drove by a field in late summer; the crops were ripening and nearly ready to be harvested. I couldn't believe how many birds were flying about in the fields, though; fat ones, fast ones. When we slowed down, I got a better look. They were not live birds at all; they were fake ones, on poles and strings—bogus birds of prey to scare away the true grain predators. Clever! It reminded me of the fake owls on poles I had seen near some blueberry fields months earlier.

A farmer puts a lot of energy into his crops—time, love, care, attention, and affection. And he's hoping for a good return on the investment. But there are those who do not work at all and yet want to poach the fruit of another's labor. The farmer doesn't always have to rely on a force of strength or firepower to repel an enemy. In this case, the farmer used pure cleverness. The birds who might have eaten the crops never even landed because they didn't want to be attacked themselves!

God loves you very much; he has showered you with time, love, care, attention, and affection. And you're of much greater value to him—made in his image and bought by his Son—than any mere crop. He promises to protect you and to rescue you, and he is true to his word. Keep an eye open for the clever means he employs to do just that. Not only will it boost your faith to see him at work in your life, guarding you, but it will boost your admiration when you see just how creatively he does it!

The LORD says, "I will rescue those who love me.
I will protect those who trust in my name."

PSALM 91:14, NLT

TABLE MANNERS

One day when my children were young, we had fun making homemade place mats out of laminating sheets. On some of them we placed information about missionaries we supported so we'd remember to pray for them at mealtimes. On a few we put rules for table manners, as I was trying to teach them which fork to use for each part of a meal. On others we put the word *grace* to remind us to say grace over the meal.

I'm happy to say that these little tricks worked and instilled good table habits in my children. I noted in my own life that, while I was always sure to say grace before every meal, it had begun to be more of a ritual. My mind wasn't in it, and I said pretty much the same thing every time. Was that thankfulness?

Christianity is the upside-down faith: the one who is last becomes first, the master serves, the person seated at the foot of the table is the one likely to be asked forward. In the same way, Philippians 4 reminds us to say thank you before we say please. It may be that God, as a great parent, wants us to develop our manners, but it also may be that he is reminding us of his faithfulness before we ask for anything more in order to reassure us: *See? I heard you before. I'll hear you this time too.*

I do not want to be among the nine people who did not thank the Lord after their pleas had been answered. I want to thank him for everything, every time, from the heart. To that end, no more canned, ready-made grace before dinner for me. I'm going to put as much thought into the grace I'm saying as I do into the food I'm serving.

One of them, when he saw he was healed, came back, praising God in a loud voice. He threw himself at Jesus' feet and thanked him—and he was a Samaritan. Jesus asked, "Were not all ten cleansed? Where are the other nine?"

LUKE 17:15-17

HAIR IN THE SHOWER DRAIN

I'm guessing that this is the first devotional you've ever read about hair caught in the shower drain. Stick with me. I looked down one morning before turning on the water. What I saw was not inviting. The water from the shower just before mine (my husband's) was not really draining. I was about to yell something about personal responsibility when I saw that it was long, dark-brown hair that was clogging the drain. Not short, graying, reddish hair. So it wasn't Hubs's hair that was causing the problem. It was mine.

I admit it; I didn't want to pull it out. You know how it is. It's all wet and stuck together and has soap scum on it and doesn't come out with one clean pull. But the fact of the matter was it was my hair clogging the drain, so it was only fair that I clean it up. I got a piece of toilet tissue and grabbed the wad of hair, then threw it away. I really enjoyed my shower afterward; the hot water was refreshing and went right down the drain.

It's really no fun to admit our wrongs, but we only make things worse when we try to either pin the blame on someone else or even just share the blame. We simply have to own up to our own messes. Scripture tells us that we are to truly repent of our sins—by owning and turning from them without blaming others and not repeating the sins over and over. When we do, we are refreshed, renewed, and made clean.

In order for things to keep working right, I've got to clean out that drain—admit my sins and learn to find them as disgusting (really, more disgusting) than that slimy hair in the shower. The good news is, God can wash me clean.

Repent, then, and turn to God, so that your sins may be wiped out, that times of refreshing may come from the Lord.

ACTS 3:19

GOOD EXCUSES

A while back, we had some friends over for dinner. Because we all lead busy lives and they live hours away, we don't get to see them very often. So we sat around the fire pit long into the night, looking for good excuses for them to remain with us. More coffee, more dessert, another important conversation, anything. We wanted to give them an excuse to tarry . . . to stay, to abide with us a while longer.

A few months later our son had to return to his apartment after a holiday with us. Although we didn't want him to drive while tired, I kept wishing he would stay a little longer—for one more meal, even one more hour. I wanted a good reason for him to tarry, to stay with us, to abide.

To abide means to remain together, to linger in love, to be comfortably entwined, twisted together gently like ivy and oak, or like the branches of wisteria. Scripture tells us, "Whoever loves his brother abides in the light, and in him there is no cause for stumbling" (1 John 2:10, ESV). It's easy not to stumble when the light is on—you can see where you're going. Loving our brothers and sisters, our fellow believers, is a sign that we are remaining in the light of Christ. In 1 Corinthians, Paul tells us, "Faith, hope, and love abide, these three; but the greatest of these is love" (13:13, ESV). It's a gentle, pleasant thought to imagine faith, hope, and love tarrying at my home, lingering in and after my conversations, pressing in for one more hour, like trusted, beloved friends.

I wish to abide with my friends, and Jesus calls us his friends. He lingers among us. I'm honored that he chooses to abide with me; I must continue to choose to abide in him.

Abide in me, and I in you. As the branch cannot bear fruit by itself,
unless it abides in the vine, neither can you, unless you abide in me.

JOHN 15:4, ESV

DEADHEADS

One of the regular tasks for the flower gardener is deadheading. It has nothing to do with the band from the '70s! In essence, deadheading means taking gardening shears in hand and confidently snipping off the head of a spent blossom—sometimes all the way down the stalk. Why deadhead? Flowers were created to reseed themselves—lots and lots of energy goes into making seeds so that the flower can self-propagate. Once the seed is made and dropped, the plant can rest.

Oh, we evil gardeners. I don't want my plants to rest. I want to trick them into blooming over and over again, so I don't let the flower heads stay on the stems long enough to go to seed.

Deadheading is tricky, though. Often the new, tight bud is growing right alongside or nearby the one that has exhausted itself. Snipping carelessly or too close to new growth will cut off the emerging flower before it ever gets a chance to unfurl its beautiful petals.

I don't know about you, but I have experienced people cutting a little too close to my blossoms. Maybe they shut down a new idea before I'd had a chance to fully explore it, or offered some advice—"I just want to be honest"—that resulted in a few bruises. This is a particular pitfall for parents (Hey, we're guiding and correcting all the time, right?) but also for those of us who teach and mentor, and even for all of us in honest and loving friendships. I want to help snip away, when asked, everything that is preventing new blooms, but I also want to aim my pruning shears gently, with love, discretion, and care. There's nothing as disheartening as looking down to see you've mistakenly sheared off a blossom just getting ready to pop out into the sun.

Let the message of Christ dwell among you richly as you teach and admonish
one another with all wisdom through psalms, hymns, and songs from
the Spirit, singing to God with gratitude in your hearts. . . . Fathers,
do not embitter your children, or they will become discouraged.

COLOSSIANS 3:16, 21

August 31
PILL DRAWERS

It had been some time since I cleaned out the bathroom drawers, and we were having to look through the medicine bottles in the pill drawer every day in order to find the ones we now needed. There had been a recent time or two when we'd almost taken the wrong medication, and it was time to throw those old, no-longer-needed ones away.

Some were expired, no good in any sense and possibly unstable. Some medications were for conditions that had been resolved. A few were pain medications for pain that had subsided. I looked at one empty bubble pack for an antibiotic that had cleared up a stubborn infection. I remember taking it for two days and thinking, *Why isn't this working already?* But after the full course of time, the full dose, it did its work, and I learned to be more patient with healing. It often takes time to become ill, and it takes time for health to rebuild too.

I realized that, as with the pills, I often hold on to strategies and tools that have worked in the past but are no longer useful in my job, my personal life, or my spiritual walk. I can be reluctant to let go, but in many cases, the "cure" addresses a condition that is no longer present.

We might have used avoidance in the past but have now learned how to deal with difficulties head-on. Maybe we've used food or alcohol or other substances to blunt our pain, but over time we've developed new coping skills. Perhaps we've had a lifetime of anxiety, now somewhat quelled by faith. How wonderful to discover that God has healed wounds, and we can back off the substances and find true vitality. There is a prescription in the Bible for what troubles our hearts; it never expires or loses its effectiveness, and it's good for any situation.

Do not be anxious about anything, but in every situation, by
prayer and petition, with thanksgiving, present your requests to
God. And the peace of God, which transcends all understanding,
will guard your hearts and your minds in Christ Jesus.

PHILIPPIANS 4:6-7

SEPTEMBER

Cupcakes in a Jar

These are fun to send to a kid at college, a service member, or friends and family who live far away. Any kind of cake mix works, but it's fun to use food coloring to make team-color cupcakes, or tie-dyed cupcakes, or any favorite color of the recipient. Red velvet cake with cream cheese frosting looks especially lovely. Tell your recipients to eat these with a spoon!

WHAT YOU'LL NEED

1 cake mix, any kind

8 to 12 half-pint canning jars with lids

1 recipe of butter cream or cream cheese frosting

Something to pipe the frosting onto the cupcakes with—either a pastry bag or a plastic sandwich bag with one corner cut off

DIRECTIONS

Preheat the oven to 325 degrees. (Because you're baking in glass, 325 degrees works better than a higher temperature.) Make the cake mix as directed, then fill each jar about halfway with cake batter. Place jars on a cookie sheet and bake for about 30 minutes, till an inserted toothpick comes out clean.

Let cool completely, then pipe frosting onto the cakes. (If shipping overseas, don't add icing.) Add sprinkles if desired. Screw the lids onto the jars and freeze the cupcakes completely. (If the cupcakes are a little too tall, just give them a little trim before you ice them; the frosting will hide your edit!) Wrap in bubble wrap, then place into a sturdy shipping box. Mail away and await the coming applause!

For this month's free printable, go to http://tyndal.es/homeandgarden.

BLOWING ON EMBERS

An emergency was brewing. The campfire was about to go out, and we hadn't made s'mores yet. The children sat with pleading eyes, sticks and marshmallows in hand, as Dad bent over the fire and blew on it till he was dizzy. The fire came back, first a little, and then, with some dry kindling and a few more dragon puffs, to a full, s'more-cooking roar.

I recall that scene whenever I read Isaiah 54:16, where God says, "See, it is I who created the blacksmith who fans the coals into flame and forges a weapon fit for its work." Sometimes, when we're on a busy train or bus, packed into a room with hundreds of others, or among 2,300 social-media friends, it's hard to remember that we are individually created, made with specific thought and purpose. When my husband was questioning his purpose and wavering about going into ministry, there came a time when he felt the Lord impress upon him that he needed to follow that call now or the Lord would move on and give the call to someone else. Fish or cut bait, as my husband would say.

Each of us feels fear when stepping into a new ministry or a new venture, or when one we're involved with grows or changes. But God has enabled and encouraged us to step up. He could have done the job himself, but by partnering with us, he enables us to feel fulfilled and satisfied and to meet our destinies. Eric Liddell of *Chariots of Fire* fame said, "I believe God made me for a purpose, but he also made me fast. And when I run I feel his pleasure."

We are the blacksmiths. God has given us the gift. Lean over, blow on those coals, and then run, fish, teach, give, serve, whatever it is that you've been created to do!

Fan into flame the gift of God, which is in you through the
laying on of my hands. For the Spirit God gave us does not make
us timid, but gives us power, love and self-discipline.

2 TIMOTHY 1:6-7

DRIPPING WATER

I stepped onto the back porch one day and saw just one wet spot on the dry, cobbled path. When I went to examine it, I saw that it was a moist cobblestone standing alone; the concrete grout around it had been completely worn away. A drainpipe clogged with debris had focused a stream of tiny, persistent drips on that small area. Over time those little drops, each no bigger than a sunflower seed, had worn away the tough, cured concrete.

The power of little drops. Water, it's been said, carved the Grand Canyon. Water smooths huge, sharp rocks into the round pebbles we walk on at the beach. It breaks those stones into even smaller particles of sand. Water—a little at a time, over a long period of time—can break down even the sturdiest material.

Remembering something about a leaking roof in Scripture, I sat down in my comfy chair and looked it up. Proverbs says that a quarrelsome wife is like the dripping of a leaky roof. I had always imagined how annoying that would be. A dripping bathroom faucet will make even a tired person haul out of bed to shut it off. But I had never given any thought to the destruction that those annoying drips can cause.

The verse talks about a wife, but I've also been annoyed by (and have annoyed, I am certain) quarrelsome people outside of a marital relationship. There are times to gently pursue a topic or conversation, and there are times to simply let it go. I need to remember to ask myself, *Will this matter in three days? Is this a persistent problem or a one-off? Am I just overtired? Is she?*

Love is not easily provoked, I'm reminded. And perhaps love does not easily provoke, either. It's a lot easier to shut that faucet off or clear the gutter than it is to fill in a grand canyon between me and someone I love.

A quarrelsome wife is like the dripping
of a leaky roof in a rainstorm.

PROVERBS 27:15

SWEPT AWAY

You can call me Miss Muffet, even though I'm not really sure I know what a tuffet is or if I've ever sat on one. I am, though, seriously freaked out by spiders. September kicks off spider season in our area.

I know they're mostly harmless. But they can be big and hairy and intimidating, and they show up when and where you least expect them—and they scurry! Frankly, I'm afraid of anything that scurries. If someone else is around when I see a spider, I have no shame in calling for reinforcements to kill the thing. But mostly I work from home by myself and have to face the beasts alone. I've tried spraying them (there's a funny meme about spiders who have been sprayed with hair spray showing up at discos) and hitting them with shoes, but I've found the best tactic of all is vacuuming them up. Then I set the vacuum in the garage. For someone else to empty.

The beauty of the vacuum, besides the fact that I don't need to touch the spider, is that it sweeps up the entire web, too. Not only is the perpetrator gone, but there is nothing for him to return to. The enemy has been vanquished—that one anyway. Freedom for now!

No matter what enemies face us, big or small, God is close at hand to help us vanquish them or even to vanquish them for us. When we call upon him, he not only takes care of the matter at hand; in his great love, he makes a clean sweep so we can be at peace. The funny thing about those big spiders—once they're dead, they shrivel up and reveal themselves to actually be very, very small. That's true, too, with the enemies the Lord conquers on our behalf. It reminds me of an old VBS song: "My God is so big, so strong, and so mighty; there's nothing my God cannot do!"

In your great love, vanquish my enemies;
make a clean sweep of those who harass me.
And why? Because I'm your servant.

PSALM 143:12, MSG

September 4

WHERE'D THAT SPIDER COME FROM?

Some family and friends were hanging out in the living room one night watching a movie together, when our peace and enjoyment were assaulted by an uninvited guest who made a silent but impressive appearance. He was, yes, scurrying around the TV.

"A spider!" I called out, pulling my feet up from the floor and onto the couch. "Where did it come from?"

My son, who is also not too fond of spiders, answered, "When a mommy and daddy spider love each other very much . . ." Ha-ha. Yes, I threw a couch pillow at him. But I'd taught him well; he was prepared with the vacuum cleaner to rid us of the little guy.

The truth is, trouble often seems to sneak up on us when we're not looking for it. It creeps into what we thought was a good relationship, a steady and secure job, a happy neighborhood. It arrives quietly, and when it does, it startles us.

Problems and troubles are not surprising to God, though. He sees the past, the present, and the future, all rolled out like a carpet before him. He knows every one of your days and has numbered the hairs on your head. He is not startled by the appearance of trouble, and he always has the remedy. If trouble comes barreling in and you see it from a mile away, or if it scurries in and is difficult to see in the dark, no matter. God is prepared.

You can go to bed without fear;
you will lie down and sleep soundly.
You need not be afraid of sudden disaster
or the destruction that comes upon the wicked,
for the LORD is your security.

PROVERBS 3:24-26, NLT

SOLAR POWERED

I was pushing my cart down the wide aisle of the big-box store when they caught my eye. A box of eight outdoor lights, solar powered, that would make the perfect finishing touch to the small path alongside our driveway. After a minute of mental math, I returned the French macaroons ($14) and a magazine ($6) so I could add the $20 lights to my haul.

Once home, I measured out exact spacing, installed the lights, and waited. It was an unusually sunny day, so I hoped they would charge quickly and be on display that very night. "When do they come on?" my son-in-law asked. "As soon as it's dark," I answered. But, that night, they did not.

"Maybe they need more time to charge?" I asked my husband. He shook his head, went outside, and took the plastic sticker off of the top of each one. The overlooked stickers, it seems, had been blocking the lamps' ability to take in the sunlight.

The next day the lamps charged right up. As soon as dusk fell to darkness, each of the lights blinked on. Delighted, I ran outside to see that yes, they *were* the perfect touch and lit up the path nicely.

Scripture tells us that from the very beginning, God did not leave us in the dark, neither physically nor spiritually. At night the moon, of course, reflects the light of the sun, and my solar lights absorb the sun's energy and release it, as it were, when it's dark.

I love the play on words and concepts—absorbing the light of the Son and releasing it when it's darkest. Each of us has dark moments; even some of Jesus' friends rejected him, his family thought he was unbalanced, the leaders of the time hated him, and he had nowhere to lay his head.

"Don't forget in the darkness what you learned in the light," Christian author Joseph Bayly exhorts. The key, I believe, is taking off whatever barriers prevent you from absorbing and storing sunlight during the best of days so you have power reserves when darker times arrive.

In him was life, and that life was the light of all mankind. The light shines in the darkness, and the darkness has not overcome it.

JOHN 1:4-5

September 6
WHAT'S YOUR ESSENCE?

I'm trying to cut back on the sugar I consume in food and in drinks. Strangely, it's harder for me to cut back on beverages than on food—I love lemonade and pumpkin-spice lattes. A friend turned me on to infused water, which is just as it sounds: water that has been infused with the essence of a fruit, vegetable, or herb. I've tried a lot of combinations: orange with vanilla bean, cucumber and lemon, and lemongrass all by itself. My favorites, though, always include mint.

In order to get that mint flavor, one must firmly press the leaves before submerging them in the water. When pressure is applied, the cells release the pure mint properties. It's not the outside of the mint leaves that holds the concentrated mint flavor; it's the inside. It takes only a few leaves to add zip to a whole pitcher of water because of that concentrated flavor. When you pour the water into a glass, though, it looks just like plain tap water. You have to interact with it—smell it, drink it—in order to sense the vibrant difference.

Jesus says that our faith can be summed up this way as well, into its "essence," if you will. We're to love the Lord our God with all our hearts, souls, minds, and strength and to love others as we love ourselves. Oftentimes, we're called to do just that under pressure or what seem like crushing circumstances. That's when our flavor comes through most strongly. We look like plain water on the outside, but when we interact with others, they can sense a difference. If we can emit the essence of our faith wherever we go, in whatever challenges we face, God will savor every situation.

We are hard pressed on every side, but not crushed; perplexed, but not in despair; persecuted, but not abandoned; struck down, but not destroyed. We always carry around in our body the death of Jesus, so that the life of Jesus may also be revealed in our body.

2 CORINTHIANS 4:8-10

September 7
RAISING A REBEL

I had pruned back the perennials for the season, cutting them to within inches of the ground. The daisies, which had towered more than three feet at the height of their glory, looked particularly small. A week or two later when I looked outside, I spied a new daisy perhaps ten inches off the ground. She alone had risen from the devastation of my pruning shears. She was bright and light and stood alone. I named her The Rebel.

We don't care much for the word *rebel* in Christendom; it rings of rebelliousness against God. Which is bad, of course! But what about rebelling against that which is wrong? I think of John the Baptist, a rebel for sure, a man who wandered in the wilderness and spoke honestly and freely of the Lord but also bluntly about sin—which eventually cost him his head. Elizabeth and Zechariah, his parents, were not shunned, as parents of rebels in our society often are, but honored.

What makes a rebel? A tattoo? A piercing? Questioning the way things are always done or speaking up when someone in power does wrong?

It takes confidence to speak up in a world that wants you to pipe down. Helen Keller said that nothing can be done without hope and confidence. If you're the mother of a daisy, one who pokes her head up when everyone else has their heads down, and she's speaking up for good, then take heart. You've raised the right kind of rebel!

I tell you the truth, of all who have ever lived, none is greater than John the Baptist. Yet even the least person in the Kingdom of Heaven is greater than he is! And from the time John the Baptist began preaching until now, the Kingdom of Heaven has been forcefully advancing, and violent people are attacking it.

MATTHEW 11:11-12, NLT

September 8
BIG BUCKS

Normally when someone uses the phrase "big bucks," it's in reference to money. Lots of it. But sometimes in autumn it refers to large male deer, leading their families to higher ground.

We watched a small herd of deer on a road near our house some time ago. Traffic stopped in both directions as the animals crossed from a developed neighborhood to a preserve of hundreds of acres of wooded land. The big bucks walked first, heads held high in a majestic manner. They were on constant lookout for danger, leading their families toward safety as they made their way to protected ground. As I watched, a grown buck would take a few steps forward, and then so did the does and their young behind him. When he paused and looked around, so did they, tentative. As a prey species, they knew their lives depended on following the head of their herd to safe ground, free from predators: animal and man.

We humans watching in our cars seemed to hold our breath as the deer made their way into the woods and out of our sight. We'd seen something wonderful and unusual, not soon to be forgotten. Reluctantly, I put the car in drive and moved on.

Like those deer, we are called to follow our majestic Leader, to walk when and where he walks, to stop when he stops. We, too, are stalked on this earth by a predatory enemy. Our enemy, however, can never outsmart our Leader, who bids us with the simplest of phrases: Follow me.

As Jesus passed on from there, he saw a man called Matthew sitting at the tax booth, and he said to him, "Follow me." And he rose and followed him.

MATTHEW 9:9, ESV

September 9
BIBLE GARDEN

One of the greatest pleasures I get from gardening is in the selection, purchase, and placement of plants. You've heard of the crazy cat lady who can't say no to one more kitten? My kids call me the crazy plant lady. I'm ready to adopt them all.

While some gardeners more learned than I use the botanical names with regularity, I'm a down-home girl at heart and use the common names most of the time. They're easier, more descriptive, and more interesting, I think. Among my favorites are those plants that reflect beloved passages or truths in the Bible.

I think of the lovely rose of Sharon growing against my neighbor's fence, papery pink blossoms with a dark red heart, blooming in August when the other plants are winding down. "The rose of Sharon" is used in Song of Songs to describe a woman whom a man loves, and tradition has it referring to Christ, too, the beloved of God.

I have a handful of lilies, yellow trumpets that open among long wands of grace. When I look upon them, I remember God's constant care for me— the lilies of the field are splendorous, and yet, he reminds me, he loves me even more than he loves them.

Other plants that turn my thoughts toward faith include the red-orange burning bush, which reminds me of God's holiness as he warned Moses not to look upon him but to remove his shoes in God's presence. The thorns on my barberry remind me of Christ's painful sacrifice. And although I know Eve's fruit was likely a pomegranate, the crab apple trees in my neighborhood remind me of the consequences of sin.

My garden isn't Eden, and this world is not heaven, but I am blessed when I can look around me and see God in the ordinary.

Since the creation of the world God's invisible qualities—
his eternal power and divine nature—have been clearly
seen, being understood from what has been made.

ROMANS 1:20

September 10
LOCUSTS

A few years ago, the people of a small farming town near where my husband grew up watched as a giant, black cloud moved menacingly close. Suddenly, the buzzing cloud dropped to the ground, and millions of grasshoppers began chewing up any and all living plants—stalks of grass, dandelions, and worst of all, the carefully tended wheat crop. Imagine the menacing hum of all of those jaws devouring a year's worth of the farmers' work. The bug-covered roads seemed to move. The insects would part—like the Red Sea—only when a car (with its windows tightly rolled up) would drive through.

As quickly as they came, the bugs departed, but only when there was nothing left to eat. The land was completely mowed down, the air stank, and a gloom hovered over the devastation. The farmers had no harvest that year. They were discouraged, scared, and broke. We've all been there, haven't we? All our hopes and dreams chewed up by circumstances completely beyond our control.

The next winter was so cold that most of the grasshopper eggs did not survive. When summer came, the crops grew thick, and that autumn brought the most tremendous harvest ever—enough to make up for everything that had been lost the year before. Because there had been a crop shortage the previous year, the prices were higher, which meant more income.

What hard things have happened in your life that you are discouraged about? Do you believe that God is willing and able to restore them when the time is just right, even when you stand among the ruins? Hold on, because a year of harvest will soon follow. He promises.

The LORD says, "I will give you back what you lost to the swarming locusts, the hopping locusts, the stripping locusts, and the cutting locusts."

JOEL 2:25, NLT

SHAKEN

Washington state is apple country. Johnny Appleseed must have dumped whatever was left in his bag when he reached us, the westernmost continental state, before dipping his tired feet in the Pacific Ocean. Each year, Washington harvests over 100 million boxes of apples. That's a lot of fruit!

A few of those apples are for eating, and they are handpicked slowly and carefully. Most, however, are destined to be juiced. The fastest, most efficient way to harvest a huge load of juicy, ripe fruit is to use a tree shaker.

The shaker is a machine that pulls up to the tree, clamps around the trunk, and then shakes with amazing might. The ground surrounding the tree shakes too, like an earthquake. The fruit rains down on the ground (don't stand too close!), and soon the land is carpeted with luscious apples, the air perfumed for miles around.

Orchardists may get a few apples here and there by handpicking, but they'd never be able to harvest all they need without the trees being shaken. The act of shaking brings the bounty, although both good and bad apples fall from a tree in the process.

In our spiritual lives, too, it seems that we drop our fruit, whatever it may be, when we are shaken. When things go wrong, do I drop bitter fruit, crab apples of anger and doubt that I have been nurturing through my sense of entitlement? Or do I drop the nutritious, fragrant fruit of faith and hopeful expectation?

Like the apple trees grown for their valuable crop, we're going to grow fruit of some kind, and we're also going to be shaken by life, perhaps annually. What will be found on the ground around us? Sweet stuff, I hope!

By their fruit you will recognize them. Do people pick
grapes from thornbushes, or figs from thistles?

MATTHEW 7:16

September 12
DORMANT

Every year, come September, I finish watering and feeding my plants. After that, the rain takes care of the maintenance watering, and the plants shouldn't need to eat again till they start a new growth period in early spring. Autumn and winter are periods of dormancy for garden plants. They don't grow taller, or fuller, or develop leaves or blossoms. What energy they do have they put into pushing their roots deeper and wider. Or sleeping.

Dormancy is a tough season for plants. The weather is colder and windier, and they have less protection. There is little sun to bless their branches and lots of ice to curse them. It's a time when they put their heads down and bear things out.

When spring arrives at last, the plants begin to let loose. I watch them as they leaf out, each in its own season, and pop out little buds ready to blossom. Last year's perennials grow another several inches, or maybe even a foot if the plant is a fast grower. This is the time to feed them again.

We, too, have periods of dormancy in life. We've got our heads down and our teeth clenched, and we are doing what we can to get through a cold, icy season. But all the time, whether we realize it or not, our roots are growing stronger against the whipping wind, our branches growing tougher bark against that ice. When it comes time for us to blossom again, when the sun shines once more—and it will—we'll be ready to face the new season in beautiful grandeur.

Is this a cold season for you? Hold on. Sunshine is on the way.

Yes, my soul, find rest in God;
my hope comes from him.
Truly he is my rock and my salvation;
he is my fortress, I will not be shaken.

PSALM 62:5-6

MAY I HAVE SOME ICE CUBES?

One of the most important appliances in my kitchen is my ice maker. I am truly and completely American in my love for iced drinks. When I travel to other countries where drinks are served without ice, I often ask for it. Good waiters and servers will comply with the wishes of the customer and usually arrive with a scant one or two cubes, probably thinking, *Who could want more than that?* When I politely ask for a few more, more are delivered, almost always cheerfully.

It's the essence of good service to help those we are called, appointed, or have decided to serve without an "attitude." But it's hard sometimes, because servers aren't chefs, whose work is more highly lauded. The world, like the church, is made up of many more servants than rock stars, but the rock stars get the accolades and the servants do not.

God does not look upon work that way. The book of Acts records a gathering of church leaders who realized that people were doing too much work and were working outside their areas of gifting, which wasn't helping the overall mission. They selected deacons—those chosen to serve—and made it clear that worthy servants are those who are filled with the Spirit and with wisdom.

Even knowing that, it's hard to be a servant in a world and in churches that often exalt the high-profile people. But Jesus speaks to all of us who serve, telling us that when we offer a cup of cold water to his disciples, it will not go unnoticed or unrewarded.

I'm thinking cold water has ice cubes in it, no?

The Twelve gathered all the disciples together and said, "It would not be right for us to neglect the ministry of the word of God in order to wait on tables. Brothers and sisters, choose seven men from among you who are known to be full of the Spirit and wisdom. We will turn this responsibility over to them.". . . So the word of God spread.

ACTS 6:2-3, 7

PILGRIM'S PROGRESS

The verse that starts popping into parents' heads when their child is about eighteen months old is "Train up a child in the way he should go; even when he is old he will not depart from it" (Proverbs 22:6, ESV). Depending on the training, and how old is "old," there may in fact be a departure from training in the bathroom department, but that's another discussion!

When our second child was born, I decided that I just couldn't be changing diapers for two; it was time for the older child to be toilet trained. He liked the idea—conceptually—but sitting still for long periods of time waiting for something to happen wasn't his strong suit. We made progress when I placed an M&M's machine in the bathroom. For every four minutes he sat on the toilet, he got to turn the crank, and a victory was rewarded with two turns. But what really did the toilet-training trick for both kids was when they decided they did not want to sit in their own messes anymore.

That's how it is sometimes, in non-potty-training life too. I can make bad decisions, and only when it starts to feel icky or smell bad do I feel motivated to make the effort toward long-term change. Once the kids realized that not only was it relatively easy to stay clean but also that it felt much better, there was no going back. Bad habits can be cleaned up, and replaced with good habits that bring us satisfaction. It feels good to act holy, to act righteously, to love well, and to do good and imitate our God, because that's how we were created to work.

No one in the family has regressed from their potty training, and we're all making good progress in becoming more like Christ—even without the M&M's.

Train up a child in the way he should go;
even when he is old he will not depart from it.

PROVERBS 22:6, ESV

September 15
LOVE LANGUAGES

I'm sure you've heard of the book that discusses love languages—how each of us best receives and understands love from others, and how to show others we love them in the language they speak. I'm here to tell you something startling.

Food is my dog's love language.

There is no number of comfy blankets that can do what a slice of turkey can do, no number of belly rubs or Frisbee tosses that means as much as a squirt of whipped topping. When she's truly ill she refuses a treat, and that's when we know to call the vet. When we feed her, she knows we love her.

My husband's love language is touch, so a back rub means more to him than a gift. Mine is acts of service, so when someone cleans the kitchen or mows the lawn, I feel loved. My kids have their own love languages, and it's been a pleasure to learn about those of my friends, too. I want them to know how much I care for and appreciate them, and it's not too much trouble to learn how they'd like to hear that.

God has a love language too. It's faith. Hebrews 11:6 tells us to have faith not only because it's good for us (and it is!), but because it is how we can show love to God. We ask him hundreds of times a week to show his love for us: care, provision, encouragement, forestalling problems, etc. It's so good that we know exactly how to show our love in return. By faith! We can have faith that he will provide for all our needs.

⚬⚬⚬

Without faith it is impossible to please God.

HEBREWS 11:6

PLUMB LINES

I have always loved boxwoods, mainly because they're easily shaped. We shape ours in spring and in autumn. They can be trimmed into strange shapes—I've seen a bush trimmed to look like a golfer teeing off—but I prefer them neat and square, like birthday gifts without the bows on top.

We had some boxwoods lining our driveway, and I wanted them to be even in height. In order to prune them straight, I could not rely upon my eye alone. The eye, one person's perspective, can play tricks. Something can seem right, and when you step away from it, it's off. If you've already pruned . . . uh-oh. There's no gluing back the branches and leaves already lying on the ground.

I consulted a garden manual to discover exactly how to measure and cut to get the results I wanted—so my boxwoods would look the way I wanted them to look. The book suggested that I use a plumb line, stringing it from one shrub to the next till the hedge is exactly aligned. Then I should look at the shrubs on the other side of the driveway and make sure they align. Then I should ask someone else to come and look. When all methods of measuring match up, *then* I can fire up the power trimmers and prune away.

Like any good parent, God has expectations for his children, and those expectations are for his glory and our good. He doesn't just leave us wandering around wondering what to do, though. He not only gives us explicit instructions (the manual) or nudges from within (his Spirit), but he gives us examples to align ourselves with—faithful plumb lines, as it were, and not just one, but a whole cloud of them. Aligning myself with them, I can see where I need pruning and where I need growth.

Love the LORD your God and keep his requirements, his
decrees, his laws and his commands always.

DEUTERONOMY 11:1

MUDDY FEET

My daughter had been where she wasn't supposed to be, and by the time she made her way up the street and to our house again, her clothes and feet showed it; they were covered with mud. We hustled her into the house, and I held my tongue (this time!). I didn't ask her why she'd gone out of bounds or point out that this mess was the consequence of the action—a consequence that other people were going to have to help her clean up.

Instead, in a moment of true inspiration (and after she had changed from the muddy pants), I took a washcloth and some warm water and washed her feet. *Say nothing*, the Holy Spirit prompted me, and I obeyed, glad he'd made it so clear. After my daughter's feet were clean, she reached up for a hug. I hugged her back and knew that nothing would ever need to be said. She already knew that what she'd done was not right, and she wished it undone; although I couldn't help with that part, I could help her make it right again.

"Do you understand what I have done for you?" Jesus asks us, and the answer truly is no. We can't yet understand the breadth and depth and width of his love for us, the fullness of consequences avoided, and all his examples of care and concern. But what we *do* know is that we've done wrong, we don't like the feeling of crusted mud, and we need someone to help us clean it off.

I don't know for sure that my daughter "learned a lesson" that day, but I do know that she felt my love. And in the most powerful of ways, I understood Christ's love for me.

"Do you understand what I have done for you?" he asked them. "You call me 'Teacher' and 'Lord,' and rightly so, for that is what I am. Now that I, your Lord and Teacher, have washed your feet, you also should wash one another's feet. I have set you an example that you should do as I have done for you."

JOHN 13:12-15

September 18
MOLD

We live in a region where damp is a state of being at least six months out of the year. Our clothes are moist from running in and out of the car and in and out of buildings (umbrellas are for tourists!), rugs are damp from wet shoes, the dog sometimes smells like, well, wet dog. The back patio, overshadowed by trees, never really catches any sun, not even in the summer. The cobblestones making up the patio are now a beautiful gray, aged and lovely, but for a long time we didn't spend any time on the patio because the stones were slippery and slick with green. They didn't smell good. Back there, where they were, was not only damp, it was dark. Here's something I learned:

Mold grows in the dark.

In order to get rid of the mold, we not only had to dry things up, we had to lighten them up too. Once the tree branches were trimmed way back and the cobblestones were exposed to the sunlight, the mold began to dry up and wither till eventually I could quick-broom it off. It did not return. The sun had made this possible. No more slipping and sliding when walking outdoors!

There is mold in our lives, too. The parts of us that we don't want to grow, that aren't healthy, that we believe to be ugly—well, they thrive in the dark. We keep secret the things we consider to be shameful about ourselves. Would our friends still love us if they knew? Would we be taken out of a ministry?

The truth is that light heals, light strengthens, light brings life. Start small—open up a little corner of vulnerability to someone you trust. Just sharing a little bit will lighten your load, and before you know it, that shame will be quick-whisked away!

I have come into the world as light, so that whoever believes in me may not remain in darkness.

JOHN 12:46, ESV

September 19
LAZY EYE

The day had come. The junk drawers were so full of junk that I couldn't even find the junk I wanted. A purge was in order. I found a collection of hair bands, leaking pens, batteries (Burned out or new? I had no idea.), and way in the back of the drawer, my daughter's first set of glasses.

I remembered the day we'd found out that she needed glasses. All the preschoolers had been dismissed to their parents, except for two. Another parent and I waited, nervously, while our kids underwent free vision and hearing screening. Finally my daughter came out of the testing room. She had lazy eye.

Lazy eye is a condition in which one eye wanders and doesn't exert itself strongly enough, which forces the other eye to work much harder. This becomes a bad cycle wherein the strong eye becomes stronger and the weak eye becomes weaker till it eventually goes blind. In order to stop the progression, you have to patch the strong eye, forcing the weaker eye to work harder and grow stronger.

I used to be known in my family as Wanda Worrier. If nothing presented itself to worry about, I went in search of something reasonable. And it usually wasn't hard to find something. I've learned that it's the easiest thing in the world to focus on your problems—both those that *are* and those that *might be*.

What happened, though, was that my "worry eye" grew too strong. I could see all the problems in clear, sharp focus. I visualized the anxieties from far off. But my other eye, the one attuned to pleasures, blessings, hope, and joy—well, it grew weaker. In order to bring things back into balance I had to "cover" the worry eye, refuse to let it dominate. How? Well, I'm glad you asked. Read the verse below. It works!

*Now, dear brothers and sisters, one final thing. Fix your thoughts on what
is true, and honorable, and right, and pure, and lovely, and admirable.
Think about things that are excellent and worthy of praise.*

PHILIPPIANS 4:8, NLT

September 20
GRIPPER

We put a few new rugs in our house after moving in. One was in the hallway on slippery tile. I didn't realize exactly how slippery that tile was till I stepped on the rug, in a hurry and with my head down, and went hurtling into the next room like Aladdin on his magic carpet. I went to the local home improvement store in search of a product to help and found Grip-Its—not the stick covers for video controllers, but pads to go under rugs.

A Grip-It rug pad is a mat that can be cut to any size. It's a little tacky (in the sense of holding on to things, not poor taste!), and it has some cushion to it. I brought one home, cut it to the right size, and put it on the floor underneath the new rug. Voilà! No more slipping and sliding.

Most of the things that send me flying in this life aren't things that I expect will do so. I put a step forward, and suddenly I'm in an unpleasant and slightly scary situation. For the Christian, there is good news. We have one who is always with us—sticks with us, if you will—in every situation. He's there with a ready hand. I'm guessing that there have been dozens or even hundreds of times in which I took a misstep—physically, emotionally, or spiritually—and God undergirded me in such a way that I didn't even realize a disaster had been averted.

And when I do realize danger is ahead, I know what to do. Look up. God's help is coming!

I lift up my eyes to the mountains—
where does my help come from?
My help comes from the LORD,
the Maker of heaven and earth.

He will not let your foot slip—
he who watches over you will not slumber;
indeed, he who watches over Israel
will neither slumber nor sleep.

PSALM 121:1-4

September 21

CLAIMING A STAKE

I love topiary. I have fun little silk boxwood twists inside the house, and I wanted some living topiary outside, too. So one year I bought four for the front yard: two pink Tinkerbelle lilacs, a fragrant white camellia, and a yellow witch hazel. Part of the topiary charm is the slender stalk upon which rests a large, tousled head of untamed leaves and puffs of flower. That pliable stalk, though, is weak for a number of years, often the result of having been grafted onto the rootstock of a hardier plant.

My house faces a windy bluff, and therefore my lovely little topiaries needed a helping hand. I put thin stakes into the ground and then used landscape fabric to tie the topiary trunks to those stakes. The supports gave my plants backbones, if you will, to help them withstand the first few years in the ground while they adjusted to their new home.

A master gardener warned me to remove the stakes after a number of years, just before autumn winds begin to blow. If I didn't, the plant would remain weak and dependent upon the stakes, unable to grow the strong roots and thick trunk required to face those winds on its own. Developing the strength to stand alone was what would help it to live long and prosper. I felt a little nervous at first when I removed the stake and waited for the first sustained winds. Would the plant snap? It did not. It stood straight, tall, and strong.

That seems to me a good analogy for all those we train, teach, and mentor. Whether they be our children or our students, or even when we ourselves are being mentored, the idea is not to grow dependent upon the stake, but to rely on it while we get strong. And then—take the stake away. Once strengthened, we can face those winds on our own.

I will instruct you and teach you in the way you should go;
I will counsel you with my loving eye on you.

PSALM 32:8

FINDING MARIE

One night my daughter was driving home from work when she saw two little lights by the side of the road. She pulled over and heard something rustle. Was it a raccoon? She heard a tiny meow. It was not a raccoon. It was a kitten!

The kitten was fearful and did not show herself right away, but she did keep meowing out in distress. Eventually my daughter found her, scooped her up, and took her home. After ascertaining that the little cat had been abandoned, she took her to the vet for care and then kept her. She named her Marie. I'm telling you, there is no cat as loved and spoiled as that one. Marie rules the household.

There was nothing about the cat, at first, that drew my daughter's eye. It was my daughter's own qualities—her compassion for animals, her response to the distress calls, her desire to lavish her love upon a pet—that led to Marie's adoption.

God's love for us is like this. When we were in distress before we knew him, he came looking for us first. When we responded and became his own, he did not stop looking out for us. He is near at hand, listening for a distress call, ready to scoop us up and protect us.

If an abandoned animal can stir so much compassion in a person, how much faster and more lovingly will your Father, who cherishes you, respond to your calls? The Israelites faced danger and called out for help. God rescued them. He will surely rescue you and me, too.

They said to Samuel, "Do not stop crying out to the LORD our God
for us, that he may rescue us from the hand of the Philistines."

1 SAMUEL 7:8

September 23
STORM CHASERS

One humid, late-summer night, our family gathered on the front lawn as lightning shot across the sky. It was a spectacular, focus-fixing display of God's power. As the thunder rolled in, we reluctantly went inside, where we continued our discussion of weather. Both my husband and I grew up in areas that had tornadoes, and we remember taking shelter in school hallways, books over the backs of our necks for protection. My kids recalled being in elementary school when we had a large earthquake. I recalled it too. I had run outside, dog in my arms, and watched as our flat street undulated like a shaken bedspread.

When such displays of power suddenly strike, completely out of our control, our minds naturally turn to the God who both allows and calms such storms. Truth is, though, those storms don't happen very often. I've experienced only one large earthquake and a couple of small ones, and I can remember about only five tornadoes. Even thunderstorms are scarce.

Instead, my life is made up of days on end of quiet and gentle rain, or a soft evening breeze to cool an after-dinner walk. The moon as it rises over the mountain makes no sound; it does not call attention to itself in any way and yet is undeniably majestic. A sunrise serenaded only by morning birds can easily be overlooked. So often we look for God in the big moments, the thunder or the lightning of life. And he's there, to be sure. But I don't want to miss the majesty of the daily moments, as he quietly whispers his love to me, which I must still myself to hear.

The LORD said, "Go out and stand on the mountain in the
presence of the LORD, for the LORD is about to pass by."

Then a great and powerful wind tore the mountains apart and
shattered the rocks before the LORD, but the LORD was not in the
wind. After the wind there was an earthquake, but the LORD was
not in the earthquake. After the earthquake came a fire, but the
LORD was not in the fire. And after the fire came a gentle whisper.

1 KINGS 19:11-12

September 24
SOWING AND REAPING

Our lawn was balding quicker than, well, quicker than someone who lives at our house and shall remain unnamed. Bald is beautiful, though! Unless it's your yard.

So we decided we'd reseed it, taking advantage of the autumn rains and trying the cheaper route before investing in sod. First, we had to kill the weeds and remove them. Then, we scattered grass seed. After that, we rolled over the yard with a prickly machine that was designed to push the seeds into the ground, often splitting the seed as it did so. Weeks later, thin, green blades of grass began to thread their way up through the soil. Our new lawn looked to be a success.

As we washed off that seed-piercing machine to store it away, I thought about Scripture. The book of John tells us that unless a grain of wheat dies, it remains alone; it cannot grow or reproduce. An early church father, Tertullian, proclaimed that "the blood of the martyrs is the seed of the church." We live in a time when it seems that there is more global violence against people in general, including Christians dying for their faith. We know that there would be no salvation for any of us without shed blood. The word *martyr* means "witness," and those who die for the name of Christ are witnessing to their faith in this reality; a more powerful testimony cannot be found.

The Lord still calls, "Can I get a witness?" to some. Let's pray today for those courageous enough to answer, "Here I am, Lord. Send me."

Very truly I tell you, unless a kernel of wheat falls to the ground and dies,
it remains only a single seed. But if it dies, it produces many seeds.

JOHN 12:24

I'LL JUST DO IT MYSELF

Have you ever assigned a household chore to your child or spouse and then decided you wanted it done differently or more quickly? Or maybe you were unwilling to let go of the control, the timing, or the outcome?

Whenever I decide that something needs a little kick into action from me, one of two things usually happens: debt or disaster.

Debt occurs when I decide I want something before the resources have been provided. I'm not talking about medical care or emergencies; I'm talking about the portrait of Mozart at Versailles that I want for the powder room. When I rush ahead of my resources, I don't truly enjoy my purchases, because I've incurred trouble. Scripture tells us that the blessing of the Lord brings no trouble with it..

Disaster results when I'm trying to rush things to happen on my schedule, which is not always (in fact, is rarely) God's timing. I lack patience.

When Abram's wife, Sarai, decided to stop waiting for God and take action to provide a son for herself though her handmaiden, Ishmael was born. God, however, kept his promise to Abram and provided Isaac through Sarai. The consequences for Sarai rushing ahead have had terrible ripples through the ages and impact our world even today; the descendants of Isaac and Ishmael are still in conflict in the Middle East today.

I don't like debt, and I don't like disaster! So I've got to keep working on the discipline of patience.

Sarai, Abram's wife, had borne him no children. But she had an Egyptian slave named Hagar; so she said to Abram, "The LORD has kept me from having children. Go, sleep with my slave; perhaps I can build a family through her."

Abram agreed to what Sarai said.

GENESIS 16:1-2

September 26
SEASONS

Many of my friends have favorite seasons—the most popular seems to be autumn! It's difficult for me to choose just one, though. Winter brings some favorite holidays and cozy evenings with books and movies with its early-setting sun. Spring is the time to plant, and I love getting my hands dirty and looking forward to a new bounty as the days lengthen just a little, week by week. Summer is hot and sunny and usually holds a vacation; my favorite part, though, is the stunning displays of shooting stars. I still make wishes—or often turn them into prayers. Autumn is the time to slow down and enjoy the majestic display of copper, yellow, and red leaves. But the best part of autumn, to me, is the brilliant, unusual moons.

Two special moons mark the season of harvest. In September there is the harvest moon for bringing in the crops, and in October there is a hunter's moon, lighting the night for hunters to procure meat for winter. It has been said that these full moons seem to last longer and shine brighter than full moons at other times of the year to allow harvesters and hunters a few extra hours of light so they can provide food for the long winter ahead.

In some ways, the passing of one season and the start of a new one, year after year, is comforting. God has made the world and everything in it, and the seasons tick along according to plan, month after month, year after year. The very regularity of the seasons, even down to the annual harvest and hunter's moons, reminds me that God is the same yesterday, today, and tomorrow. He is dependable to each generation that passes through its series of seasons. He is the one thing that never changes.

You made the moon to mark the seasons,
and the sun knows when to set.

PSALM 104:19, NLT

September 27

ON DISPLAY

We had befriended a young couple; one of them had family members who'd been mired in paganism and other dark practices. As this couple began to turn more and more toward the Son, they simultaneously experienced more and more spiritual attack and oppression. Many times we prayed with them, and they grew stronger. Yet when we left their home, we often felt like we were leaving them vulnerable, unattended in a shadowy neighborhood.

One time shortly after we'd left, the Lord reminded me that our friends were not unattended; he himself remained, as did the angels Scripture tells us are sent to minister to those who will inherit salvation. I wanted these friends to have a tangible reminder of that, day and night. The Spirit brought to mind that this couple, who lived on a tight budget, did not have a cross in their home.

I had one. But it was my *special* cross. It had been a gift from a group of people I work with, made from stone quarried in Jerusalem. It was mounted on a wall in a location I walked by often. It was a treasure to me, like he whom it represented. I had even remarked about the cross to this young couple.

I wanted to give it to them. And yet, I did not want to. As I stood in front of it, a thought came to me: the cross was not meant primarily to be displayed, whether on our walls or around our necks, but to be given away.

We took the cross down from the wall, drove to that couple's home, and gave it to them; they were overjoyed. They hung it on a prominent wall in their own home. As we drove away, I was glad that the Holy Spirit had nudged me to act and that I'd been obedient to follow his instruction—something I don't always do.

I trust that in the right way, at the right time, I will find another cross to treasure. Till then, the spot on my wall remains bare but for the nail, which reminds me of the true cost of sacrifice.

Do not withhold good from those who deserve it
when it's in your power to help them.

PROVERBS 3:27, NLT

DINOSAUR BONES

One of the great things about having kids is that you get to do kid things all over again, sometimes even things you didn't get to do on your first go-round. When our scientist son was small, he wanted to be a paleontologist. So one night, we took the skeleton of the roasted chicken we'd just eaten for dinner, boiled it clean, and buried the pieces in the backyard.

We gave the kids helmets and shovels and sprinkled some chalk powder around, just like a real dig site. Imagine their delight when they uncovered "dino" bones in the backyard! They knew that some animal was buried there (we told them later it was a chicken), because they could see it plainly before their eyes. They were gathering evidence.

So often we hear that it's hard to believe in God because we can't see him, and that's true. But Romans 1:19-20 tells us that we can see the evidence of him all around us: "What may be known about God is plain to them, because God has made it plain to them. For since the creation of the world God's invisible qualities—his eternal power and divine nature—have been clearly seen."

Sometimes it's easier to believe in God in the big sense (*Sure, someone had to create all this*) than it is in the personal sense (*Does he love me? And if so, then why?*). We all have those *then why?* moments. And the antidote to them is to look around. Counting blessings is just as easy as counting problems, only we slide into one more easily than the other. Chicken bones weren't evidence of a dinosaur, but my son knew they were evidence of parents who loved him and believed he could be a scientist. And today, he is one! Our God, too, created us for a purpose and wants us to live up to our potential. He leaves the evidence all around us in the form of our passions, blessings, and sources of joy.

Do you not know?
Have you not heard?
Has it not been told you from the beginning?
Have you not understood since the earth was founded? . . .
The Lord is the everlasting God,
the Creator of the ends of the earth.

ISAIAH 40:21, 28

September 29

LABORERS, CRAFTSMEN, AND ARTISTS

After a couple of bad experiences, my husband and I decided that from now on, the people we hire to work on our home need to come with good training, good reviews, and professional credentials. It's not that beginners can't be good; they can. And when beginners work under the guidance of a mentor, their work can be both fresh and solid. It's just that we've had a few experiences with those wanting to make a few bucks on the side without having the proper training.

My favorite people to hire are those who are nerds about their professions. They know all the ins and outs of the plumbing pipes, why some paints set better than others, or how some plants will sprawl and some will not. You know them—the kind of people who talk on and on while your eyes glaze over. I have to admit to being the cause of glazed eyes sometimes too. I've been known to drone on about historical or biblical accuracy or how not to drop a soufflé, because I care about those things.

I love this quote from Louis Nizer: "He who works with his hands is a laborer. He who works with his hands and his head is a craftsman. He who works with his hands and his head and his heart is an artist."

You, too, are an artist. You were created to create, to love, to excel. You have gifts and interests and skills that intersect in a unique way. What are you passionate about? Where do you share that passion?

Whether you eat or drink or whatever you do, do it all for the glory of God.

1 CORINTHIANS 10:31

September 30
WELL DRESSED

The other morning I was riffling through the drawer that holds my, er, foundations, and I thought, *Wow. There's a lot more substance to some of these things than the ones I wore when I was younger.* I'm not quite to the whalebone-corset stage yet, but I am getting close. The breastplate of righteousness has to be made of sturdier materials as one gets older! Support hose and constriction garments round out the wardrobe of a properly attired middle-aged woman—even, I hope, a fashionable one.

The truth is, no matter our age, it's important to be well dressed. Career women are often advised to dress for the job one rung up the ladder from theirs. It's even more important to pay attention to your spiritual wardrobe. The enemy doesn't bother targeting ineffective malingerers, but once you move forward with a purpose—loving the unlovable, caring for those on the margin, speaking the truth, coming alongside the hurting—you transform into a beautiful target.

My husband is former military, and the military outfits we civilians generally call "camo" are really referred to as BDUs—Battle Dress Uniforms. God has given us Battle Dress Uniforms too. We can take a lot of time on our hair, our makeup, our clothing, and our shoes when we prepare for the day. I admit I'm not quite as good at ensuring as I leave home each day that I'm dressed for spiritual battle. I've gotta change that. You?

Put on the full armor of God, so that when the day of evil comes, you may be able to stand your ground, and after you have done everything, to stand. Stand firm then, with the belt of truth buckled around your waist, with the breastplate of righteousness in place, and with your feet fitted with the readiness that comes from the gospel of peace. In addition to all this, take up the shield of faith, with which you can extinguish all the flaming arrows of the evil one. Take the helmet of salvation and the sword of the Spirit, which is the word of God.

EPHESIANS 6:13-17

OCTOBER

Lots-to-Love Lasagna

As autumn winds and rain reintroduce themselves and the nights
get cozy and cool, I'm ready to set salads aside and indulge in comfort food. This recipe is for the ultimate lasagna. Don't stint on the
ingredients; use the best you can find. The recipe makes two large
batches; they freeze beautifully for a busy night or as a delivery to a
sick friend. Smaller pans, say four 8 x 8 pans, work too. Just watch
your baking time, taking it out after perhaps 30 minutes instead
of 45. This is an all-day project, though for most of the time the
sauce simmering or cooling, so it can be going in the background,
perfuming your house, while you're doing something else.

Lasagna is very forgiving. Like olives? Add some. Like mushrooms? Stir fry them with the onions. More cheese, less cheese? It's
your call.

WHAT YOU'LL NEED
3 cups chopped onion
3 tablespoons minced garlic
8 ounces finely chopped pancetta, or American bacon if you can't
    find pancetta
3 pounds ground Italian sausage
5 cans (28 ounces each) of whole, peeled tomatoes
12 ounces tomato paste
2 tablespoons Italian seasoning with sea salt
Fresh lasagna noodle sheets (You can find these in the deli section.
    If you can't find them, use regular noodles, parboiled and patted
    dry.)
1 pound sliced provolone cheese
4 fresh mozzarella cheese balls (6 ounces each), thinly sliced
2 cups grated parmesan cheese
Fresh basil leaves, if desired

2 9x13 pans (I use disposable—that way I can give the lasagna
  away or freeze it for my own use. I can pop the frozen lasagna
  out of the disposable dish and put it in a nice dish if necessary.)

DIRECTIONS

Heat large frying pan over medium-high heat. Add the onions,
garlic, and pancetta (or bacon) to the pan. Cook, stirring constantly, till meat is crisp and onions are brown, about 10-12
minutes. Remove from heat.

Heat a very large pot over medium-high heat. Add the sausage
and cook till brown and cooked through. Break the sausage up
with a wooden spoon as you go, but try to keep it in dime-sized
chunks. Drain.

Add the onion mixture to the sausage pot. Then stir in tomatoes, tomato paste, and seasoning. Bring to a simmer, then turn
heat to low and let cook for 2 hours, stirring occasionally and
breaking up the tomatoes as you do. Continue to season to taste.
Let cool completely. The sauce will thicken as it cools.

Ladle sauce onto the bottom of each pan till it's about 1 inch
deep. Add a layer of fresh lasagna noodles. Layer sliced provolone
on top, slightly overlapping the pieces. Layer mozzarella on top,
the rounds barely touching. Sprinkle with parmesan. Add another
layer of noodles, all three cheeses again, and then ladle sauce over
all of it. Add any other cheese slices that are left over, and sprinkle
with a light layer of parmesan and sea salt. If you're feeling fancy,
slice some fresh basil leaves and scatter on top.

The lasagna you're saving should be frozen unbaked. Thaw
before baking.

The one you're eating should be baked at 350 degrees for
about 45 minutes. Let it sit for 15 minutes after you take it out
of the oven. This helps it keep its shape when cut and not be
runny. Enjoy!

For this month's free printable, go to http://tyndal.es/homeandgarden.

DRAW NEAR TO GOD

One of my favorite things is to sit on the couch with people and pets that I love. I especially love it in the autumn, with throw pillows and blankets and a fire in the fireplace. Even though our couch is pretty worn out and has a rip in the arm, I don't want to replace it, because it sinks into coziness in all the right places.

If my husband is home, we sit on it together and read or watch TV, cuddling sometimes. When my daughter comes to visit, we lean against each other and watch movies. My son and I read side by side, and my friends and I sit close enough to share prayers and coffee. If I'm the only one home, I simply have to pat the couch a few times, and my dog jumps up and sitsthisclose to my leg. She comes near.

The Lord has told us that he wants to be close to us; in fact, he paid the ultimate price to make that happen. People have often asked, if he wants to get close to us, why does the verse say that you have to come close to him, then he will come close to you? Why not the other way around? But here's the deal: he has already made the first move by making a way to cover sin and create intimacy. It's as if he is saying, "I cleared the space on the couch. Your move next—want to come over?" And then when we do, we feel him and his presence.

God has made a space for you. Scoot a little closer.

Come near to God and he will come near to you.

JAMES 4:8

October 2

SLOW LEAK

Over the course of winter, I had become very sick to my stomach several times. I had no other symptoms of illness, so the diagnosis was stress. A month or two later, a member of my family who had never been prone to headaches began to have them fairly regularly. Cause assigned? Stress.

Spring came, and with the sunshine our symptoms cleared up. Or so we thought. Once it grew cooler out and we turned on the heat again, the symptoms returned. Diagnosis? There was a slow leak in our furnace; the gas had been leaking into the house, making us sick. Eventually, it could have caused someone to die.

The gas was odorless and tasteless, and initially the meter designed to detect it didn't sense it. But our bodies were telling us something was wrong, even though we couldn't pinpoint just what it was at first; it took time and discernment. I thought about how much this is like other situations I sometimes find myself in. Things may seem natural and good at the outset, but along the way, I begin to sense that something just isn't right. Over time, as I begin to suffer the consequences—in body, spirit, and mind—my eyes are opened, and I discern the problem. The *aha!* moment. Once I figure out there's a problem, I must either fix the problem or forsake the situation.

So often we start with good intentions—a job, a ministry, a church, a relationship—but then along the way it becomes clear that something is wrong. Perhaps the people turn out to be other than who they had represented themselves to be; the job requires you to bend your ethics or morals, if not the law; a relationship is toxic (there's a reason for that phrase); or the ministry takes more than you have to give or does not advance the cause of Christ. Once diagnosed, the problem must be remedied or the situation abandoned! And then . . . you will be well again.

Do not be misled: "Bad company corrupts good character."

1 CORINTHIANS 15:33

October 3
A TIME FOR EVERYTHING

I was outside raking, which was hearty exercise and actually felt good—warm hoodie and cold breezes. The sky was bright blue; the leaves fluttering down were shades of wine and gold. I found it kind of sad that they were at their most beautiful on their way to death. I picked one up. It had lost its pliable nature and was becoming stiff and crispy. And yet what a way to go out, in a blaze of glory, which most of us (though we are not leaves) might choose to do as well.

The thought struck me: the tree must release that which is dead, or dying, in order to bring new life in a new season. I have held on to jobs for too long, past the time when I knew I could be serving better elsewhere. I've stayed in relationships out of nostalgia, even when they were no longer healthy. I've retained habits that weren't working, and I have had to transition from mother of children to mother of adults, which is harder than it sounds. But without the ability and willingness to let go of that which has had its time, I would not be able to make room for new people, new ministries, new phases—perhaps even grandchildren someday.

Don't be afraid to let go of something whose time has passed. It can go out in a blaze of beautiful glory, long remembered and treasured. Letting go makes way for new buds, new shoots, new flowers, new leaves. As something old passes away and something new takes its place, the tree grows year by year. And so do we.

There is a time for everything,
and a season for every activity under the heavens.

ECCLESIASTES 3:1

HIGH-POWERED BLOWERS

Do you know about high-powered blowers? I do. We bought a leaf blower when we moved into our first house, and it's still with us. I use it every autumn to corral those pesky leaves into a pile for the dog to frolic through and for us to bag up and compost. We use it to blow the dust from our driveway and walkways, too. I never have huge piles of dirt to blow away, but whenever I use the machine, I end up covered in a fine shroud of dust. The place I've aimed the machine at is clean and clear, but one look at me and you'll know what I've been up to.

People who speak ill of others are not so different from high-powered blowers. They may think they are spreading juicy nuggets of gossip or casting doubt on another's character, but mainly they are drawing attention to their own weakness. And they're not winning any friends; if they'll gossip to you when no one else is present, they'll gossip *about* you when you're not there—and who needs a "friend" like that?

I used to think I had to defend myself to those who had blown dirt my way. Now I know I don't need to. Instead, I work hard to keep my own mouth and motives pure, knowing that character speaks louder than words. If I don't gossip and my behavior reflects the fruit of the Spirit, those who malign me will not be believed; their dust will stick to themselves. But if I join in blowing that hot air, then when ill is spoken of me, it will be easier to believe. It's hard not to stick up for yourself. But keeping silent isn't running scared. It's trusting that your integrity is known and seen.

Do not worry when others speak ill of you. Your own actions are your best defense.

Keep your conscience clear. Then if people speak against you, they will be ashamed when they see what a good life you live because you belong to Christ.

1 PETER 3:16, NLT

October 5

SOWING AND WEEPING

Without rain, nothing grows. Instead, plants dry out, wither up, and blow away. It's not often that I see this lesson play out in the Pacific Northwest, known for its rain, but one year was particularly dry. Even sprinklers, tossing hose-fed drops hither and yon, could not provide the deep soaking required for real growth. Many young landscapes perished, but Hubs and I still planted a few favorite plants, in faith and with care.

Our young family was undergoing a trying season that year, too, and the drought seemed an apt metaphor. Things were going wrong on many fronts, and as most people know, fighting a battle on more than one front leads to exhaustion and the potential for failure. Eventually, brought to our knees, we spent the next few months praying and crying, praying and crying. At long last came the rain.

The rain of our tears watered the seeds sown during that season: seeds of faith, perseverance, and hope in spite of discouraging odds, and wondering without wandering. God restored our fortunes in ways we could not have dreamed of; he filled us with joy. If we had not planted the seeds before the rains came, nothing would have grown. If there were seeds but no rain to water them, nothing would have grown either. But both—seeds and rain, working together—brought sheaves of blessing in good season.

Hold on; joy is coming. Do not be afraid to let the tears fall, but sow good seed too.

The LORD has done great things for us,
and we are filled with joy. . . .
Those who sow with tears
will reap with songs of joy.
Those who go out weeping,
carrying seed to sow,
will return with songs of joy,
carrying sheaves with them.

PSALM 126:3, 5-6

FULLY CHARGED

In our kitchen we have a recharging station with ports and cords for the various gadgets critical to modern living, but we don't always make the best use of it. Too busy to wait for recharging! Unfortunately, multitasking drains the batteries rapid-fire fast.

Sometimes I plug my phone in when the battery is at a 15-percent charge and then yank it out to use it again when it's at only 25 percent because, you know, I've got stuff to do, and I can't wait all day!

That's not enough of a charge, though. Applications malfunction. I worry about a phone call being cut off or the GPS shutting down just when I need directions on the road. I've missed important calls and texts because the battery died. In order to make the phone work as it was designed, I need to be patient and let the battery fully charge.

It's hard to wait. It's hard to see those you love suffer when it seems like the cure for their ills would be so easy for God to provide. It's hard to see a loved one deal with a financial meltdown, or a lonely person endure a broken heart while all her friends seem happily partnered. I want to solve their problems now, solve *my* problems now. But rushing into the solution with only a 25-percent charge will just cause more trouble, because I'll short-change what God has planned for the long term. At just the right time he will make a way for what we've been waiting for, if it's in his will. Till then, he'll be giving us the patience to wait till our strength—or others' readiness—is at 100 percent.

Those who trust in the LORD will find new strength.

ISAIAH 40:31, NLT

GATES AND WALLS

The traditional Japanese home—at least one owned by wealthy people—has a series of what could be considered either entrances or barriers. The first is a locked gate in the wall surrounding the house and garden. Someone invited through the gate proceeds to the house, where a sliding door provides entrance to a partially enclosed room that serves as both a place to sit and a hallway to the more private rooms of the house. In each of those rooms, sliding screens can be erected to create yet more barriers or entrances to the inner space of the house.

There is a Japanese parable that uses the house as a metaphor on how to relate to others. For someone you don't know well, or who has proven unreliable or untrustworthy, you may let her in the front gate but no further. A longer-standing friend, who has become more trustworthy, may be allowed through the screen into the sitting room. Family members and friends who have proven themselves may be allowed in further, into the heart of the home.

Keeping everyone out of your heart for self-protection—at the outer gate—is not wise, but neither is letting everyone in all the way. If you've developed friendships over time with people who have proven trustworthy, kind, and reliable, you let them in through the gate, to the front room, and perhaps further. Other friends or family might break trust or prove to be unreliable, exploitative, or dishonest. They should be kept at arm's length, if allowed to remain in your life at all.

It's pretty lonely keeping up walls so that no one gets near your heart, but it's emotionally dangerous to let everyone close. Keep close only those who prove to be real friends.

There are "friends" who destroy each other,
but a real friend sticks closer than a brother.

PROVERBS 18:24, NLT

HOT ROLLERS

When I pulled my hot rollers out of a drawer to plug them in, I found a lone pink, fuzzy sponge roller in the drawer. What memories that brought back: I would roll up my daughter's slippery, blonde hair in fuzzy rollers; she would complain that she could not possibly sleep on them. But she did, because she wanted curly hair for a special event and she was deathly afraid of hot rollers and curling irons, having once burned herself.

As I rolled up my own hair, I considered a difficult situation the Lord was allowing my daughter to undergo. People want to know: If God is good, why does he allow bad things, both little and big, to happen? In truth, we may not understand for sure till we see him face to face. I do know, though, that he promises to be with us and that he will make all situations, easy and grinding, work out according to his goodness and great plan.

Heat can burn, of course. But if it's controlled, heat from rollers or flat irons shapes the hair the way we want it to go. Sometimes difficult situations are like that. The heat from them could burn us if it were allowed to, but heat can also shape us into the women God wants us to be. When you or someone you love is suffering, remember that although you'll feel the heat, God won't let the iron get too close.

I took the rollers out of my hair twenty minutes later, asking myself, *How is God shaping, styling, and molding me into the woman I am meant to be?*

Do not be afraid, for I have ransomed you.
I have called you by name; you are mine. . . .
When you walk through the fire of oppression,
you will not be burned up;
the flames will not consume you.

ISAIAH 43:1-2, NLT

October 9

PLANTING AHEAD

I looked out my window at the landscape, turning brown and dry with the season, and I spied a squirrel running off with a bulb, newly dug up (and probably recently planted!), twice the size of his mouth. Would he eat it on the spot, store it in the ground and eat it later, or perhaps bury it and forget it?

Next spring, I had an answer. To one side of the front door I had a lovely display of neatly arranged bulbs—crocus and daffodil and tulip in a steady procession. To the other, a few yards away, a crazy quilt of colors and flowers grew where bulbs had been removed, reburied, and forgotten. I have to say, knowing the story behind that pretty patch and its unexpected splendor, I enjoyed it just as much, if not more, than the one so thoughtfully planned and prepared for.

Sometimes we wonder if our efforts in this world—whether at home, at work, with friends, in church, or the many other endeavors we pour ourselves into—will bloom. When I don't see the results I hope for, I often wonder if squirrels came right behind me, digging up and destroying my efforts. And sometimes, they do. But other times my little efforts—the single hour of time I offered as a volunteer, the simple meal or quick hug I gave, the small check I wrote to an organization—grow beyond all reasonable expectation. Sometimes we won't even see our efforts blossom in the people and organizations we pour our hearts into. Instead, those people will love others, who will love others, and that faith and love will bloom several stages down the road.

The body of Christ is both orderly and planned, and a crazy quilt of unexpected joys and blossoms as well. There's a certain pleasure in watching both gardens realize their beauty, so keep planting.

Sow your seed in the morning, and at evening let your hands
not be idle, for you do not know which will succeed, whether
this or that, or whether both will do equally well.

ECCLESIASTES 11:6

October 10

MESSAGE IN A BOTTLE

I was sorting through movies in the DVD drawer to see which ones we might want to offer to a movie-swap service. I came across a favorite, in which a man stranded on a desert island spies a message in a floating bottle. Thrilled to have some contact with other humans, he splashes out to retrieve it only to find, sadly, that it is the desperate message and plea for help that he himself had written and tossed out some time earlier.

SOS. Help me! Need rescue. Is anyone there? These are some of the messages a castaway might write on that tiny, rolled-up scroll before throwing it into the sea. However, the ocean rarely cooperates. It very often brings the bottle right back to shore, carried in on the waves that roll back to the island. No help can come if the bottle never makes it across the sea.

Giving our problems to God and then taking them right back in worry is very much like sending an e-mail to ourselves asking for help or throwing an SOS bottle into the sea to have it pitched right back at us again. God tells us he is pleased to help us with all of our worries and cares. But when we hand them to him in prayer and then take them right back again through worry, we're telling him that we can solve them better or quicker than he can. So then why send the SOS at all?

God deeply cares for everything you're concerned about. Mail the letter to him, in prayer—and don't take it back! Watch for him to work. He will!

Give all your worries and cares to God, for he cares about you.

1 PETER 5:7, NLT

October 11
NEITHER LEFT NOR RIGHT

I walked up the long, damp street with my friend's little boy; we were collecting autumn leaves to press between layers of waxed paper, transforming them into homemade stained-glass windows. He swung the bucket we were collecting them in, and we picked leaves as we went. Each house on the street had deciduous trees, so we chose one from the left, then one from the right. This allowed us to get a better selection of leaves . . . and tired the little man out before his nap time.

I couldn't help but notice how beautiful the houses on this street were. No cookie cutters here; each one was custom built and beautiful in its own right, landscaped impeccably to match the style of the home. There were no yard waste containers parked at the edge of the driveway (*must put mine away*), and there were no weeds poking through the moist earth. It was hard not to wish my own home looked like one of these.

As I held my companion's little hand and marveled at his glee and delight in the free, beautiful leaves, I cracked a smile myself. I recalled a quote ascribed to Teddy Roosevelt: "Comparison is the thief of joy." My young friend's joy was pure, instant, and immediate. I could have that joy too, and suddenly I did. Scripture implores us not to look to the left or to the right, but forward, where we're called to walk, on the path that has been carved out for us alone.

We did do some comparisons later that day—yellow leaves compared with red ones compared with coppery-orange ones. It was a wonderful way to spend a day—a life, really. The weeding would wait till tomorrow.

Each one should test their own actions. Then they can take pride in
themselves alone, without comparing themselves to someone else.

GALATIANS 6:4

October 12

LIVING 3-D

We went to a 3-D movie recently, and I brought the glasses home, thinking they looked kind of cool and hipster—or that at least they might look funny on the dog. When you put on 3-D glasses—one blue lens, one red—a static picture or a movie comes alive in a whole new way.

A short time later, I ran across a contest in a magazine. In order to decipher if you were a winner or not, you had to view the page through a piece of red film or cellophane. When you did, the cellophane blocked out all of the camouflage and allowed the true picture underneath to appear. I ran to the office to grab those 3-D glasses. I knew I'd saved them for good cause! I scanned the ad. Was I a winner? Not that time. But in that contest I found an important lesson.

So often we think about how we fail, what we do wrong—besetting sins we constantly struggle with, never seeming to fully overcome; bad decisions, choices we regret. If we let them, these kinds of sorrows will drag us under, and that's not at all what God wants for us. When I get caught in that cycle, I need to remember that after I repent, God looks at me through a set of red glasses, the blood of Christ. When God sees me, he doesn't see the sins he's forgiven and forgotten nor the flesh I wrestle with. He sees the righteousness of Christ. When I remember that, I come alive in a whole new way.

If anyone is in Christ, he is a new creation. The old
has passed away; behold, the new has come.

2 CORINTHIANS 5:17, ESV

TEMPORARY GENERATORS

In my neck of the woods, the lights go out from time to time. We have regular windstorms in autumn that can cause tree branches, burdened with ice, to snap and take down power lines. We've got to be prepared to live for a short while with no power.

So we invested in a generator. Now, some people have whole-house generators, but we have a little, noisy one that runs on lawn-mower gas out in the backyard. It keeps the refrigerator going (can't afford to lose all that food) and the phones charged. Yeah, I admit it. I need my phone.

Our little generator pretty much keeps the basics going till the storm passes and life can get back to its regularly paced craziness. It's a help for a short, dark time. And I appreciate that. So why is it so hard for me to accept help from real, loving, warm human beings? I enjoy being the one to bring a meal or offer a shoulder, but it's much, much harder for me to call someone and say, "I'm in trouble. Can you help?"

By resisting help, I'm not only feeding some unhealthy pride, I'm also denying my brothers and sisters in Christ the opportunity to extend a hand to me, to be a temporary aid in a dark time, to fulfill an important role in the body. We're not meant to be independent. Christians are created to be *inter*-dependent.

Don't be too proud to call a friend for help to keep the basics going till the storm is over. It'll draw you closer than ever, and then she'll be close enough to call out to you sometime too.

Carry each other's burdens, and in this way you will fulfill the law of Christ.

GALATIANS 6:2

SLIVERS IN MY EYE

I decided it was a good day to tidy the garage and blow the debris down the driveway. I was wearing earbuds, but I did not put on protective eyewear. A few days later, the garage was clean, but my right eye was not. It watered, and it hurt. I went to the eye doctor, and she found a sliver of copper embedded in my eye. After numbing the area, she used tweezers to pull the sliver out.

I went home and told my family. "You would never have let me do yard work without protective goggles," my son reminded me. True. I guess that *do as I say and not as I do* thing doesn't work.

"Did the doctor take the log out of her own eye before removing your sliver?" Hubs joked.

Although my eye began to feel better immediately, those two comments, said in jest, resonated with me. Why had I been willing to give good, important advice to my child and yet failed to follow through with it myself? Perhaps I thought I wouldn't be harmed. Or maybe I don't take care of myself as well as I do others. Either way, I had been hypocritical, failing to walk my talk.

The weight of our testimonies is not in what we say, but in what we do. People watch more than they listen; or perhaps they watch *before* they'll listen. A few months later I popped on some yellow goggles before heading out to mow the lawn. On the way out, I passed my son, who grinned. I lifted the goggles for just a second and winked in response, with my healthy right eye.

How can you say to your brother, "Brother, let me take the speck
out of your eye," when you yourself fail to see the plank in your own
eye? You hypocrite, first take the plank out of your eye, and then you
will see clearly to remove the speck from your brother's eye.

LUKE 6:42

QUARANTINE ROOMS

One of my favorite parts of writing novels is the research. I love finding little bits and pieces of life gone by and then including them in my books. I recently learned about quarantine rooms, often found in larger homes of the Victorian era.

Before hospitalization was commonplace, most people were sick—and then got well—at home. Of course, others lived in those homes too—others who did not want to share the patient's ailments, many of which were easily transmitted. So the quarantine room was developed, a small room where an infected person would be kept isolated till she recovered . . . or died.

The goal was not to punish the unwell but rather to protect others from contracting disease. We understand that not everyone in this world is healthy; it's a world rife with physical sickness. And with sin. It's important for us to understand that not everyone in this world is spiritually healthy either.

Some don't know they are sick, and it's good for us to speak of—and to—them patiently. There are others who intend to do harm by spreading illness or not warning others to protect themselves—what we would call criminal transmission of an illness. Christians have the heart of the Lord, which means we are tenderly disposed toward and forbear much from others. Still, anyone who cares for a person with a contagious illness must take precautions not to get sick herself.

In our faith and in our emotional lives, we must likewise protect ourselves. Speak up to someone who is harming you (or yours), and if there is positive change, you have won a brother or sister back. But if someone insists on causing trouble, unwellness, or division, it's perhaps better to remove yourself from her malignant presence than to catch something deadly yourself.

Warn a divisive person once, and then warn them a second time.
After that, have nothing to do with them. You may be sure that
such people are warped and sinful; they are self-condemned.

TITUS 3:10-11

October 16

PUMPKIN CRISIS

A few years ago, the suppliers of the most famous brand of canned pumpkin had a crop failure. Because of that, canned pumpkin was in short supply, and the store shelves were empty before the end of October—and I had plans for pumpkin bars, pumpkin bread, and Thanksgiving pumpkin pie. What could I do?

Muttering Proverbs 31 over and over to myself, I drove from store to store and found a few cans. There were cans of organic pumpkin, but for some reason, we just didn't like it. Different brands of pumpkin tasted funny. We'd developed a taste for one brand of pumpkin and one brand alone. (I ended up buying a case online!)

Likewise, I took great pride in baking homemade cakes for my children and was shocked when my daughter told me she liked the little, wrapped snack cakes in the grocery store aisle better. "But they're full of preservatives!" I informed her. "I *like* preservatives!" she responded. She always requested those snack cakes in her lunches. She'd developed a taste for them!

With regular consumption, we can train our taste buds to prefer that which is good for us or that which is not. "Sow a thought and you reap an action; sow an act and you reap a habit; sow a habit and you reap a character; sow a character and you reap a destiny," says Ralph Waldo Emerson. There's nothing wrong with preferring a type of pumpkin or snack cake, but my family's insistence that we do what we've always done made me look at my other habits. A few situations immediately fell under consideration—for example, my overconsumption of TV. Was I training myself to hunger for non-nutritious media rather than God's sweet Word?

Are you?

◦⟋⟍⟋

How sweet are your words to my taste,
sweeter than honey to my mouth!

PSALM 119:103

FAMILY CONNECTIONS

My family tells a funny story about a young cousin who was asked to hold a flashlight for our grandfather while he looked into a dark area. The cousin took the flashlight in hand and vigorously shook it up and down. When someone asked what she was doing, she replied that it was what Grandpa did when he held the flashlight, so she was doing likewise.

Our grandfather had what's called an essential tremor. I have it, too, as do several other family members. It runs in families. Families can be prone to have straight teeth, have a disposition toward mental illness, or have an innate ability with language or numbers, or all of these things. Often these traits are passed on from one generation to the next.

An inheritance can be monetary as well as genetic. Good parents save money, if they can, enabling them to bequeath something to their children, who will go and do likewise.

As pleasant as it is to receive a financial or personal bequest, nothing measures up to the spiritual legacy left by godly parents. God's commandment not to worship idols comes with a promise and a warning. Do not bow to idols; if you do, punishment will come to your children and grandchildren. But if you worship and love God and keep his commandments, future generations will be blessed.

We don't have much control over the physical characteristics we pass on to our kids, nor sometimes over the financial bequests we might make. But each of us has the choice to pass along a precious legacy that will live long after our names are forgotten. Let's make that choice!

You shall not make for yourself an image in the form of anything in heaven above or on the earth beneath or in the waters below. You shall not bow down to them or worship them; for I, the LORD your God, am a jealous God, punishing the children for the sin of the parents to the third and fourth generation of those who hate me, but showing love to a thousand generations of those who love me and keep my commandments.

EXODUS 20:4-6

October 18

FRUITFUL AND WITHERING BRANCHES

The sky was that clear blue peculiar to autumn—or maybe the sky just looks bluer against the dry, wheat-colored grass it bumps up against. In any case, it was a perfect day for a drive to a local fruit stand. My dessert menu was ready to move on from berries to pears!

After parking, I noticed a wild pear tree next to the little market. Its branches were absolutely burdened with fruit, and the sweet, ripe scent drew not only me but some yellow jackets as well. I walked as close as I dared. Although the tree wasn't carefully tended, it was lush; the weight of the pears pulled the branches toward the ground—easy pickings. There were even pears growing on the suckers sprouting from the tree's base.

We made a purchase, and then I took my haul home and wandered out to the backyard, where I'd just begun to dig up the summer squash plants. The night before, I'd plucked a vibrant yellow squash blossom, but now it was wilting, withering, and beginning to go brown and dry. If I had left it, could I have had just one more squash? I thought so.

Anything connected to the main plant continues to bear fruit, sometimes even without careful tending. But once removed from the life source, it begins to die and decay immediately. I walked back into my office, where I dedicated myself anew to staying connected with God. I placed my Bible where I'd see it each morning and programmed worship music into my playlist.

I am the true vine, and my Father is the gardener. . . . If you do not remain in me, you are like a branch that is thrown away and withers.

JOHN 15:1, 6

A HEFTY RETURN ON INVESTMENT

When our kids were younger, we had "memory-verse theater," in which they got to jump on the beds while reciting memory verses from a children's Bible; we would shine a flashlight on them so they'd have the spotlight for themselves. Twenty years later, it was such a blessing for us to hear our son recite back to us one of those verses. He's not jumping on the bed any longer (that I'm aware of!), but deep within him, dormant, are all of the verses he took to heart. They're at the ready when he needs them.

A few weeks ago someone dinged my daughter's car while she was at work. When she came out, she found a note on the windshield. Someone had seen it happen, wrote down the offender's license plate number, and offered to be a witness. The note was signed, "A Good Samaritan." Was this person a Christian? I don't know. But it's a pleasure to see Scripture remain part of the common culture.

We don't know which of our deeds—toward our friends or family, in our jobs, or online—will sprout and grow into a healthy plant and bear fruit. Sometimes it seems like we're sending hope and love forward into a dark hole. But there is at least one time that we can be assured our efforts will bear fruit: when it involves the Word. God says it never returns to him empty; it always accomplishes what he desires it to. And when we pass it on, in large ways or small, we, too, can be assured of a hefty return on our investment.

*As the rain and the snow come down from heaven, and do not return
to it without watering the earth and making it bud and flourish,
so that it yields seed for the sower and bread for the eater, so is my word
that goes out from my mouth: It will not return to me empty, but will
accomplish what I desire and achieve the purpose for which I sent it.*

ISAIAH 55:10-11

October 20

TOFU

Our daughter is a vegetarian, so we've learned to cook food that doesn't have meat in it yet still tastes very good. (Some members of our family still don't believe this is possible, but we'll hush them for now.) One of the most common vegetarian proteins that we use is tofu. Now the thing about tofu is that it pretty much tastes like nothing. But that is not a bad thing! Instead, it readily and easily takes on the flavors of whatever you cook it with, or season it with, or spice it with. Versatile, right?

Tofu can be made into sweet smoothies (add fruit and honey, and top with granola), or it can be made into a savory Asian stir-fry (add vegetables, rice noodles, and soy sauce). It can be made into a fine lasagna. It can be made into cheesecake. You cook it alongside whatever you want it to taste like.

We humans are like that. We readily take on the "flavor" of whatever we spend the most time with. Ever come back from a visit to a foreign country or a state far from where you live, y'all? You pick up the regional speech habits and accents. Hang out with friends who like big accessories? I foresee bling in your future. This adaptability is a good thing; we're able to change when circumstances require it. But it can be a bad thing, too, if we're not careful. Scripture forewarns us: do not be misled—bad company corrupts good character.

I don't mind being a character, and I'll bet you don't either. But we want to keep ours healthy and holy. I've got to surround myself with people whose "flavor" I don't mind taking on, and that way we'll all be a part of a tasty, healthy dish.

Let us consider how we may spur one another on toward love and good deeds, not giving up meeting together, as some are in the habit of doing, but encouraging one another—and all the more as you see the Day approaching.

HEBREWS 10:24-25

October 21

TIMES AND SEASONS

Late autumn is a lovely time to take a walk; I can see things in fall's stark beauty that I can't see at any other time of the year. Once, while walking through the woods, I could see a "widow maker," a tree that had fallen and was resting, unstable, against another thin tree. I knew that when it fell the rest of the way, it would do so quickly and take down whatever or whoever was in its path.

In my backyard, after the leaves had all fallen from the Japanese maples, I spotted an elaborate bird's nest in the upper branches. I had seen its residents but had not seen where they lived . . . till then. I like to prune my shrubs and trees in late autumn, because without the cover of leaves, I can clearly see where they need clipping to take on the shape I'd like them to have.

The starkness of the dormant season reveals things to me that I can't see in the dense lushness of spring and summer.

Although I don't like undergoing dormant seasons in my own life, times when I wonder if God loves me still or has a purpose or a plan for me, I know that those quiet seasons allow both of us to make assessments and adjustments where needed. Seasons are completely within God's control, both on earth and in my life. He rearranges as he sees fit, and it's always for his good—and mine. The changes he makes are always beneficial: remove the fallen, dangerous tree; show me life where I'd not seen it before; help shape me in the way we both know is best. I have come to love our quiet seasons.

He changes times and seasons;
he deposes kings and raises up others.
He gives wisdom to the wise
and knowledge to the discerning.
He reveals deep and hidden things;
he knows what lies in darkness,
and light dwells with him.

DANIEL 2:21-22

BABY GATES

I bought our baby gate before the baby was even born. I wanted to be ready! We also bought snaps to lock toilet seats down and plugs to go into electrical sockets so little hands couldn't poke little toys into them and get a shock. We made sure that rugs were taped down, and trinkets that could be swallowed were all put away.

The gate proved useful much longer than the other safety devices. When our kids were toddlers and even once they were in elementary school, they would wander, kind of blindly, in the middle of the night toward the bathroom. The bathroom was located right next to the stairs, so to avoid a midnight tumble, we kept the baby gate up for a few more years. No harm in being safe!

We once knew a couple who wanted to care for our children, and their backyard had a steep drop-off to train tracks. There was a gate, but when we politely asked if they'd please lock it while our children were there, they laughed at us and refused. It was not a place I felt comfortable dropping off my children.

As people of faith, we're not to panic over what might be, what may come, or what-ifs. God will not let us tumble down the stairs or off a cliff. We can trust him to lead us in the dark. But because we are made in his image, he has also gifted us with reason, and he expects us to use it. Pray, prepare, progress!

A prudent person foresees danger and takes precautions.
The simpleton goes blindly on and suffers the consequences.

PROVERBS 27:12, NLT

October 23
BURNING OUT

Before that glorious day when my neighbor Toni gave her little-used Kitchen-Aid mixer to me, I used a handheld mixer. It was easy to use and didn't take up a lot of space on the counter. One problem, though—it wasn't very powerful. It was fine for cookie dough or cake batter, but one day when I tried to plow through some heavy, bread-like dough, it protested. After whining for a few minutes, it belched smoke and then went quiet. I had burned it out by asking it to do more than it was designed to do.

I thanked it for its many years of service, laid it to rest, and took a few months off from baking—which actually turned out to be okay, because I was a little burned out too. By the time Toni gave her mixer to me, I was reinvigorated and excited to be back in front of an oven. Time away had helped me to realize how much I had missed baking, allowed the creative part of my brain to begin thinking of new recipes, and helped me reclaim baking as a want-to—not must-do—activity.

When the Lord tells us—not asks us—to rest, it's in our best interest. Just as the brain clears the junk out when we sleep, our lives need the revitalization that rest allows. Observing the Sabbath by resting shows trust, too. We are not depending on our own constant, wearying efforts, which lead to burnout. We're trusting in God's endless store to provide the right "recipes" to us at the right times. All things become a joy again!

The new KitchenAid has a powerful motor and has not yet burned out. But I don't turn it on every day, either.

I gave them my decrees and regulations so they could find life by keeping them. And I gave them my Sabbath days of rest as a sign between them and me. It was to remind them that I am the LORD, who had set them apart to be holy.

EZEKIEL 20:11-12, NLT

DESIGNER SHADES

What's the first thing you do when you walk into a dark room on a dull autumn evening? Turn on the light! Lights allow us to enjoy books, company, and evening activities. Soft light is pleasant at dinner. Night-lights help us not to be afraid of the dark when we're kids or not to trip on the way to the bathroom at three in the morning when we're adults.

Rarely do plain bulbs just hang from the ceiling—they'd be an ugly fire hazard. There's almost always a cover—lovely etched glass, maybe, or a beautiful shade. I have several faux Tiffany lampshades in my home. Before the lights are turned on, you can see that the shade is pretty, a rainbow of cut glass held together by strips of lead. But it's a little dull, and really, in a large room you don't notice it at all. But when I tug the toggle and turn the light on, the stained-glass beauty shines. It's beautiful *and* useful.

Like light, Jesus shines in dark places so they aren't fearsome anymore. When he lives in us, we become his light too. Your life is like a lampshade. You're beautiful and unique, but you were made to look your best when the light of Jesus shines brightly inside you and through you to illuminate whatever room you are in. Then you not only help people see so they don't stumble anymore, you light up every room you walk into.

Be sure to let everyone see your beautiful lampshade by turning your light up just a little brighter.

You are the light of the world—like a city on a hilltop that cannot be hidden. No one lights a lamp and then puts it under a basket. Instead, a lamp is placed on a stand, where it gives light to everyone in the house.

MATTHEW 5:14-15, NLT

October 25

LESSONS FROM SQUIRRELS

One week a really big storm blew into my town. The electricity kept flickering on and off, and the howling wind made me think of all the unfriendly things that could be outside. Then suddenly, the lights snapped off, and a terrible cracking noise stopped us in our tracks. We all stood absolutely still before running to the window to see what had happened.

A huge tree had cracked and fallen, just missing our house. We thanked God for keeping us safe . . . but what about our chubby animal family that had been squirreling away nuts in their home in that tree?

The next day we stepped out onto the patio to see what had happened. The largest tree in our backyard had broken nearly in half. All that was left was a jagged, sharp-edged stump. The rest of the tree had thudded into our yard and spilled over into our neighbors' yard. The squirrels, who had been faithfully storing nuts in that tree in preparation for winter, looked as confused as we did.

Why that tree? they seemed to ask. *It seemed so strong. We never expected this to happen.* But then we watched as they carted their stash of nuts out of that tree and into another one standing firmly nearby. They were busily starting over, in an even stronger tree trunk—one that had many more warm fir branches and had proved its superior strength by surviving the storm.

Life is often worrisome and dangerous. The "tree" we don't expect to fall does. And we scratch our heads and wonder why. But soon we see that the roof wasn't hit and everyone is safe, and while it may not be what we planned for, we are able to move forward with a new plan and stash our acorns somewhere new, stronger, and even better.

If you say, "The LORD is my refuge,"
and you make the Most High your dwelling,
no harm will overtake you.

PSALM 91:9-10

SQUIRRELING THINGS AWAY

I love the phrase "squirreling things away," because it's so wonderfully evocative; anyone who has watched a squirrel scamper to a hidden nest or hollow tree, cheeks heavy with acorns, knows just what it means.

Some people don't squirrel anything away. They eat their acorns as soon as they get them and then have nothing left to get them through the wet and windy winter. Some people squirrel *everything* away for a rainy day that never comes. By faith we are led to a happy medium between these two extremes. Hoarders come to understand that acorns buried and forgotten can rot and be of no use. Spendthrifts come to understand that while the Lord will provide pleasure and joys today and tomorrow, we must save a little for that proverbial rainy day.

I love to look out my kitchen window and watch squirrels working together. One finds, another brings back to the nest. They are partners, each doing his share. I think we're to be like those squirrels. From what I have, I save some and share some. And you do the same. Jesus tells us we will be known by our love for one another, and James says our faith is proven by our deeds. When we have faith that the Lord will provide tomorrow as he does today, we needn't stuff our cheeks. When we have faith that he will bring joy tomorrow as he does today, we needn't party like there's no tomorrow.

Do not worry, saying, "What shall we eat?" or "What shall we drink?"
or "What shall we wear?" For the pagans run after all these things,
and your heavenly Father knows that you need them. But seek first
his kingdom and his righteousness, and all these things will be given
to you as well. Therefore do not worry about tomorrow, for tomorrow
will worry about itself. Each day has enough trouble of its own.

MATTHEW 6:31-34

October 27
WHAT'S NEXT?

Why me? Why now? Why this? I'm embarrassed to tell you that I have these phrases down pat, and that's because I say—or think—them more regularly than I wish I did. They kind of sound like whining, which I hate when my kids do it, but I don't seem to feel as bad about it when my own lips utter the words.

We were having guests over for dinner, and the food I'd made had all gone wrong. Burned, dry, and oversweet in turn. Pridefully, I had tried to make new things that I thought would impress. Well, my cooking was certain to make an impression—just not the one I had hoped for.

After my *Why me?* chorus, I felt a nudge in my heart to replace that with *What's next? What good can come of this? Show me.* As I said that prayer and set the disasters out on the serving counter, a certain peace overcame me. Our guests came, and no one raised an eyebrow, although I did pull one woman aside to confess how bad I felt that I'd ruined the meal. "Oh, this isn't ruined," she said. "To tell the truth, it had made me nervous to have you over before this because everything you served seemed so perfect, and our meals are rather plain."

My desire to be seen as a successful cook—and the pride that went along with it—had actually pushed away my greater desire, a deeper friendship with this woman. I'm not saying God wanted my food to go wrong, but he did show me that imperfection is tastier than perfection, and that seeking what good may come of something is more productive and peaceful than worrying and whining. Since then, we've had circumstances arise that were much more complex and painful than a spoiled meal, but the truth still holds. *What's next? What's good? Please show me.*

Show me the right path, O LORD;
point out the road for me to follow.
Lead me by your truth and teach me,
for you are the God who saves me.
All day long I put my hope in you.

PSALM 25:4-5, NLT

October 28
BREAD BASKET

You know that old joke, "I know what to make for dinner: reservations"? Having someone else make the food, serve the food, and clean up after is an absolute dream.

Many of the restaurants we visit serve a little appetizer: maybe chips with salsa, or a basket of bread with dipping oils. One favorite eatery serves hot rolls drenched in garlic butter. Or sometimes it's biscuits with butter and jam, or cornbread with honey. The best part? They'll refill the bread basket as many times as you want. For free!

Therein lies the problem, and I'm not just talking carbs. The meal is still ahead.

By the time that delicious and delightful meal arrives, we're full. We stick our forks in our entrees and take a few bites, but the food doesn't taste as good as we remembered. The bread had seemed like a treat at the time, but because we ate so much of it, we have no room left for the nourishing parts of our meals.

This happens in our spiritual lives, too. We fill ourselves up on TV, movies, books, or social media, using up our time and even our daily dose of concentration. By the time we turn our attention to God's Word—well, we're stuffed! Instead of having a little of the bread and a lot of the meal, we eat a whole basket of garlic rolls, and there's no room left for dinner.

Go ahead. Choose one biscuit: one TV show, something interesting on the Internet, or a few chapters of a great book. But be sure to save room for the main course every day. I'm trying to consume less of the empty entertainment so that I'll still be hungry for the Word of God.

<hr>

A person who is full refuses honey.

PROVERBS 27:7, NLT

DIAMOND OF GREAT PRICE

One morning during the course of my normal chores, I cast a glance at my wedding ring. I did a double take and looked more closely. And as I did, a cold feeling coursed through me. The center stone was missing.

That stone was the most valuable gem in the setting—the centerpiece, the main attraction. Beyond its monetary value, the diamond ring signified something more precious: since the day it was placed on my finger, it had been with me through every better and worse, sickness and health, richer and poorer. I needed to find that diamond.

I prayed and asked God to help me locate it. He doesn't always answer my prayers quickly or affirmatively, but this time he did. I made my way back into the bathroom and into the shower, where I found the gem resting right on the edge of the drain. I took it to a local jeweler, who reset the stone and advised me to have the prongs, which hold the diamond in, examined regularly to avoid this in the future. You can bet that I do that now!

Scripture tells us that the Kingdom of Heaven—all that is associated with God—is worth our leaving everything else we own to acquire. Because without it, nothing else matters. Once acquired, it cannot be lost. Jesus is our Bridegroom, there to see us through better and worse, sickness and health, richer and poorer. But it is still prudent to do a little checkup now and again to ensure everything is holding firm!

The Kingdom of Heaven is like a merchant on the lookout for choice pearls. When he discovered a pearl of great value, he sold everything he owned and bought it!

MATTHEW 13:45-46, NLT

GRACE-FILLED HOMES

There are any number of women's magazines that illustrate how to have a gracious home. Some women seem to have an instinct for this. They have the right amount of family photos and knickknacks about—enough to show you that theirs is a family home, but not so many that you're worried the next episode of *Hoarders* will be filmed there.

I've come to appreciate even more the women I know who have grace-*filled* homes. You are always welcome, whether or not the place is tidy. Honest fears and tears can tumble freely because you know you won't be judged. Children's friends run about, and if there isn't enough food, Mom or Dad have smaller portions. Furniture is meant to be used and people meant to be hugged. There aren't many magazines that talk about this kind of home, but they're the homes we want to return to.

I do want my home to be lovely, to have it reflect the habits and interests of my family. But even more, I want it to be a place with doors wide open, a place where people can come for a hug or a tissue or a meal or a night away. I want the things we talk about to be more important than the rooms we say them in. I want to wrap friends and family in the warm blanket of the Lord and show them that they are loved. Scripture admonishes us to love one another, since love is from God; God is love. Sharing that, I think, is the essence of a grace-filled home. My goal is to create a home that is both gracious and grace filled.

Do not forget to show hospitality to strangers, for by so doing some people have shown hospitality to angels without knowing it.

HEBREWS 13:2

CONDEMNED HOUSES

We drove by a plot of land that had recently been rezoned for a small shopping center. The trees had already been cleared, and we could see the older homes awaiting their executioner as well. They looked nice enough to me, actually, but someone had determined that they were in the way, so they, too, would be demolished. There was a notice posted on each—a condemnation notice—warning others to keep away.

Condemnation is such an ominous word that reading or saying it aloud weighs heavily on the heart. We have all been recipients of condemnation. Perhaps our work has been slammed; or our characters maligned; or we've been told through word, deed, or nonverbal communication that we are no good, of no value, unloved. Although it's difficult to bear when it comes from someone we know only casually or professionally, it's crippling when it comes from someone we had counted on to be there to support and not tear down: a spouse, a parent, a loved one, someone from our faith community.

Often, sadly, we Christians are known for our condemnation of others. In some cases the accusation is exaggerated, but sometimes we've earned it. It's too often said that we Christians are known more for what we're against than what we're for. We're quick to wag a finger and slow to offer a hand. I know I can be. But Jesus was not.

We're familiar with John 3:16; it's printed at the bottom of retail bags and held up on banners at sports stadiums. Less familiar are the verses that follow it. Jesus didn't come to wag a finger at the world, he tells us, but to save it. I'm going to rush to put my arm around the next person I know who thinks she is condemned and wrap her in love instead.

God did not send his Son into the world to condemn the
world, but to save the world through him.

JOHN 3:17

NOVEMBER

Twinkly Topiaries

Sometimes when the weather outside is cold, it's nice to have living greenery in the house. A topiary project is especially rewarding at this time of year because you can spread some battery-operated twinkle lights among the leaves.

WHAT YOU'LL NEED

Planter or flower pot (Terracotta pots are nice to use because they look good with French-inspired topiary, and they are relatively inexpensive.)

A topiary frame (found at craft stores or online)

Planting soil

A plant with 6 to 8 vines, about 6 inches long (Ivy works well because it doesn't require a lot of light; some herbs work well on smaller frames.)

Twinkle lights

DIRECTIONS

Fill your planter about halfway with soil. Place your plant into the pot, making sure to break up the roots a little at the base. Settle it in tightly, then pack soil around it till the pot is full.

Next, stick the topiary frame into the pot. Gently wind the vines through the frame.

Water your plant completely. As the vines grow out, continue to wind them through the frame. You can snip and trim with scissors, and as suckers start to grow from the base of the plant, wind those around the frame too!

Once your plant is grown enough, add some twinkle lights. Just remember to take out the battery before you water!

For this month's free printable, go to http://tyndal.es/homeandgarden.

November 1
THANKSGIVING TABLE

I've always said it takes a month to plan Thanksgiving dinner, a week to shop for it, a day to prepare it, and fifteen minutes to eat it. At least that's what it seems like on the work end of things. And yet, nothing brings me more pleasure than planning, preparing, and presenting my family's favorites for them. I'm already thinking about preparing this year's smoked turkey and estimating how many butternut soufflés it will take to ensure sufficient leftovers.

I had a friend who grew up in a family in which holidays were not celebrated. There was no turkey, no holiday meal—ever—and when they ate out, it was done for sober sustenance and not cheery celebration. There was no real presence of God in the family either. Perhaps the two circumstances were related? It's hard to celebrate if you feel discouraged, disheartened, and unloved. All of us feel that way some time or another; those of us who believe, though, have a God who unfailingly comes alongside us to offer comfort, grace, and companionship.

Even though it's cheap and easy, I would not eat a peanut butter and jelly sandwich on Thanksgiving. It would not satisfy me. It's worth the sacrifice to eat less expensively during the weeks beforehand and to spend time preparing for the celebration so that I can enjoy it to the full with loved ones.

Jesus offered us an expensive gift, a tremendous sacrifice, at great cost. He invites us to come near him to listen, to take in what is good, and to delight in the richest of fare—a life with him. Thanksgiving table, indeed!

Come, all you who are thirsty,
come to the waters;
and you who have no money,
come, buy and eat!
Come, buy wine and milk
without money and without cost. . . .
Listen, listen to me, and eat what is good,
and you will delight in the richest of fare.

ISAIAH 55:1-2

SALTY AND SWEET

I love holiday candy. I especially love M&M's, and we try to buy a bag of the specially colored "holiday" variety each season. No, not the little fun-sized bags. The king-sized bags! But I've learned something: although the first little disc is delicious, chocolaty, and sweet, and the tenth and even twentieth ones are pretty tasty, they get kind of dull after that. My taste buds become numb, I think; I taste almost nothing. Here's a sad truth: even the best sweets don't taste sweet, or even good, when you've had too many of them.

The same is true with salty snacks. A snack-sized bag of chips or pretzels is tasty. A family-sized bag all to myself? No thanks. The salt starts to hurt my tongue, and after a while the formerly tasty snacks just taste like paste. A way around this, for the inveterate snacker, is to blend sweet and salty together:

- a chocolate-dipped potato chip or pretzel
- a caramel with sea salt on top
- trail mix with nuts and candies mixed together

In life, if we have too many things that sweetly go our way, we eventually stop appreciating what we have. We can become greedy or impatient when something doesn't go the way we want. We lose the ability to wait or even share. Too many sad things—which cause salty tears—can bring a person down. But happy and sad, mixed together, actually enhance one another. The sad times make me grateful for what I have and make the happy times that much sweeter.

"The LORD gave me what I had, and the LORD has taken it away. Praise the name of the LORD!" In all of this, Job did not sin by blaming God.

JOB 1:21-22, NLT

BONSAI

One of the great pleasures of having adult children—once you get past the empty-nest mourning period—is to watch them kit out their own apartments. Although my son was understandably disappointed that we would not pull the engine from our dead SUV so he could have a *Top Gear*-style coffee table, he was able to indulge another interest: bonsai.

We went together to a bonsai nursery that employed master growers and gardeners. It was clear that they took their art seriously. They even offered bonsai babysitting for customers who purchased from them. If owners needed to go out of town, rather than leave their bonsai with an untrained stranger, they could drop it off for the best possible care. I half expected to have to undergo a background check before making our purchase.

My son selected a planter, the proper soil and food, and finally, a deciduous bonsai tree. It came with a lengthy instruction sheet that provided quite a bit of detail about pruning. Bonsai, after all, are known for their carefully controlled shapes, and what makes them unique is the precision required to shape each little tree in just the right way. According to the instruction sheet, pruning should be done in autumn during the tree's dormant season, and there were likely to be wounds after the shearing. A healthy tree could withstand the pruning, but the instructions also recommended applying a wound paste afterward to protect the tree from infection and to speed healing.

I thought about the Lord, who describes himself as a gardener. A more careful gardener could not be imagined. God tells us that he prunes us; he shapes us into the people he's created us to be. Pruning can be painful, as it often comes in the form of correction, rebuke, criticism, redirection, or withholding of things we think we want and need. And yet, he also applies the wound paste of love, of comfort, of patience, of fellowship. The tree that does not undergo regular pruning and shaping cannot be a bonsai.

Blessed is the one whom God corrects;
so do not despise the discipline of the Almighty.

JOB 5:17

AFTER THE CUT

After our bonsai master had convinced us that a bonsai plant requires regular, careful cuts, he showed us how to do the pruning.

"When you make the cuts," he said, "it's important that you use a special concave cutter. It limits the indentations on the base when you remove a branch. Then in order to prevent scarring and infection, you must gently apply wound paste." He showed us his wound paste, which was carefully measured and mixed.

The Lord himself is often the one who wounds us; this is a hard truth. Better the wounds of a friend than the kisses of an enemy, Scripture reminds us, and the person who does not discipline his child does not love him (see Proverbs 27:6; 13:24). But the discipline and training of a beloved child by a good parent is always carefully planned for growth and health, does not cause permanent damage, and is tended to afterward.

I want my body to be healthy and have a certain shape, but I do not always like the self-discipline and exercise that are required to get me there. I like to have Scripture spring to mind when advising a friend, but I can be lazy about memorizing and reading it. I want to be the person who offers shelter, love, and wisdom, but I don't always want to undergo the troubles necessary to earn that wisdom. God knows how to help me grow into the shape he has planned for me. While he sometimes allows painful circumstances to help me take that shape, he is also the binder and healer of my wounds, applying comfort and protection with his own hands.

[God] wounds, but he also binds up;
he injures, but his hands also heal.

JOB 5:18

PICK UP YOUR FORK

Our pastor was preaching a few weeks ago on church (in church!), and he said that people sometimes leave churches or ministries because they are not being fed. Now, that's definitely valid if you attend a church that does not use Scripture or doesn't have teaching available in addition to worship, fellowship, service opportunities, and all the other things we look for in a congregation. But what does "not being fed" really mean?

When we're infants, we are completely dependent upon our parents to feed us. As we grow, we begin to gain more autonomy in feeding ourselves. When we're toddlers, food is cut up for us in little bite-sized pieces and placed on a high-chair tray, perhaps, or a small plastic plate. Kindergarten sees us advance to sandwiches that we can help make, and high school students should be able to provide their own meals, even if they prefer Mom's cooking.

So why do we expect to be spoon-fed in our spiritual lives? If you're new to faith, then of course you need help. We all do then. But as we mature, we need to learn to feed ourselves. Finding a good church is a start, but nothing is stopping us from picking up and reading a Bible, finding a great teaching book, asking to be discipled, or listening to sermon podcasts. Pick up your fork! We've got a buffet to enjoy!

We have much to say about this, but it is hard to make it clear to you because you no longer try to understand. In fact, though by this time you ought to be teachers, you need someone to teach you the elementary truths of God's word all over again. You need milk, not solid food! Anyone who lives on milk, being still an infant, is not acquainted with the teaching about righteousness.

HEBREWS 5:11-13

AUTUMN-BLOOMING LILACS

First one bud appeared, and then a second. Within the week, my lilac trees were covered with tiny flower buds—again—and in November! Maybe it was the warm weather or something in the water, but to me it was a miracle. I love lilacs, and to get an unexpected double dose was a blessing indeed. It reminded me, just as winter was beginning to set in, *Don't worry, spring is coming around soon.*

That day I was recalling a friend who had died too young. And social media had passed along several other bits of bad news, things that seemed to unfairly strike good people already having hard times. Although I've been a believer for a long while, I admit to still asking God, "Why? What good can come of this? Why them?" Reading through Isaiah last week, I found one answer: "The devout are taken away, and no one understands that the righteous are taken away to be spared from evil" (57:1). Things will not always make sense to us, but they do to God. We have to trust him to do the right thing, all the time, even when we don't understand.

I *don't* understand more than I *do* understand, but this is one thing I know and can testify to: God is good, all the time, in all places, and all circumstances are filtered through his fingertips. "We know that in all things God works for the good of those who love him, who have been called according to his purpose" (Romans 8:28).

Is anything too hard for the Lord? No. He is able to bring good from bad, peace in times of hardship, beauty in place of ashes. The truth of it is, he answers yes many more times than he answers no. So go ahead. Ask. Why not? He can even make lilacs bloom in November!

I am the LORD, the God of all mankind. Is anything too hard for me?

JEREMIAH 32:27

MAKING A LIST, CHECKING IT TWICE

In November many of us start planning for the Christmas gifts we'll buy. I write out a list of everyone I'll need to buy for and review the money I budgeted and set aside months before to see how much I can spend. After years of overspending, I decided to start planning ahead. Hey, it's not like buying Christmas gifts at Christmas is a new idea. I know it's coming.

I've had times when I just headed to the mall with a credit card and started shopping without planning ahead or looking at my bank balance. One time an embarrassing thing happened. I went to the checkout counter with my haul of Christmas gifts and the cashier said, "I'm sorry, but your card is declined." I'm sure I mumbled something about a problem with the magnetic strip on the back of my card, but the truth of it was I hadn't planned ahead, and I'd hit my credit limit without realizing it. Christmas red and green is not supposed to represent my red face resulting from not enough green!

Planning ahead is important in many areas of life. I might want a new hobby, but do I have the time? I might want to redecorate my bedroom, but do I have the money? I might want to quit my job, but is there another one readily available? I might want to give everyone I love excessive gifts (I do, I really do), but I don't want to overspend. With anything you undertake, count the costs. That way, when the hard times come, you won't be surprised, burned out, overspent, or embarrassed.

Don't begin until you count the cost. For who would begin construction of a building without first calculating the cost to see if there is enough money to finish it? Otherwise, you might complete only the foundation before running out of money, and then everyone would laugh at you. They would say, "There's the person who started that building and couldn't afford to finish it!"

LUKE 14:28-30, NLT

RIGHT AT HAND

Here are some things it's okay for kids to say:

- "Teacher? Teacher! Teacher!" while sticking their hands way up in the air, needing help or recognition.
- "Mom? Mom? Mama? Mother? MOM!" when something has gone wrong and the solution is out of their range of experiences and abilities.
- "Dad? Can you come and look at this, please?"

It's a little sad when you grow up and are expected to care for things all by yourself. Is that really a good or valid expectation? I've mentioned that one of the things most comforting about renting a home rather than owning it is that when something goes wrong, you're not expected to fix it yourself. You dial 1-800-Landlord and someone comes over—soon, one hopes—to fix the problem and take care of the financial consequences. Mechanics, friends, doctors, dentists: all are at the ready to help in specific circumstances.

The good news is that even if we own our homes, are no longer in school, or don't have living mothers, we have someone we can call upon. God doesn't think we're too old or too mature for help, and he doesn't put our trouble back on us, saying as the world often does, "That's your problem, not mine." Instead, he is the finest teacher, parent, and landlord—he tells us he is happy to help. He calms our hearts, telling us not to fear, and then reassures us that he will assist, heal, and mend. We're never too old, too mature, or too independent—and we should never be too proud—to call on his name.

What is troubling you? What do you need help with? Come on, think of one thing, and then call upon him. He is right at hand.

I am the LORD your God
who takes hold of your right hand
and says to you, Do not fear;
I will help you.

ISAIAH 41:13

SIPPY CUPS

We were preparing the house for a visit from friends who were bringing their young children. We borrowed a crib and a high chair, and I went out and bought something my kids loved when they were little. Sippy cups!

I nursed both of my children, but by the time they were about nine months old, they became more interested in looking at what was going on around them during mealtimes than in nursing, so they graduated to sippy cups. I bought the lidded ones at first, and then—when the babies developed a sturdier grip—the cups with the built-in straws. Eventually the kids moved on to regular glasses and mugs, like the rest of the family.

As a joke, I put one of the newly purchased sippy cups up to my mouth. My grown kids didn't laugh—their mouths hung open in a combination of shock and embarrassment. "It's a joke!" I insisted.

Sippy cups are for wee ones, and it looks, er, unusual at best to see an adult drinking from one. First Peter tells us that newborn spiritual babies crave pure spiritual milk, but we're expected to move on, grow up. We move to soft foods, and then to having our meat cut up for us, till finally we can cut and consume meat on our own. It's the natural progression of healthy children—and of healthy Christians, too.

That day was a good reminder to me. Am I still eating pre-mashed food, soft teaching that is heavy on humor and illustration but thin on the Word? Am I drinking milk, which is easy to swallow and digest but leaves me feeling hungry? Or do I seek spiritual meat, which requires more effort to prepare and chew, but which nourishes for much longer and is necessary for growth? Adults, after all, choose and prepare their own meals!

Anyone who lives on milk, being still an infant, is not acquainted with the teaching about righteousness. But solid food is for the mature, who by constant use have trained themselves to distinguish good from evil.

HEBREWS 5:13-14

COOL BREEZES

It had been a really hard day in a really hard month. Everything that could go wrong *had* gone wrong. Bills were left unpaid, for now. Jobs looked iffy. My kids were struggling with their schedules and were crabby. A friend was going through a divorce, and another friend's child had been diagnosed with a mental illness. The house was in a wee bit of disarray. Or maybe not such a wee bit. I decided to do the only thing I could think of at that moment. I went to bed.

Once in bed, I lay there, thinking. The blinds were open, and as the sun set, the late autumn evening winds moved in, blowing a cool breeze over my sweaty forehead. Breezes always remind me of Jesus teaching Nicodemus that the Holy Spirit goes where he wants, like the wind. This gentle wind cooled and refreshed me, reminding me that when the big things are going wrong, I can be thankful for the small things.

This won't last forever. The hard things will pass. Just for this one minute, I need to find little things to be thankful for.

A cool breeze. A bed in a house that protects me from the elements. Clean water. Clean air. Antibiotics. Books. Jokes. Chocolate. Warm socks. Toothpaste.

My hands began to unclench a little, and I allowed myself to drift toward sleep. I'd wake in the morning with the same problems, but God had reminded me, in a breeze that continued throughout the evening and night, that he is there, he is present. He would be with me the next day, too, helping me face those things that seemed unsolvable, and I knew that those problems, too, would pass.

Meals with family. Good music. Indian food. My faith. My Savior.

Let all that I am praise the LORD;
may I never forget the good things he does for me.

PSALM 103:2, NLT

EASY STREET

I've moved many, many times in my life, but I keep wondering why I've never had a house on Easy Street! When we're going through tough times, it's easy to get angry at those who seem to have permanent residence on said avenue. Why don't they have it as hard as I do, or—even better—why don't I have it as easy as *they* do? Then I remember that Christianity is the upside-down faith. Jesus says that the first shall be last, and the last shall be first. Sometimes that means putting off now what we're going to be given eventually. Last now, first later.

The year is moving toward the end, and it's getting colder out. Plants go dormant, kind of like hibernating. This time of year, you might be mowing your lawn for the last time before winter comes, or pruning and deadheading spent blossoms. Are those wilted flowers worth much? They might be good in a compost bin, but that's about it. That's what God says will eventually happen to all the achievements of those who depend on their riches for their value. Later on, they won't be worth much at all. It's not that being rich is bad—the Kingdom needs those with resources to share with those who have little. But ultimately, wealth doesn't last.

Do you believe, deep inside, that everything will work out fairly someday?

Those who are rich should boast that God has humbled them. They will fade away like a little flower in the field. The hot sun rises and the grass withers; the little flower droops and falls, and its beauty fades away. In the same way, the rich will fade away with all of their achievements. God blesses those who patiently endure testing and temptation. Afterward they will receive the crown of life that God has promised to those who love him.

JAMES 1:10-12, NLT

POWER TOOLS

Christmas must be coming, because I've been seeing a bunch of ads on television for power tools.

I'm not sure if men are generally ripped off and don't get gifts the rest of the year, or if advertisers have figured out that if wives want more accomplished on their honey-do lists, buying cool tools is the way to go. Whatever the motivation, a few months before Christmas I start seeing ads in print, on the Internet, and on TV for large toolboxes topped with giant, red bows, and men in their pj's happily wielding new drills.

Besides being sleek and fun, those new tools truly are effective. Hubs was scraping out old grout from the shower surround with a pocketknife (!) till we bought him a multipurpose machine that had a whirring sanding head. With that, he got the job done in no time at all.

I finished early, ready for the game, he thought. *He finished early, more time for another project*, I thought. (He won.)

Not only was that job done more quickly but it was done better. Every little bit of grout was cleaned out, along with some underlying mold. The knife could not have done that. When the project was finished, it was perfect.

Just so, when the Lord calls us to something—missions, giving, serving, teaching, encouraging, or any of the thousands of other ways he may choose to use us—he equips us with exactly what we need. He doesn't send us into a large project with just a pocketknife. Oh no, he will provide the very best tool—his Spirit to guide, empower, and provide. Do not be afraid when you sense he is calling you into a new season, a new arena. If he's given you the vision, he'll provide the power!

You will receive power when the Holy Spirit comes on
you; and you will be my witnesses in Jerusalem, and in all
Judea and Samaria, and to the ends of the earth.

ACTS 1:8

MAKING THINGS PALATABLE

My son's friend was joining us for dinner, and he announced that he absolutely could not eat the polenta and prosciutto I was serving that night. It sounded awful to him. "How about ham and grits?" I asked. "Sure," he replied, happy. Polenta vs. grits, prosciutto vs. ham—exactly the same foods, but renamed in order to make them palatable.

There was no harm done in this case, and we laugh about it to this day, but renaming things isn't always benign. One thing many of us are tempted to rename is sin. *He's not arrogant; he's moody. It's not a lie; it's stretching the truth. It's not wrath; it's a short temper.* We soft-pedal the sins of others because either we don't want to face the truth about those we love or we're afraid to confront them. We change the names of our own sins because we don't want to own them. Owning our sins, we mistakenly believe, condemns us.

Sin stands between us and God, and his love and sacrifice make it clear that he desires to be near us and to have us draw near to him. John 3:17 tells us that Jesus did not come into the world to condemn it but to save it. Confessing our sins does not condemn us—it saves us. It frees us not only for intimacy with our Lord but for intimacy with others we do not want to push away by our bad behavior.

The way to reinstate that intimacy is to own our sin, call it what it is, and humbly ask those who have sinned against us to own their sin. Then repentance is at hand, forgiveness is available, and often reconciliation is possible. Which is what we all want, isn't it?

Woe to those who call evil good
and good evil,
who put darkness for light
and light for darkness,
who put bitter for sweet
and sweet for bitter.

ISAIAH 5:20

SERVE THE SHEPHERD, NOT THE SHEEP

We once cared for an Australian sheepdog, a canine that was bred to care for sheep. Sheepdogs are working dogs. The Aussie was most unhappy in our small backyard.

Sheepdogs round up sheep when they go astray. They're not afraid to nip at the sheeps' heels when they're breaking away from the pack or heading in a direction where they would be in danger. Sheepdogs are tireless in their work; they're willing to climb steep hills and run long distances in order to care for the sheep, keep them safe, and direct them to green pastures. The thing is, they do not do this for the praise or affection of the sheep they care for. They do it for the affection and praise of the shepherd they serve.

We live in a people-pleasing world. Good manners, while important, do not preclude gentle biblical honesty in the right context. Scripture tells us that those who teach will be held to a stricter standard. What does that standard measure against? Biblical truth. And who teaches? Truly, all of us at some time, place, and circumstance.

Being nice, which means always being agreeable and avoiding confrontation or offending anyone for any reason, is not a fruit of the Spirit. But kindness and gentleness are. Sometimes the kindest thing we can do for a friend heading for a ravine is to run after her and warn her, even if it feels to her like a nip on the heel. As for my part, when I'm the recipient of such a nip, I'll remember that a good friend is bravely risking my displeasure to serve our Shepherd and protect me from harm.

The LORD is my shepherd, I lack nothing. . . .
He guides me along the right paths
for his name's sake.

PSALM 23:1, 3

November 15

RIKER!

Once during a sermon, our pastor spoke about the importance of a father's role in a child's life and mentioned that a child's first word is often *Dada*. On the way out to the car after the service, I asked my husband, "So what does it say about our parenting that our kids' first words were *dog* and *Riker*?"

Dog we can understand; our daughter loved animals—and still does. But *Riker*? It came from my letting our son sit on my lap while I watched *Star Trek: The Next Generation* when he was a baby. He'd heard the character's name over and over and liked it, and he would throw his fat little fist in the air and shout, "Riker!"

As the kids grew, I noticed them fighting quite a bit. They'd been watching a TV show with two aardvarks, brother and sister, who constantly bickered. Once I banned the show, my kids' bickering quieted down too.

In later years, we all loved watching *Sherlock Holmes* on TV. After a few episodes, I noticed we were saying "I shall" more than most of our fellow Americans, a habit that persists to this day.

Truth is, we pick up the word choices, habits, and intonations of people we watch and listen to. Sometimes this is relatively harmless, but sometimes—for instance, when gossip, condescension, verbal abuse, or sarcasm are involved—it is not. That is why we are commanded to estrange ourselves from unrepentant people who persist in harmful habits and methods, lest we become harmers ourselves.

Do you have a few "God with skin on" people—mature believers whose language is tempered with grace and salt—in your life, whom you can pattern your speech after? And who is listening to you, and what habits and methods are they picking up? It's worth thinking and praying about. So I shall!

Follow my example, as I follow the example of Christ.

1 CORINTHIANS 11:1

INCENSE BURNERS

I love homey scents—potpourri, fragrant candles, linen water gently misted over the sheets. I love incense, too; its heavy, scented smoke reminds me of weightier matters.

We humans are sensory beings. A whiff of cologne on a passing stranger might call to mind a long-forgotten friend who wore the same scent. The smell of fresh apples summons recollections of autumn; the fragrance of lilacs evokes the memory of a beloved, deceased grandmother. Incense is used throughout Scripture as a sensory reminder of God's presence.

Exodus 30 records that the Lord instructed Moses, "Make an altar of acacia wood for burning incense. . . . Put the altar in front of the curtain that shields the ark of the covenant law—before the atonement cover that is over the tablets of the covenant law—where I will meet with you" (verses 1, 6).

In Revelation 8:2-4 we read, "I saw the seven angels who stand before God, and seven trumpets were given to them. Another angel, who had a golden censer, came and stood at the altar. He was given much incense to offer, with the prayers of all God's people, on the golden altar in front of the throne. The smoke of the incense, together with the prayers of God's people, went up before God from the angel's hand."

Some churches incorporate incense into their celebrations and services, but even if yours does not, bringing incense into your home from time to time can serve as a reminder: God is here!

Make an incense blended as by the perfumer, seasoned with salt, pure and holy.
You shall beat some of it very small, and put part of it before the testimony
in the tent of meeting where I shall meet with you. It shall be most holy
for you. And the incense that you shall make according to its composition,
you shall not make for yourselves. It shall be for you holy to the LORD.

EXODUS 30:35-37, ESV

WHO'S LEADING WHOM?

My husband thinks it's really funny when he sees a dog walking its owner. The dog pulls the owner along at its own pace, out in the front, in the direction it wants to go. If it's a big dog, it can be stronger than the owner, and it's really a sight to behold when the master is being tugged along.

What we call a dog *leash* the British call a *lead*. It makes good sense— whatever is on the end of it is meant to be led by the master. When a dog gets ahead of its master, we know something isn't right. Who's leading whom?

I have to admit, it was convicting one day when I considered this. I had a number of legitimate concerns in mind, and I was letting those fears lead me down all sorts of dark paths. I let one tug me down into worries of what might happen financially; I let another pull me down the dark corridor of poor health. When I finally caught my breath, other fears pulled me down the road of concern for my children's futures, for my friends' marriage.

Who was leading whom? I knew. Fears were leading me.

For a Christian, this is as wrong as the dog pulling the master down the road. Love drives out fear, Scripture says, and we are led by God himself, who loves us, is good and in control, and can be trusted. As we rest in God's love, we can follow him without fear.

God is love. Whoever lives in love lives in God, and God in them. . . .
There is no fear in love. But perfect love drives out fear, because fear has
to do with punishment. The one who fears is not made perfect in love.

1 JOHN 4:16, 18

REFLECTED LIGHT

There are many long, dark months where I live in the Pacific Northwest. Months in which most days have very little light. Gray days, days with drizzle and rain that start dark and end dark with some tiny pinpricks of light in between. Our friends in northern Alaska have it even worse in winter. There are days when the sun doesn't shine at all! Residents in sunless or sun-deficient climates are susceptible to SAD—seasonal affective disorder. Depression resulting from lack of light.

The citizens of one Norwegian town have found a solution to their similarly dark days. Because they live in a valley that is dark five or six months out of the year, they have erected giant mirrors on the tops of some nearby mountains. They position these mirrors so that the sunlight is reflected into those dark valleys, bringing some relief, some hope, something to look forward to. See? Summer is just around the corner. Hold on!

Life on earth has some dark seasons too, doesn't it? Months where things are dark, or are bright for only a short time before depressing news descends again, trying to drag us down with it. We needn't allow it to, though. Seek some warmth from a sunny friend, a passage of Scripture, a funny movie, a book you've always loved, or a favorite song. When you're the one in the sun, reflect a little of it on your loved ones with a cheery word, an encouraging verse, a funny video clip, or a lunch date.

We will not be free of intermittent darkness while in this world, but when we reflect the Son, we're able to pass the time more cheerfully, more hopefully. One day, the darkness will be dispelled, and we'll all rejoice together. Hold on!

Now we see only a reflection as in a mirror; then we shall see face to face.
Now I know in part; then I shall know fully, even as I am fully known.

1 CORINTHIANS 13:12

TRANSITIONS

It came time to replace the worn-out carpeting in our house, and we had such fun choosing and ordering the new flooring. After we had selected the new carpet and hardwood, the sales associate led us to another set of products. "What are these?" I asked. "Transitions," she said. "They go between the carpet and the wood, or between the wood and the tile, smoothing the way so that no one will trip and get hurt."

So we bought some transitions to bridge the gaps between the different flooring materials and had those installed too. When everything was done, our floors were flawless and the pathways were smooth. As I gave them one last approving look one night as I turned the lights out, I thought about a different set of transitions—those that move us from one stage of life to the next.

Honestly, I don't like them. It makes me nervous—and excited, too—when things change from one comfortable, familiar circumstance to the next unknown adventure. New job, new town, new church, new calling, new friends or family. I rarely know where to place my foot in the new venture, and I'm worried I'll make a misstep and tumble, maybe bringing someone down with me. I don't like to disappoint. I don't like to fail. But God calls me to risk; without risk, faith would not be required.

When Jesus calls us out upon the water, he holds out his hand and bids us to keep our eyes on him. He will not let us drown or sink, and faith in Christ will never lead to ultimate disappointment. We can trust him through all of life's transitions, because he is always the bridge who smooths and protects the way.

The LORD makes firm the steps
of the one who delights in him;
though he may stumble, he will not fall,
for the LORD upholds him with his hand.

PSALM 37:23-24

November 20

BAKERY IMPERFECTS

When I was a teenager, I worked in a bakery. It was a most wonderful place to work; one of the perks was that any broken or imperfect cookies or baked goods were given to the staff to eat. I happened to love Linzer torte cookies, and it was a big delight when one was cracked or smeared. Down the hatch it would go.

The bakery owner wanted only perfect specimens for his customers. The customers were paying good money and had high expectations, and the baker had his reputation to uphold. Truth was, though, those imperfect cookies tasted just as good as the "perfect" ones. Further, the "perfect" ones being sold weren't really perfect. Some had more chips than others. Some had slightly browned edges. Some had slightly runny cream. Perhaps others had been pulled out of the oven a little too early and were soon soft rather than crisp. No one noticed, because they tasted so good. The important thing was to get them home for a snack or dessert!

I was thinking on this as the holiday baking season approached. Nearly everything we do in this life will be imperfect. If we expect our children, our ministries, our jobs, our projects, or our churches to be perfect, we will live in a constant state of unmet expectations. With the exception of God, no one is perfect, and therefore our offerings are always imperfect. Even God's creations, here on earth, are presently imperfect. And yet he chooses to love and work through them. Don't worry if you aren't perfect or if your offering isn't perfect; God cares about the heart.

So if the priesthood of Levi, on which the law was based, could have achieved the perfection God intended, why did God need to establish a different priesthood? . . .

The law appointed high priests who were limited by human weakness.
But after the law was given, God appointed his Son with an oath,
and his Son has been made the perfect High Priest forever.

HEBREWS 7:11, 28, NLT

ANOINTED

I was cleaning out the pantry one day and was amazed by the number of condiments, especially the oils, that I found therein. Sesame seed oil for Asian dishes, walnut oil for salads, apricot kernel oil, almond oil, canola oil, olive oil. The bottles sat quietly in the dark, waiting to be summoned forward into the bright kitchen for good use.

Throughout history, oil has been dear—costly—because it takes so much of something to produce just a teaspoon of the oil, the essence that is squeezed out of it. Extra virgin olive oil comes from the first press of the olive and is the purest, and therefore the most expensive, kind of olive oil. We read in 2 Kings that when Elisha wanted to bless the widow who had cared for him, he asked for God to supernaturally provide oil till she could pay her debts.

Oil can also represent the Holy Spirit; Luke 4 tells us that the Spirit of the Lord *anointed* Jesus, evoking images of kings, prophets, and priests who were anointed with precious oil. Like oil, the Spirit is dear and precious, and it came to humanity at a great price. Living within us, the Holy Spirit fills us with the essence of God.

Perhaps the most poignant use of oil is when Mary poured a pint of the essence of spikenard over Jesus' feet as a way to show extreme honor and value. While Martha served (something we might do easily and willingly), Mary gave sacrificially in a way that others may have been embarrassed to do. And yet that gift perfumed the whole house and has lived on as an example of devotion.

What can I offer, something close at hand and dear to me, as a freely given expression of my devotion?

Mary took about a pint of pure nard, an expensive perfume; she poured it on Jesus' feet and wiped his feet with her hair. And the house was filled with the fragrance of the perfume.

JOHN 12:3

November 22

WAKE UP, SLEEPYHEAD!

One of my friends recently used social media to ask for advice on how to get her teenage son out of bed in the morning. The suggestion we deemed most likely to succeed was a mild cattle prod. That made me giggle—but not too loudly, because I have been known to hit the snooze button on our phone's alarm clock time and time again myself. I can set the alarm to sound like nature calls, to quote funny lines from a movie, or—a recent favorite—to play Spanish guitar music. As a result, though, I don't find my alarm all that alarming anymore.

When Scripture speaks of waking up, it's mostly as a response to danger—creditors coming, the devil chasing, or a thief in pursuit. I don't know about you, but with any of those trailing me, I think I'd definitely be awake—and alarmed.

When alarms are quiet or gentle, they lull us into complacency till it's too late: we've already missed a class or an appointment, or we're late for work. The Lord reminds us several times to be awake and alert. He will return like a thief in the night, quickly, unexpectedly. Our lives may be demanded from us this very day—so be prepared! Those intending to do harm do not warn us in advance, of course, but those who want us to be ready to face a new day with gladness send reminders. It's good when we turn them up loud enough to get our attention!

Everything exposed by the light becomes visible—and everything that is illuminated becomes a light. This is why it is said: "Wake up, sleeper, rise from the dead, and Christ will shine on you." Be very careful, then, how you live—not as unwise but as wise.

EPHESIANS 5:13-15

MONOGRAMS

We have a few personalized things around our home: a rug with the letter *B* in the center, and a plaque or two with our names on them. Not much, though. So I was somewhat surprised when my son told me that he would like some monogrammed clothing. I teased at first. "You mean, JBQ—Just Be Quiet?" or "CYR—Clean Your Room?" This was not met with gales of laughter nor with agreement. After the gentle teasing was over, I did order something monogrammed—it was a reasonable request—and upon its arrival it brought great joy and fulfillment.

I'd never much liked monogrammed towels or cuffs, because in some way they seemed stuffy or snobby. But looked at from another angle, they simply express gentle pride in oneself and especially in one's family. Many a child has grown up being told, "We don't do that in this family." Said appropriately, it's not meant to shame but to guide the child into good and righteous behavior as they identify those behaviors in the people around them. When you're loved, cherished, and welcomed, it feels good to identify with your family.

When I got married, I took my husband's name. It took some getting used to, but it's the only name I identify with now. When I became a Christian, my name didn't change, but my identity did. Now I can barely recall a time when I did not identify myself by that family name, *Christian*. It's my name, it's my identity, and I'm very happy that my name is monogrammed onto Christ's heart, and his onto mine.

I [the LORD] have written your name on the palms of my hands.

ISAIAH 49:16, NLT

WE'LL LEAVE THE LIGHT ON

The day after Thanksgiving, I put candles on all of our windowsills to begin the celebration of Advent in advance of Christmas. The candles aren't actual flame-burning candles; they're battery operated and firesafe. But they flicker, and they are golden, and when you drive up to the house when it's dark outside (and it's getting dark pretty early by the end of November), they cast a welcoming glow. I have a dozen or more of them. They're hard to miss.

As I placed fresh batteries into the candles this year, I was reminded of an old commercial for a hotel chain, which said, "We'll leave the light on for you." I've been on many a road trip where we've pushed it for one more hour, one more town, one hundred more miles. A place beckoning in the distance with a warm light and a warm room was a most welcome sight.

Jesus tells us that we who believe in and follow him are the light of the world. He puts us on a hill—meaning he raises us high enough in the culture, in one way or another—so that our deeds and lives can be seen, even from a distance. When we behave badly, that is seen. But when we use our light to beckon the weary, the worn out, those who are feeling a little uneasy because it's getting dark out again, then we are doing exactly what we were created to do.

This little light of mine, I'm going to let it shine. How about you?

You are the light of the world. A town built on a hill cannot be hidden.
Neither do people light a lamp and put it under a bowl. Instead they
put it on its stand, and it gives light to everyone in the house.

MATTHEW 5:14-15

BATTERY OPERATED

Till last year, I had known nothing of the wonder of Swedish batteries. You can buy them at the big-box store that started in Sweden. The batteries do what the bunny ones promise to do: they keep going and going and going. And they're cheap!

Because the little lights shining in my windows throughout the holiday season don't have automatic timers on them, they often stay on for many hours each afternoon and evening. That uses a lot of juice, because they're working hard. I had been thinking of giving up my beloved candles because of the cost of the batteries, till the Scandinavians came to my rescue. Now a couple of large boxes of batteries gets us through the whole season. The batteries, hidden and unseen, are the keys to the whole light-giving operation. Without them, all is dark.

So often I try to power through a spiritual assignment. I push through on my own energy, on my own insight, taking on too much. I have too many things pulling on my limited energy. I don't shut off often enough. And finally, I flicker, waver, go faint, and then burn out. I call out to God, and he rescues me.

I have found it is better to install a powerful source of energy ahead of time rather than let it become a rescue effort. I say yes only to projects I feel the Spirit is leading me to. I put limits on the amount of time I'm "on." I don't have to light the whole world. Only God does that. He'll give me just enough power, though, to light the little corner that he's asked me to shine in.

We have this treasure in jars of clay to show that this all-
surpassing power is from God and not from us.

2 CORINTHIANS 4:7

BE PREPARED

Many people have had bad dreams about being in a place or circumstance in which they find themselves naked. Perhaps these dreams reflect the vulnerability they feel in their everyday lives. I don't have many dreams in which I'm unclothed, but I do have a persistent dream of a different sort. I'm back in college, and I have either forgotten or decided not to attend a class for an entire semester. I didn't drop the class, though, so I have to show up for the final exam, completely unprepared. I sit through the exam, completely humiliated and certain to fail.

When I wake up, pillowcase wet with sweat, I still feel the pounding-heart emotion even as I reason with myself that it didn't happen and, even if it did, it wasn't that bad. Perhaps for me, being unprepared and then failing as a result is what makes me feel vulnerable.

I care about doing good work. I'll bet you do too. And for all of us, the most important work in our lives involves carrying through with the tasks the Lord has lovingly appointed us to do.

There are many ways he prepares us for these works. He softens our hearts through the Holy Spirit and makes us whole again through the blood of Christ. He sends good and wise people to teach us, if we'll listen. But there is something we need to do too: show up to class (wherever that may be!) prepared.

Preparation mostly involves knowing God, through prayer, through experience, and through his Word. I know he shows up prepared for his part; I've got to ensure I show up prepared on my end too.

Do your best to present yourself to God as one approved, a worker who does
not need to be ashamed and who correctly handles the word of truth.

2 TIMOTHY 2:15

WE'RE ALL WRENCHES

One Sunday morning when my husband was a young boy, he listened intently to the hymn being sung. He wasn't always sure why people were singing what they were singing. Angels have prostates? All of us, every last one of us, are wrenches?

On the way home that afternoon he asked his father, "That song we sang in church. If we're all wrenches, what kind of wrench am I?"

Without missing a beat, his dad answered, "A monkey wrench."

It has been preached that we're all tools in God's toolbox. Certainly I have known Christians who have felt it was their calling to be the Christian version of Thor, Hammer of God. There are plenty of loose screws in the church, for sure. I'm very certain there are people who have met me and thought they had found the lost nut for some bolt. The truth is, we're all a little off sometimes, which is why all of us wrenches need that amazing grace. Grace is necessary for salvation and for a life of joy and peace.

Amazing grace! how sweet the sound
That saved a wretch like me!
I once was lost, but now am found;
Was blind, but now I see.
'Twas grace that taught my heart
*   to fear,*
And grace my fears relieved;
How precious did that grace appear
The hour I first believed!
Through many dangers, toils and
*   snares,*

I have already come;
'Tis grace hath brought me safe thus far,
And grace will lead me home.
The Lord has promised good to me,
His Word my hope secures;
He will my shield and portion be,
As long as life endures.
Yea, when this flesh and heart shall fail,
And mortal life shall cease,
I shall possess, within the veil,
A life of joy and peace.

—JOHN NEWTON

God saved you by his grace when you believed. And you can't take
credit for this; it is a gift from God. Salvation is not a reward for the
good things we have done, so none of us can boast about it.

EPHESIANS 2:8-9, NLT

NIGHT-LIGHTS

I love night-lights. In the powder room I have one that looks like Marie Antoinette, of the large bird's-nest hairstyle. A sleek black-and-white Paris skyline night-light graces the guest bathroom. I have tiny, pink track lights in my own bathroom, and under-the-counter lights shine softly in my kitchen. When my daughter moved into her own home, I bought her a night-light with bright red poppies, which matches her style.

Night-lights are sweet. They say, *Here, don't trip. Don't be afraid.* They give enough light to show you there is nothing to fear, but not so much as to startle you. Night-lights are gentle and comforting, and they bring a bit of hope into dark places. There's a reason toy makers are now inserting night-lights into stuffed animals; when little ones squeeze a bear or a baby doll, a bulb goes on, providing comfort and light at the same time.

We believers are night-lights too. We carry within us the greatest light the world has ever known, the one who created light and separated it from the darkness in a physical sense as well as in a spiritual, eternal sense. When we walk into a room, we dispel a little of the mist and fear by our presence and the presence of the one we carry with us. We take the hands of those who don't know the way and walk with them so they don't stumble, so they can see where they can safely walk.

You may have a Marie Antoinette style, or you may be a poppy or a skyline or the world's softest teddy bear that everyone wants to love on, and that's okay. Your night-light is just right no matter what it looks like.

Whoever walks in the dark does not know where they are going. Believe in the light while you have the light, so that you may become children of light.

JOHN 12:35-36

PAPER PLATES

What's the point of doing dishes all the time? Why don't we just eat off paper plates?

I decided that it's okay to use paper plates sometimes; they were made for quick meals. Picnics wouldn't be the same without them, nor would backyard barbecues. But paper plates are not used for special times, to win people over, to make guests feel special. Who wants to invite a new friend over to eat on disposable dishes? Who wants to eat Christmas dinner on paper plates?

Pretty much no one. Beautiful dishes with lovely patterns, rimmed in gold, and filled with special foods are what many families use for Easter, or Christmas, or even every day. To feel special. To feel like time together as a family or with friends is set apart. People don't throw away good china, and they don't store it under the sink. They take good care of it. It's expensive!

The Bible tells us that we Christians are very much like those pretty dishes. God has made us for something special, something wonderful and important. Our words and works are not to be disposable, throwaway, of no account. It takes more work to hand wash beautiful dishes than to throw away paper ones. And it takes some effort to keep our lives pure. It's okay, though. Better to be a pretty plate than a dirty dish. We and our good works were not destined to be paper plates.

In a wealthy home some utensils are made of gold and silver, and some are made of wood and clay. The expensive utensils are used for special occasions, and the cheap ones are for everyday use. If you keep yourself pure, you will be a special utensil for honorable use. Your life will be clean, and you will be ready for the Master to use you for every good work.

2 TIMOTHY 2:20-21, NLT

CATHEDRALS

Like many women, I hate mirrors. I avoid them if I can. There's a reason my full-length mirror is hidden behind my always-open bedroom door.

If you've ever taken a trip to Europe, you'll remember the many cathedrals. They are skillfully crafted, using the finest stone, wood, marble, and glass. The light filters through windows and arches and casts gorgeous shadows everywhere. Cathedrals are built to be beautiful because they represent where God lives and provide a place to worship him.

Can you imagine how people would react if someone spat on the floor of a cathedral? Stuck chewed gum on one of the windows? Littered it with candy wrappers? Docents and other worshipers and admirers would be outraged—and rightly so. The culprit would likely be hustled right outside. Everyone would understand: this is not how you treat a piece of art, and certainly not God's house and a place of worship.

Scripture tells us that we, God's people, are temples of the Holy Spirit. In fact, we are even more beautiful than those European cathedrals because we are made in his image. We are his home—he lives within us. We use our beautiful bodies to work for and worship him.

Take good care of yourself, sister, not only because you deserve to be treated with honor and dignity but also because your beautiful body is God's home. I'll try not to avoid the mirrors if you'll do the same.

Do you not know that your bodies are temples of the Holy Spirit, who is in you, whom you have received from God? You are not your own; you were bought at a price. Therefore honor God with your bodies.

1 CORINTHIANS 6:19-20

DECEMBER

Heavenly Scented Sea Salts

Dead Sea salts are said to have healing and restorative properties, and I'm a believer because I've experienced it. These salts will help you relax and unwind during a typically overextended month. Even better, you can share them with friends for welcome and inexpensive Christmas treats. If you don't have time for a bath, just open the jar, inhale for a few seconds, and be calmed or energized depending on which oils you've chosen!

WHAT YOU'LL NEED

Glass jars with lids (Blue or green canning jars work really well for this and are festive.)

Large bag of Dead Sea salts (You can find these online.)

Essential oils of your choice (Lavender or citrusy scents work well for this.)

DIRECTIONS

Place 1½ cups of sea salt and 25 drops of oil into each jar. Place lid tightly on jar, and shake to mix. For each bath, place ¼ to ½ cup of salt in the tub while water is running. Swirl water before climbing in.

For this month's free printable, go to http://tyndal.es/homeandgarden.

December 1
BATHS

There's a reason cats get hairballs—they groom themselves quite often. Fastidious as they may be, though, they can never get themselves completely clean on their own. Sticky fur usually means a cat needs a bath.

This process can be painful for the person bathing the cat, because the cat does not go gently into that warm, soapy spa. She'll scratch, meow like she's dying, and make everyone around her uncomfortable throughout the whole process. (Note: it's better to trim kitty claws before the bath.) The neighbors will certainly be clear on the fact that the cat does not like baths. Yet baths are necessary for the cat's health and well-being.

We people, cat owners or not, think we do a pretty good job keeping ourselves clean, and to some extent, that's true. But we cannot remove our own sins. We can repent of them; we can apologize for them; we can avoid them as much as possible. But we cannot make ourselves clean, because total purity requires complete holiness. Only one Person qualifies to offer that.

Old Testament law showed that a blood sacrifice, representing life given, was required for the cleansing of sins. The new covenant, through Christ, provided one perfect sacrifice for all time: Jesus Christ, whose blood is sufficient to cleanse us from every sin.

We, like cats, may believe ourselves to be clean and self-sufficient, but that just isn't the case. We must be cleansed by the forgiveness accessed only through Christ. It's much easier on everyone around us if we receive it willingly!

In fact, the law requires that nearly everything be cleansed with blood,
and without the shedding of blood there is no forgiveness.

HEBREWS 9:22

December 2
CHRISTMAS COOKIES

When my kids were young, one of our favorite activities was making Christmas cookies together. They loved decorating them and loved eating them. Making the dough? Waiting for it to chill? Rolling it out? Cleaning up? Not so much!

I understood that there were limits to their young attention spans and that there were many other days during the year when I might teach them lessons about patience and duty; baking day was a day for fun. So I prepared the dough in advance and let it chill overnight. I made sure the countertops were cleared so there was room to roll the dough, and I bought lots of fun-colored sugars and cinnamon buttons for decorating. On cookie-making day, we all had a good and productive time, and the kids made cookies they were proud of. No cookie looked like another, although all were delicious.

In the same way, the Lord knows just the kind of tasks we're suited for, those things we will love to do. He prepares these good works for us in advance, not just because we're children (although we *are* his children), but because he is setting us up for success, so to speak. When we undertake the task he's set apart for us, we can feel the excitement and pleasure that comes from working alongside him.

Yes, there are days for learning lessons and performing duties. But much more often we have the delight and joy of working alongside our Father. After all, we are his handiwork, which he planned for and designed and lovingly brought to life—not just for one season but for eternity. We're uniquely different—no cookie-cutter Christians among us!

We are God's handiwork, created in Christ Jesus to do good works, which God prepared in advance for us to do.

EPHESIANS 2:10

TOO HEAVY

We were moving—again—at what seemed like the worst time of year. It was time to move everything from the current house into the moving van. Once we arrived at the new house, we'd have to move everything into the garage and the house. There were lots and lots of boxes, but we were determined to do the job ourselves, reluctant to ask our friends to help us move once again.

Our kids tried to help, but mostly all they could handle were pillows and little bits and pieces that couldn't fit in boxes. We made some progress, but we soon grew tired.

A large box tumbled down the stairs. Our weakened arms were unable to stop its fall, and it became clear we needed help. So we dialed some friends, and most of them were happy to come and help, in spite of our early misgivings. Many hands make light work, the saying goes, and alternatively, pride goes before a fall. Had we been too proud to ask for help? Maybe.

Late that night, sleeping on mattresses on the floor, we recounted how glad we were that we had reached out. No person is meant to pull a load alone. We, like oxen, are team animals, as it were. There is no shame in asking for help.

What could you use help with today, this week, this month? Reach out.

What you are doing is not good. You and these people who come to you will only wear yourselves out. The work is too heavy for you; you cannot handle it alone. Listen now to me and I will give you some advice, and may God be with you. . . . Select capable men from all the people— men who fear God, trustworthy men who hate dishonest gain—and appoint them. . . . If you do this and God so commands, you will be able to stand the strain, and all these people will go home satisfied.

EXODUS 18:17-19, 21, 23

December 4
REGIFTING

Everyone wants to know—is it okay? Will they know? Would I know? You already know not to pass along a fruitcake; everyone will assume it's been passed along for years—the high alcohol content may preserve the fruits and nuts but still won't make it edible. One distant relative came to our wedding bearing a lovely box, nicely wrapped. When we opened our gifts later, we found a set of four mismatched drinking glasses, scratched from years of use. We got a good giggle out of that for some time. Perhaps they had nothing else to offer, and we were glad they had attended our celebration.

If you want very much to give a present to someone but you have little money and are offering something of your own, sacrificially, then regifting is not tacky. Sometimes people will "regift" something that was offered to them in love but just doesn't fit their size or their style. If the item is something you truly believe that a friend would enjoy, there's nothing wrong with regifting it. And if you received something that you absolutely loved and want to share it with a friend, then go ahead! Just don't try to pass it off as new. Be up front and honest about the gift you're passing along.

The best thing to "regift" at Christmas, of course, is the good news that Jesus Christ was born! You'll be passing along something that is good for everyone, and you don't even need to give it up to do so. It's the gift that, as they say, keeps on giving!

Whatever you give and share, remember that you will be blessed for doing so, because it shows the generous, God-shaped heart inside you.

You should remember the words of the Lord Jesus:
"It is more blessed to give than to receive."

ACTS 20:35, NLT

ONE GLOVE

I have a deacon's bench in which I store winter clothing, out of sight and out of mind through another gloriously warm season. Away with the parkas; on with the sunglasses instead! For some reason, one of a pair of gloves always seems to disappear. I only buy those cheap little sets in the drugstore, so it's not a huge financial loss, but still, where do they go?

I stared at one lone glove, ready to pitch it. A glove sitting by itself looks odd. It's the shape of a hand—we see the palm and the fingers and thumbs. But when there is nothing inside a glove, it can't do much. A hand can pick up and move things; it can give a pat on the back or a hug. A helping hand can be lent to someone who needs it. A hand can do work. A hand can show love. A well-designed glove may be pretty and warm, but on its own, it has no power to do anything.

God designed us to be beautiful, useful women. We're not exactly like gloves, of course. We can do things, we can show love, we can help others. But there are limits to what one person can do. God doesn't have any limits. He loves to work with you, and in you, and through you, and he most often works most powerfully when we join together with other believers to accomplish his will. When two or three are gathered together, he is there in our midst. His spirit, alive inside of us, is like the hand inside the pair of gloves that is my Christian sister and me working together for Kingdom good.

*God is working in you, giving you the desire and
the power to do what pleases him.*

PHILIPPIANS 2:13, NLT

RED WALLS

We had bought the house knowing that it would need some painting. It had been rather hastily prepared for sale, and many of the rooms had been sloppily painted. A room painted in neutral beige had lickings of Palace-of-Versailles gold around the edges. At least those edges had received paint—the edges in some rooms hadn't, giving a few walls the look of a ripped newspaper, ragged at the margins. Worst of all, perhaps, were the rooms that had been painted in deep magenta before being lightly washed in white. Red bled through nearly everywhere, resulting in a color that can only be described as wounded cotton candy. There was no hiding it: the walls had been red.

Words from the old hymn flashed through my mind: "Though your sins be as scarlet, they shall be as white as snow." There would be no hiding the red "sins" with quick strokes of white paint in this house; it just didn't work. And it doesn't work in our spiritual lives either. We can't just lightly cover over the things we've done. Water under the bridge and letting bygones be bygones are not biblical concepts, not without repentance first. Doing "nice" things for people will never replace the biblical mandate to repent, ask for forgiveness, and change what we do. While the once-over may be okay for home buyers, it doesn't wash with those we've harmed.

Past offenses must be removed by the method instituted by the Lord—turning from sin and living a life that reflects our repentance. We may pretend to be sorry because it's the religious thing to do—but soon enough, the red bleeds through. It is only when we let Christ completely transform us that we truly become white as snow.

"Come now, let's settle this,"
says the LORD.
"Though your sins are like scarlet,
I will make them as white as snow."

ISAIAH 1:18, NLT

HANDMADE, HEARTFELT GIFTS

There have been a number of years when I've made homemade Christmas gifts for my friends and family—sometimes out of financial necessity, sometimes because I wanted to create something special that says, "I love you!"

I have made baked goods, wreaths, and scrapbooks. I'm not too handy with needlework, but once I even did embroidery. Other years, I have spent a long time, perhaps months, searching in stores and online for just the right gift. It takes time, and there have been years when I have been tempted to just give cash or gift cards. But for me, that doesn't tell someone, "I know you. I care for you."

At the end of one fruitless shopping day, I spied a plaque in an antiques store. It said, "I'm not telling you it's going to be easy; I'm telling you it's going to be worth it."

That's right. Sometimes we hit the sweet spot and the thing we want most in life, in a job, or on a shopping trip just happens to fall into our laps. More often, though, we have to reach for it, work for it, pray for it, seek it out. But the pleasure of finding just the right gift for a friend—whether it be a word of praise or comfort, a dozen cookies, or a piece of vintage jewelry—makes it all worthwhile.

What do you have to offer your Lord this season? What is precious to you? A portion of your carefully saved Christmas money? Thirty minutes in a day for prayer? Service to your church instead of enjoying a festivity? Go ahead, give. It's not easy, but it's definitely worth it.

I will not sacrifice to the LORD my God burnt offerings that cost me nothing.

2 SAMUEL 24:24

A DENTAL-CHAIR MOOD

Everyone has some ongoing challenge in life, a perpetual thorn in the side. My thorn is dental issues.

I don't know why my teeth are prone to issues, but in spite of my obsessive care—flossing, brushing, and regular dental visits—things go wrong. And when they go wrong, they go really wrong. What starts as a tiny cavity turns into a root canal. A crown needs to be replaced (an out-of-pocket expense). A root canal ruptures into an infection, requiring an extraction and, later, an implant. Yada yada. You get the picture.

One day I was walking around with my teeth clenched (another problem!), and I wondered why. I soon figured it out. My husband was in another room stabilizing some shelves using . . . his drill. Just the sound of the drill, even when my mouth felt fine, evoked bad memories, tension, and fear for what might lie ahead.

After the drill was put away, I asked myself if I have been going through all of life in a dental-chair mood. I know that my dental issues aren't over, and they likely won't be till I can toss all my dental crowns at the feet of the Lord. But there are many great days ahead of me too. We often tell people who have passed through deep water not to let their past problems steal their present joy. Worrying about the future is the same problem in reverse. Concern about what may come—in a dental office or otherwise—steals the pleasures at hand.

We're not in heaven yet, so problems will occur, but when they do, our God will provide just the right remedy to deal with them so we can move through, past them, and into a new season of delight.

Why, my soul, are you downcast?
Why so disturbed within me?
Put your hope in God,
for I will yet praise him,
my Savior and my God.

PSALM 43:5

December 9

CHRISTMAS CANDLES

At our church's Christmas Eve service, each worshiper is given a small candle with a brass holder. The final order of worship is to sing "Silent Night" while passing a flame, each person's lit candle lighting the candle of the person standing next to him or her. The lights are dimmed so only the flickering candles light the way out and into the dark night.

A favorite Christmas tradition in various churches around the world is the Christingle, often made by children. A Christingle consists of an orange, which represents the whole world, with a red ribbon around it, signifying that the blood of Christ has completely encircled the world. Bits of fruit on toothpicks that have been pushed into the orange stand for the fruit of the Spirit. Last of all, a lit candle is pushed into the center, representing Jesus, the Light of the World.

The Lord bids us, "Follow me," and just as his righteousness made a way through the darkness, we, too, are to be a light to the nations. There is no child too young to hold a Christingle with a little help from an adult, no adult too frail to hold a Christmas candle with a little help from a loved one. Let's join hands this Christmas and celebrate the coming of the Light of the World.

I, the LORD, have called you to demonstrate my righteousness.
I will take you by the hand and guard you,
and I will give you to my people, Israel,
as a symbol of my covenant with them.
And you will be a light to guide the nations.
You will open the eyes of the blind.

ISAIAH 42:6-7, NLT

STEW

I lifted the lid on the slow cooker, and a cloud of meaty, brothy aroma greeted me. Just that little bit evaporating into the winter air was enough to perfume the kitchen with cold-weather goodness. Earlier in the day I had cut up inexpensive vegetables, meat, and potatoes and thrown all the pieces into the pot with some broth and herbs to simmer. Now the cuts were tender and ready to be served and enjoyed.

The taste of herbs and vegetables commingled with meat that melts in your mouth never fails to please. Esau sold his birthright for just such a bowl; it's that good. What transforms a relatively tough cut of meat into toothsome goodness? Constant heat over a long period of time.

When tough things happen in life, our first instinct is to solve them quickly and make the pain go away, or pray for immediate relief. Sometimes, when relief doesn't come right away, I wonder if God is listening and if he really loves me. And if the answer is yes on both counts, well then, where is my rescue?

The apostle Paul tells us that circumstances that must have been difficult for him to endure over and over—time and heat—actually turned out, in the end, for his betterment and for the advancement of the Kingdom. Next time I'm stewing over something, I might ask, *Is this making my rough cut tender? Am I willing to stick out difficult circumstances long enough for them to transform me?*

I want you to know, brothers and sisters, that what has happened to me has actually served to advance the gospel. As a result, it has become clear throughout the whole palace guard and to everyone else that I am in chains for Christ. And because of my chains, most of the brothers and sisters have become confident in the Lord and dare all the more to proclaim the gospel without fear.

PHILIPPIANS 1:12-14

RUNNING HOT AND COLD

After moving into our new house, we discovered that on two of the sinks, the hot and cold taps were switched. Typically the hot is on the left, and the cold on the right. Because we've had decades to accustom ourselves to this regular pattern, we reach without thinking—left for warm, right for cool. For many months after we moved in, I would instinctively reach for the wrong handle. A few drinks of hot water and a few cold handwashings helped me to remember which was which. I had to consciously pay attention at first till the new habits were ingrained.

Our faith lives are built on distinct choices that lead to good habits over time. One of the choices is between faith and fear. For a long time, I hadn't really thought of faith and fear as opposites, but they are. In every situation, I have the option of choosing either to have faith that God will make things work out right or to fear that things will fall apart without my direct intervention. Put that way, it seems silly and simple, but it's not silly or simple at all when a scary situation is at hand!

So what can I do to try to ensure that I make the right choice? Romans 10:17 tells us that faith comes by hearing, and hearing by the Word of God. I can ensure that I have time to read the Word of God, and I can slow down long enough to listen to the Word made flesh, through his Spirit and his people, if I attune my ears to Christ.

Just like the decision to turn on the hot or cold water, I come to a crossroads every time I'm faced with a troubling situation. Do I reach right, to cold fear, or left, toward warm faith? If I've been reaching the wrong way for a while, it may take me some time to change my habits, but oh, the peace that will follow makes it all worthwhile.

"If you can do anything, take pity on us and help us."

"'If you can'?" said Jesus. "Everything is possible for one who believes."

Immediately the boy's father exclaimed, "I do believe;
help me overcome my unbelief!"

MARK 9:22-24

JEWELRY BOX

A jewelry box is a place where treasures are stored. My own jewelry box holds a variety of items. I have my high-school class ring and the earrings my husband gave me the year we first started dating. I have my first set of tiny diamond studs and a bracelet on which "1 Corinthians 13" is spelled out using the keys from an old typewriter. I also have little mementos of each of my children's baby years. They are treasures to me.

Mary, the mother of Jesus, knew before her son was conceived that his life would be unlike the life of anyone else. And as his life progressed, it would hold both great joy and terrible sorrow, all of it foretold, planned ahead, and directed by God. I'm certain that her life did not progress in the way she had envisioned as a young Jewish girl. But as she guided her young son, she took what had been planned for her and carried out her destiny with strength, dignity, and grace.

When the shepherds came to see Jesus, it must have been a sublime, almost surreal moment for Mary. And yet, she handled that with grace too. She took those sweet words, those powerful emotions, and treasured them in her heart. That's where we keep the things most dear to us, isn't it?

The greatest treasure we can have, of course, is Jesus Christ dwelling in our hearts. Without him, nothing has lasting value. With him, we are rich indeed.

I pray that out of his glorious riches he may strengthen you with power through his Spirit in your inner being, so that Christ may dwell in your hearts through faith.

EPHESIANS 3:16-17

CHRISTMAS LIGHTS

I drove through the dark streets of my small town one foggy December night. It was so dark that it seemed like midnight, but it was really more likely 7:00 or 8:00 p.m. Everyone was home from work and school, so the roads were empty. Puddles of water had formed, though, and those puddles were things of beauty. They reflected the multicolored Christmas lights strung up on houses along the streets.

Each house had joined in the festivities in some way. Some homes had many strings of lights and illuminated Santas or reindeer bobbing electronically. My heart was most cheered and brightened, though, by the houses with manger scenes, stars, angels, or signs reminding me that wise men still seek Jesus. Wise women, too. The skies cleared a bit, and soon the stars shone as well, heaven joining creation in applause and anticipation of the days to come.

I thought about how appropriate it all was. December is the darkest month in the northern hemisphere; it has the shortest days. Yet it's the month when we celebrate the birth of our Savior, the Light of the World, whose days are without end. Jesus came into the dark world and brought his light with him. And then he left the light in us to share after he left. Because his Spirit is always here, the darkness can never again overcome the world. He has won.

I did my few errands and drove home again, tires splashing through those many-hued puddles till I pulled into my own garage. I prayed and asked God, *Whose Christmas might you send me to light?*

The light shines in the darkness, and the darkness has not overcome it.

JOHN 1:5

"WHAT IF" OR "I AM"?

One of the best parts about decorating or remodeling is asking, "What if?"

"What if we move the couch over here?"

"What if we paint this room another color—or even just the ceiling?"

"What if we spend the Christmas bonus replacing that ratty carpet?"

All right, one person in the family likes the what-if questions, and one does not (the one who has to do the heavy lifting and thinks the couch is just fine where it is, thank you very much!).

Although there are many delightful what-if questions, a lot of what-if questions that float through our hearts and minds are not so happy.

"What if the test comes back positive?"

"What if I lose my job?"

"What if my child walks away from his faith?"

"What if we lose our house?"

Many of us spend quite a bit of time and energy dwelling on those anxiety-provoking what-if questions, not the good ones about buying new bathroom rugs. The vagaries of life, ever-changing circumstances, and our absolute inability to control situations that could harm us or those we love—these all make us nervous. But there's a two-word antidote for the two-word problem.

I AM.

"I am big enough to walk through the test with you and, should the test come back positive, arrange for your healing on earth or here with me. I am capable of finding another job for you or providing for you in a unique way you may not have thought of. Your child is really my child, right? I am certain I've got this one. You will gain, and lose, and gain houses in this world. But my house has many rooms, and you can be sure that there will always be one for you."

The fun-to-think-about what-ifs are good for your mind, your heart, and your soul. The panicked ones, not so much. Remodel, renew, and replace with "I AM."

God said to Moses, "I AM WHO I AM."

EXODUS 3:14

December 15
CHRISTMAS-COOKIE EXCHANGE

One of my favorite December traditions is hosting a Christmas-cookie exchange. In the early days, when I didn't know better, I just asked people to bring any old thing, and sometimes I ended up with dozens and dozens of the same kind of cookies. They tasted good, all right, and the fellowship and friendships were wonderful. But it doesn't make for much of an exchange if you have eleven dozen sprinkle cookies and one dozen gingerbread men that everyone is diving for.

In the ensuing years, I asked people what they would like to bring, and if they chose something that another lady had already spoken for, I asked them to bring another kind. No one seemed to mind; in fact, several of them went outside the cookie box, as it were, and found new favorites. Those years, each of us brought one kind of cookie but left with a dozen types to share with our families.

As people, we tend to homogenize; that is, we hang out and feel most comfortable with people who are like us. They look like us, they vote like us, they worship like us, and they agree with us. Sadly, if we keep up that kind of segregating, we'll end up like a box of delicious . . . sprinkle cookies. No variety!

I know it's hard to reach out to someone who is not like you, but why not try? Host a cookie exchange and invite members of all ages or from different churches or cultures that are not like yours. The body of Christ is made up of all nations and peoples, of all ages and backgrounds. Our gifts differ from one another in order that we may function as a beautiful whole. Variety, after all, is the sugar and spice of life!

Just as each of us has one body with many members, and these members do not all have the same function, so in Christ we, though many, form one body, and each member belongs to all the others. We have different gifts, according to the grace given to each of us.

ROMANS 12:4-6

DEEP CLEANING

Both my husband and I have some Norwegian heritage, and his mother is very proud of hers. After giving birth to my husband on Christmas Day, she celebrated by eating lutefisk—cod soaked in lye. She teases about the time she brought some lutefisk home on a crowded holiday train, and within minutes her car was cleared; others wished to avoid its stink. It smells so bad that I have never eaten it, tradition or not, but who knows? Maybe it cleanses the palate. Lye, after all, is best known as a cleanser, mostly in dish soap.

As I prepared for Christmas and thought about my mother-in-law's lutefisk, that lye was on my mind. It seems like the things that clean best are tough, abrasive, or caustic. For example, both lemon juice and bleach are acidic and very good at removing stains; lemon juice even cleanses internal organs such as the liver and the pancreas. For centuries, women have used the abrasive powers of sand, sugar, and salt to clean and smooth their skin. Sweat, brought out by intense exercise, and tears, brought out by pain, release toxins from deep inside the body. Even the painfully honest opinion of a friend can be cleansing.

There is something about difficulty, abrasion, and caustic situations that scours us, leaving soft skin, shiny hair, and a clean conscience. And who would choose to eat or serve food on dishes that had been washed in cold water with with no soap and an old rag?

I'm not promising that I'll try lutefisk this year. But I do promise not to shy away from people and circumstances that God wants to use to refine me.

Blows that wound cleanse away evil;
strokes make clean the innermost parts.

PROVERBS 20:30, ESV

VISIONS OF SUGARPLUMS

My family and I had gone out to cut down our Christmas tree, and at the register was a display of Christmas candy, free for the taking. Each of us pocketed a candy cane to unwrap on the way home.

I peeled the plastic off mine and popped the candy into my mouth, expecting a cool breeze of peppermint. Instead, I got a light coating of sweet sugarplum! The flavor wasn't unpleasant, but it was unexpected, and that surprise shocked me for a moment. After I'd reoriented myself, I rather enjoyed the sugarplum. It was different—but perhaps even better—than what I had expected, and I enjoyed it once I knew what was coming.

When I first followed the Lord, I had certain expectations. I thought all would be well from then on, that I would have little suffering and trouble, that my prayers would be instantly answered, and that I would have the answers everyone else needed. It didn't take long before reality caught up and refuted my expectations. I still suffered, in ways I had not anticipated. The longer I walk with the Lord, the more questions I have.

And yet, there is always hope. Christianity is not what I expected it to be, but once I reoriented to reality, I found it to be sweeter, better. Not all of my prayers have been answered, but I know they will be, in ways beyond what I can imagine. I hope for that, expectantly.

*I consider that our present sufferings are not worth comparing
with the glory that will be revealed in us. For the creation waits in
eager expectation for the children of God to be revealed. . . .*

*For in this hope we were saved. But hope that is seen is no hope
at all. Who hopes for what they already have? But if we hope
for what we do not yet have, we wait for it patiently.*

ROMANS 8:18-19, 24-25

December 18
TREASURED RECIPES

I love being able to access recipes online—thousands of them, with photos that show me just what the finished dishes are supposed to look like (though mine never look that good!). There are websites that show you how to make everything from gluten-free vegetarian food to raw desserts to full-fat, full-flour French treats. The recipes are often rated, and the reviewers include handy tips for their fellow cooks, which is nice!

The only downside is that the recipes online have no connection with people we love. Back in the day, when people had recipe boxes that they stuffed full of the tried and true (and tasted!) recipes from family and friends, you knew just what you were pulling out to cook. Those recipes not only delivered good meals but they also summoned good memories of those who had passed them down to you.

One neat gift I saw recently is a personalized cutting board; you can have Mom's or Grandma's famous recipe burned into the cutting board. The cutting boards are usable, but since they convey heirloom treasures, they are often hung on the kitchen wall instead. Best of all? The recipe, when copied in Mom's handwriting, is burned into the board in Mom's handwriting too, never to be forgotten.

We have a recipe of sorts too, handed down to us through the generations in the form of a book, a love letter, a collection of stories, histories, and poems. It's an instruction manual, step by step, on how to live. Stray from it and . . . disaster! But if you follow the guidance of God's Word, you can be certain of lasting success, built upon the wisdom of those who came before.

Obey my commands and live!
Guard my instructions as you guard your own eyes.
Tie them on your fingers as a reminder.
Write them deep within your heart.

PROVERBS 7:2-3, NLT

NOT-SO-BENIGN NEGLECT

One winter's day we decided to take a drive in the countryside, which isn't actually too far from us. As we drove toward the edge of our county, the land transformed from planned developments with many commercial buildings, to less developed areas with homes on acreage, to open farmland. The farmland area was truly country, practically picker heaven with old junked cars, gas-station paraphernalia, and rusted farm equipment. Two particular homes, one just down the road from the other, caught my eye.

The first had once been a beautiful house, white with green shutters. At that moment, though, it was a sad, aging beauty, falling down piece by piece, covered with mold and brambles. Clearly, at one time, it had been a proud and lovely family home. Now, however, the elements and the earth were in the process of reclaiming it, and it was no longer habitable. Had the house been intentionally abandoned, or did it—more likely—suffer from simple neglect?

Just a ways down the road was another stately home of the same age, a home that had been cared for. The siding was freshly painted, the boards all tight, plants contained within their prescribed boundaries. I thought about how life is often like that. We mean well with nearly everything in our lives— our families, our friendships, our careers, our neighbors. And yet the busyness of life often causes us to neglect the people and places that mean the most while giving our time and attention to that which is impermanent.

So often I spend my time on worthy projects or tasks, but I've realized I need to focus more on people. How much of myself do I share with them? I've decided to spend the bulk of my time paying attention to the "home" of my heart.

Do not neglect to do good and to share what you have,
for such sacrifices are pleasing to God.

HEBREWS 13:16, ESV

December 20

TODDLING TOWARD GOD

A young lady I mentor was sharing with me how her son was starting to toddle. Her life was going to be very different now that her little boy was mobile. He could decide which toys to walk toward and which to reject; he would soon be making clear his preferences. Preschool would follow with new choices, and then middle school and girls. He would become increasingly independent of her, up till the time he became a man and left home.

No, I didn't really tell her all that at once. But the journey does start with a single toddle, er, step! And it's a good journey; as much as I enjoyed my babies, I enjoy them even more as adults.

I watched as her little one steadied himself and then began to wobble toward his mom, desperate to reach her but gleeful to be moving on his own. It became clear that he wasn't going to make it all the way without tumbling, so she scooted forward a bit, closing the gap between them.

You and I are God's beloved children. He delights in us, in our continued growth and maturity. Sending Christ was the ultimate way he closed the gap between us. And as I grow day by day, he's moving his hand in powerful ways to help me succeed and to encourage me, but without doing it for me. He wants me to mature, with all the pleasures that affords both of us.

Are you toddling forward, falling into a loving Father's arms? It doesn't matter how old you are or how long it has been since you've walked toward his embrace. He's already making his way toward you.

I will arise and go to my father, and I will say to him, "Father, I have sinned against heaven and before you. I am no longer worthy to be called your son. Treat me as one of your hired servants." And he arose and came to his father. But while he was still a long way off, his father saw him and felt compassion, and ran and embraced him and kissed him.

LUKE 15:18-20, ESV

December 21

ONE ITEM AT A TIME

There are lots and lots of honey-do jokes out there, and for good reason. We wives often want more done than our husbands would prefer to do. I saw a truck in our town that offered Rent-a-Husband services "for those jobs that never get done." A friend and I were laughing about this, when she shared her technique for getting things done.

First, she tapes her request on the back of the bathroom door, so whenever her husband is, er, sitting there contemplating, he'll look over and over again at that one polite request. Second, she asks for only one thing at a time. There is no list to speak of. She doesn't want her beloved to rebel or feel overwhelmed.

I recently read that a large percentage of women feel utterly overwhelmed with the amount of work they need to do each day—job, child care, housework, caring for elderly relatives, giving time to charity and church. Like an overloaded circuit, we tend to melt down when faced with all that.

Our Lord, however, does not encourage us to become overwhelmed. I've come to realize that half the battle is in my mind—I rehearse over and over again what I have to do and how I'll never get it all done. I envision the harm those around me will suffer because of my perceived failures. It's an emotional drain and a waste of brain space.

Instead, I am learning to focus on one task at a time—the one just ahead of me that I can't escape. I'm not looking too far down the road. Today can hold just enough, and I needn't cram more into it. What do I need to do today to be faithful? You are God's beloved too, and it is never his intent to overwhelm you.

Do not worry about tomorrow. Let tomorrow worry about itself. Living faithfully is a large enough task for today.

MATTHEW 6:34, VOICE

GOLD CARDS

Sometimes when we just don't know what to get people for Christmas, we buy gift cards. We want them to have funds available for what they might want or need, at any time in any place. We don't know what those specifics might be, but the recipients definitely know. Buying them a gift card allows them to spend where they need and want to.

When the wise men came to look for Jesus, they first stopped to ask King Herod where to find him. Herod realized that people thought of Jesus as the king, and he feared that Jesus would take his kingdom, so he instructed the wise men to come back and tell him where Jesus could be found after they located him. The wise men found Jesus, but they did not go back to tell Herod. Jesus' dad, Joseph, was warned in a dream that he needed to take Jesus and Mary to Egypt, where they would be safe. But how could they live in a strange country, where Joseph had no job?

Why, the gold brought by the wise men, of course! Gold, then just like now, was very valuable, and it could be used anywhere for any need or want.

Although evil people sought to harm the Lord, it was no surprise to God. He planned in advance to take care of his Son through the wise men and their generous gift.

He will take care of us, too.

After this interview the wise men went their way. And the star they had seen in the east guided them to Bethlehem. It went ahead of them and stopped over the place where the child was. When they saw the star, they were filled with joy! They entered the house and saw the child with his mother, Mary, and they bowed down and worshiped him. Then they opened their treasure chests and gave him gifts of gold, frankincense, and myrrh.

MATTHEW 2:9-11, NLT

A FRAGRANT OFFERING

At a booth in a street market near our house, we found incense cones with unusual scents. Normally we don't burn incense, but one fragrance caught our attention, and we decided to give it a try. It was frankincense, and truthfully, none of us had known what it actually smelled like.

A second gift the wise men brought to the child Jesus was frankincense, which, like gold, was very valuable. Frankincense, when burned, has a delightful, sweet, earthy scent. We burned those cones during the month of December to help us remember 2 Corinthians 2:15: "Our lives are a Christ-like fragrance rising up to God. But this fragrance is perceived differently by those who are being saved and by those who are perishing" (NLT).

The gift of frankincense was very special in other ways as well. Starting from the very beginning with the sons of Adam and Eve, God asked people to offer sacrifices to him. Sometimes the sacrifices were grains, sometimes they were animals. The gifts were *to* the Lord, of course, but they were *for* the good of the people. The sacrifices helped people to remember that everything belongs to God. And the sacrifices represented atonement for the sins that the people had committed. Frankincense was one of the important spices that was sprinkled on those sacrifices, to make them sweet smelling.

The most important gift to God's chosen people was Jesus Christ. He came as the giver of everything and offered himself as the sacrifice for everyone. To have Jesus receive frankincense, associated with sacrifices, was a special way for God to point to the birth of the most important offering of all.

Put some pure frankincense near each stack to serve as a
representative offering, a special gift presented to the LORD.

LEVITICUS 24:7, NLT

BITTERSWEET

A lot of things I love are bittersweet. Lemonade over ice. Raw cranberries dipped in sugar. Having company, then having to watch them leave after a rich time of fellowship. Looking forward to Christmas, then having it pass all too quickly again this year.

Myrrh, one of the gifts the wise men brought to Jesus, was a bittersweet gift.

Myrrh is made from the thorny *Commiphora* tree. A sharp object is driven into the tree, piercing and wounding it till some of the sap bleeds out. The sap eventually hardens, making a pasty kind of "Band-Aid" for the tree. That sticky paste is the sweet-smelling resin called myrrh. In Bible times, people used myrrh when they were preparing a body for burial. Some of Jesus' followers used myrrh when preparing his crucified body for burial.

The gift of myrrh to the child Jesus was bittersweet. It foreshadowed the time when the Lord would be wounded by nails and spears, causing him to bleed, and then to the preparation of his crucified body. Bitter—because he would be injured and killed. Sweet—because he rose from the dead, is alive today, and will come back again!

Afterward Joseph of Arimathea, who had been a secret disciple of Jesus (because he feared the Jewish leaders), asked Pilate for permission to take down Jesus' body. When Pilate gave permission, Joseph came and took the body away. With him came Nicodemus, the man who had come to Jesus at night. He brought about seventy-five pounds of perfumed ointment made from myrrh and aloes. Following Jewish burial custom, they wrapped Jesus' body with the spices in long sheets of linen cloth.

JOHN 19:38-40, NLT

BREAD OF LIFE

God doesn't do anything by accident. Nearly 750 years before Jesus was born, Micah prophesied that the one who would become King of Israel would be born in the little town of Bethlehem.

Bethlehem means "house of bread." Back then, and even today in many parts of the world, bread was the most important part of the people's diet, the "staple" to which other things were added. Bread was so fundamental to the body's daily needs that the Lord said that his body was bread, broken for us. He commanded us to break bread together and remember his death till he returns.

God tells us that we will not live by bread alone but by every word that comes from him. The most important Word that came to earth was our Savior, Jesus Christ. He calls himself the Bread of Life. Is there a more fitting place for him to have been born than the house of bread?

Some people's Christmas dinners will be traditional, some vegetarian, or gluten free, or low carb. We can be thankful to have nourishing food available to us. Our souls need food too! Today, on this day of feasting throughout Christendom, remember to thank God for the Bread of Life, who feeds your soul and your true life!

Jesus replied, "I am the bread of life. Whoever comes to me will never be hungry again. Whoever believes in me will never be thirsty."

JOHN 6:35, NLT

December 26

NO EXCHANGES, NO RETURNS

I do try really hard to buy gifts that people will like, but you know what? Sometimes they—and I—like gift cards. Because after you've depleted your budget buying gifts for others, there may be a thing or two you'd like for yourself but just don't have the money for.

I also love the dear people who tell others, in open honesty, "If you don't like it, exchange it!" You know they mean it when they include a gift receipt in the box. The giver need never know that the gift didn't fit or didn't match.

Do you spend money on yourself? I'm guessing, if you're like most women, the answer is no. At least not without guilt for what you could be, should be, might be doing with the money for God, your family, your friends, or the poor. And of course giving to each of these is important and shows love. But one overlooked part of the great commandment, I think, is that the Lord expects us to love others *as we love ourselves*. It's not even a question. It's a firm belief.

Many women grow up believing that they don't meet others' expectations or that they have to perform well to be loved. But, by no work of your own, you are dearly, deeply loved and perfectly created. You are a gift, a gift worth dying for. It's all right to exchange Christmas gifts, but remember, the only thing that needed to be exchanged for *you* was the life of Christ, willingly given for you, his precious one.

Christ values you that much. Do you value yourself? Really? How do you show it?

"You must love the LORD your God with all your heart, all your soul, and all your mind." This is the first and greatest commandment. A second is equally important: "Love your neighbor as yourself." The entire law and all the demands of the prophets are based on these two commandments.

MATTHEW 22:37-40, NLT

SEASONALLY DISCOUNTED

All week I had been eyeing a beautiful wreath at a local grocery store. It was made of pine and other evergreens, with holly and berries, and it was flecked with gold. But the price tag—$50—was much more than I could justify for a one-season extra.

A couple of days after Christmas I returned to that same store and was shocked to see the wreath—my wreath!—on a heap of greens heading to the trash. It was still fresh and lovely, but the season was over, so it had been declared past its prime.

We women feel like that too, past a "certain age." Twenty-one? Forty? After having children? When the years mark time with smile lines on our faces? When someone a decade younger (and with much less experience) is given a job we've worked so hard for? One day we're valuable in the eyes of the world, and the next . . . not so much.

If we go looking for validation from the world—and we all do it—we'll be left empty handed and brokenhearted. The things we value—kindness, gentleness, wisdom gained through age and experience, a patient heart—are certainly given lip service by those around us, but in actuality, these qualities are often unappreciated.

Scripture tells us that people look at outward appearances, but the Lord looks at the heart. Cultivating the values worthy of notice in his Kingdom often means being overlooked in this one. But that's okay. The Christmas season lasts but a week, or perhaps a month. Christ's Kingdom will last forever.

P.S. I asked for the wreath, was given it for free, and gave it a prominent place on my door!

He stoops to look down
on heaven and on earth.
He lifts the poor from the dust
and the needy from the garbage dump.
He sets them among princes,
even the princes of his own people!

PSALM 113:6-8, NLT

ALWAYS AWAKE

The generation that experienced the Second World War is fast passing away, and with them, the memories of their courage, their actions, and their faith. Recently a woman told me a story she had heard about the war in London.

A young lady was working in her victory garden when the air raid sirens started screaming in the distance. She and her family hustled to their designated shelter and waited breathlessly. After some time, they were allowed to return to their home. In the black of night, her heart still pumping from a near miss, she lay in bed, afraid of bombs. Afraid that the bricks of her house would crumble in on her. Afraid of death, as we all would be. She prayed and asked God to bring her peace. In that lovely, peculiarly British humor, she says he conveyed this message to her: "Well, I'll be up and watching. No sense in you staying up too, and losing sleep, is there?"

Nighttime is usually when I give my fears free rein too, and December has a lot of dark nights. Freed from the daily activities that keep my mind and hands busy, the minutes or hours before I drift off to sleep too often become a fertile field in which to plant worries. We may not be consumed with war now, but there is a constant war going on in and around us—a war for our hearts and minds. Isaiah promises that God will keep in perfect peace those whose minds are steadfast, because they trust in him. The admonition to rest in the midst of war is no less valid for you and me than it was for the woman in war-torn London.

She lay down again and rested, woke up refreshed the next morning, and lived many decades past the war's end.

He will not let your foot slip—
he who watches over you will not slumber;
indeed, he who watches over Israel
will neither slumber nor sleep.
The LORD watches over you—
the LORD is your shade at your right hand;
the sun will not harm you by day,
nor the moon by night.

PSALM 121:3-6

December 29

ROUGH WATERS

A friend was to join me shortly for a walk. I sat in a light rain and watched as drops landed on the lake and then spattered and bounced in a lovely, rhythmic pattern. A month before, we'd been walking near a local waterfall; its force is so strong that it is harnessed to provide energy to be transformed into electricity. That day, the water had rushed and tumbled in great, white curls that fell with a deafening thunder.

In real life, I prefer placid waters, the kind that you can skim stones against or watch a mosquito eater skate across. I don't like circumstances and situations that feel uncontrollable, unbridled, and scary. And yet it was not in the tiny drops that great power was being unleashed; it was in the muscled waterfall.

The Gospel of John tells of a pool of water that apparently had healing properties when the water was disturbed. It seems that the first person into the water after it had been stirred was healed. Stepping into the water, not knowing why or how the miracle happened, required faith.

Similarly, Jesus did not call Peter to walk out upon the quiet waters. He called Peter to come forth into the storm, where Jesus was in the midst. He beckoned Peter to trust. Each of us feels the wind against us sometimes, even though we are under God's constant care. It is when the waters are troubled that we see God's power to transform us at work.

The boat was already a considerable distance from land, buffeted
by the waves because the wind was against it. . . .
But Jesus immediately said to them: "Take courage! It is I. Don't be afraid."
"Lord, if it's you," Peter replied, "tell me to come to you on the water."
"Come," he said.
Then Peter got down out of the boat, walked on the water and came toward Jesus.

MATTHEW 14:24, 27-29

MAKING PLANS

"For I know the plans I have for you," begins a beloved passage in Jeremiah. I love it, too, not only because I see that God has designed good things for me but because . . .

He has a plan.

I love plans. One of my favorite phrases, when I'm spending time with my family or my friends, is "Let's make a plan!" To me, a plan allows us to line up good times together, mark off space on our calendars for one another, and look forward to enjoyment. A visit to the state fair? A dinner-and-games night? Going to see a movie? Let's make a plan.

Not all planning is fun, though. Most of us keep detailed work calendars, sometimes synced with our phones, to ensure we're where we're supposed to be when we're supposed to be there. I have a long to-do list on my computer because as I get a little older, it seems I need to see it written in order to keep the details in line. Likewise, my kids grew up with chore charts. They hated them then—but they make their own now. (Mom chuckles silently, amused and gratified.) I still have charts to remind me what needs to be done for the upkeep of my home.

Those to-do lists and chore charts ensure there is time for that other planning—planning for good times and fun. Plans remind me what *needs* to be done, and plans remind me what I *want* to get done. The things I plan—for work, for friends, for taking care of my home, and for my family—are the priorities I have established. They are, in a sense, the desires of my heart. I hope they meld with the desires of my loved ones' hearts too.

Do you chart your priorities on paper or in your heart? Who knows your plan?

May he give you the desire of your heart and make all your plans succeed.

PSALM 20:4

December 31

WHAT'S OLD IS NEW AGAIN!

I admit to loving routine and structure—not all the time, maybe, but I think they make me feel like there is some order in this often-chaotic world. Each year the same routine: planting, watering, harvesting. Each year the same holidays: Valentine's Day, Easter, Christmas. Spring cleaning, autumn cleaning. And then it starts all over again, anew!

This renewal, of course, is the great hope that every Christian holds. Happy occasions come to an end; those we love die, always much too soon, before we're ready. And we, too, will find our lives passing by faster than we'd imagined. Years seem to pick up speed as we go along! But we shall see our beloveds again—healthy and renewed, without pain or fear or worries.

The last day of the year finds me packing the Christmas decorations in Rubbermaid containers to be stored in the garage till next year. Each piece means so much to me. Each ornament evokes happy memories of the past and ignites the anticipation of making more happy memories in the year just ahead. I slide the final box into place. This year held both sorrow and joy. What will the next one bring?

God says, "Forget all that—it is nothing compared to what I am going to do. For I am about to do something new. See, I have already begun! Do you not see it?" (Isaiah 43:18-19, NLT).

Are you excited to see what God will do with, through, and for you in the new year? I am!

[God says,] "I am about to do something new.
See, I have already begun!"

ISAIAH 43:19, NLT

THE ONE YEAR® WAY

Do-able. Daily. Devotions.

START ANY DAY THE ONE YEAR WAY.

FOR WOMEN

The One Year®
Devotions for
Women on
the Go

The One Year®
Devotions for
Women

The One Year®
Devotions for
Moms

The One Year®
Women of the
Bible

The One Year®
Coffee with God

The One Year®
Devotional of Joy
and Laughter

The One Year®
Women's
Friendship
Devotional

The One Year®
Wisdom
for Women
Devotional

The One Year®
Book of Amish
Peace

The One Year®
Women in
Christian History
Devotional

CP0145

FOR MEN

*The One Year®
Devotions for
Men on the Go*

*The One Year®
Devotions for Men*

*The One Year®
Father-Daughter
Devotions*

FOR FAMILIES

*The One Year®
Family
Devotions, Vol. 1*

*The One Year®
Dinner Table
Devotions*

FOR COUPLES

*The One Year®
Devotions for
Couples*

*The One Year® Love
Language Minute
Devotional*

*The One Year® Love
Talk Devotional*

FOR TEENS

*The One Year®
Devos for Teens*

*The One Year®
Be-Tween You
and God*

FOR PERSONAL GROWTH

*The One Year®
at His Feet
Devotional*

*The One Year®
Uncommon Life
Daily Challenge*

*The One Year®
Recovery Prayer
Devotional*

*The One Year®
Christian History*

*The One Year®
Experiencing God's
Presence Devotional*

FOR BIBLE STUDY

*The One Year®
Praying through
the Bible*

*The One Year®
Praying the
Promises of God*

*The One Year®
Through the
Bible Devotional*

*The One Year®
Book of Bible
Promises*

*The One Year®
Unlocking the
Bible Devotional*

TheOneYear.com

CP0145